I0187521

On Modern Poetry

On Modern Poetry

GUIDO MAZZONI

Translated by Zakiya Hanafi

THE BELKNAP PRESS OF HARVARD UNIVERSITY PRESS

CAMBRIDGE, MASSACHUSETTS   LONDON, ENGLAND   2022

Copyright © 2022 by Guido Mazzoni

First edition originally published in Italian as *Sulla poesia moderna*
(Bologna: Società editrice il Mulino, 2005)

All rights reserved

Second printing

Library of Congress Cataloging-in-Publication Data

Names: Mazzoni, Guido, 1967– author. | Hanafi, Zakiya, 1959– translator.
Title: On modern poetry / Guido Mazzoni ; translated by Zakiya Hanafi.
Other titles: Sulla poesia moderna. English
Description: Cambridge, Massachusetts : The Belknap Press of
    Harvard University Press, 2022. | First edition originally published in
    Italian as Sulla poesia moderna (Bologna : Società editrice il Mulino, 2005)—
    Title page verso.
Identifiers: LCCN 2021038963 | ISBN 9780674249035 (cloth)
Subjects: LCSH: Italian poetry—19th century—History and criticism. |
    Italian poetry—20th century—History and criticism. | Poetry,
    Modern—19th century—History and criticism. | Poetry, Modern—
    20th century—History and criticism. | Lyric poetry. | Literary form.
Classification: LCC PQ4109 .M3913 2022 | DDC 809.1 / 03—dc23 / eng / 20211213
LC record available at https:// lccn.loc.gov / 2021038963

CONTENTS

Note on Translation   *ix*

Introduction: Sundials: Literary Genres
and the Time of History   1

    Literature and the *Longue Durée*   1

    Models for a History of Culture   5

    A Theory of Genres   15

    The Topography of Genres   20

    Symbolic Forms   25

    What Is Modern Poetry?   26

Chapter One: A History of Concepts   33

    Lyric and Poetry in Modern Genre Theory   33

    Lyric and Poetry in Ancient Poetics   37

    Alexandrian, Latin, and Medieval Categories   40

    The Renaissance Breakthrough   45

    Classicist Resistance and National Differences   53

    The New Romantic Theory   55

    The Modern Idea of Lyric Poetry   62

    The Concept of Modern Poetry   65

Chapter Two: A New Paradigm   71

An Exemplary Text   71

Interpretations   78

Seriousness and Contingency   81

Three Models of Lyric Poetry   88

Public and Private   91

Transcendental Autobiographism   101

Differential Autobiographism   105

Three Historical Thresholds   108

Chapter Three: A History of Forms   115

Theories of Style   115

Poetry and Prose   122

Expressivism   124

Lexicon   131

Syntax   135

Meter   147

Tropes   155

Chapter Four: The Literary Space of Modern Poetry   166

Poetry as Estrangement   166

Lyrical Romanticism   169

Expressionism and Irony   180

Modern Lyric Classicism and Subjective Poetry   184

Beyond the Lyric: Long Poems and Theatricality   187

Beyond the Lyric: Pure Poetry   192

The Egocentric Genre   199

Invisible Choirs   202

Conclusion: Modern Poetry as a Symbolic Form   208

The Self and Fragments of Time   208

Modern Poetic Anthropology   211

The Dialectic of Expressivism   213

The Marginality of Poetry   218

Poetry and Song   226

Monads and Systems   232

Acknowledgments   239

Index   241

NOTE ON TRANSLATION

The first edition of this book came out in Italian in 2005 with the title *Sulla poesia moderna*. *On Modern Poetry* is a revised version, updated to reflect secondary sources that have appeared since then, some of which have contributed to reshaping my ideas.

Titles of foreign-language works are shown in English if the translated version has entered into common use (*Republic, Aeneid, War and Peace*) and in the original language if the translated version has not entered into common use (*Liber, Canzoniere, Un coup de dés*). In the case of a few foreign-language poems whose titles have not entered into common use but are cited repeatedly in the text, at first reference their titles appear in both the original language and the English translation; subsequently, to provide a more fluent reading experience, they are referred to by their English titles alone. The original title in both cases is shown in the note along with the original date of the text. Some foreign-language expressions have been translated into English and placed in parentheses to aid understanding; other easier-to-understand expressions have not been translated.

When passages from secondary literature are quoted, the English-language version is used whenever possible; when this is not available, they have been translated directly from the originals. In certain cases, some changes have been made to ensure that the critical passages accurately reflect the literary work under discussion. Some poems have been translated by Zakiya Hanafi so that the English translation is as close to the original as possible.

The forms of art register the history of humanity with more justice than do historical documents.

—*Theodor W. Adorno*

Introduction

Sundials: Literary Genres and
the Time of History

Literature and the *Longue Durée*

Giacomo Leopardi's complete works include fourteen series of preparatory notes written between 1819 and 1834 and published in 1878 under a title chosen by the editor: "Disegni letterari," or, in English, "Literary Designs."[1] The notes are varied and difficult to compare with each other. Some fill several pages and carefully describe the texts that Leopardi intended to work on, while others do no more than put vague possibilities to paper—ideas rarely embarked on and almost always abandoned, as suggested by the impressive number of projects listed: more than a hundred and sixty just on the sheets in our possession. Part of the list was drafted in a hurry, without much thought. Precisely for this reason, it is an extraordinary document. Setting out the texts that Leopardi had been working on for some time alongside his impromptu desires, leaving a trace of real projects as well as hazy ambitions, his "Literary Designs" describes the range of possibilities available to

---

1. Giacomo Leopardi, "Disegni letterari," in Leopardi, *Prose e poesie*, vol. 2, *Prose*, ed. Rolando Damiani (Milan: Mondadori, 1988), 1204–1220.

an Italian writer of that period and of that social class—the topography of his literary space.

I call *literary space* the set of works that writers of a particular period judge reasonable to write and believe are in keeping with the times, to use the metaphor on which every form of historical knowledge is based. Our current literary space includes the genres that are still alive, the works to which it makes sense to dedicate oneself in the early twenty-first century if one hopes to satisfy the tastes of a mass or elite audience: countless varieties of novels and poetry, some residual forms of theater, screenplays for movies and television, journalism, and nonfiction. Between 1819 and 1834, the writer who today is thought by many to be the first modern Italian poet considered very different works in keeping with his times: a novel that tells the story of a woman forced to become a nun, modeled after Denis Diderot's *La Religieuse;* the life of General Kosciuszko, in imitation of the life of Agricola by Tacitus; a historical novel according to the taste of Xenophon's *Cyropaedia,* which would have recounted the destiny of a great nation gone into decline and then restored to its former dignity; a didactic poem on the woods; the lives of illustrious Italians, in the likeness of those by Cornelius Nepos and Plutarch; a tragedy on Iphigenia; *novelle* similar to those of Ludovico Ariosto written in ottava rima; a poem or novel modeled on Alexander Pope's *The Rape of the Lock;* a prose epic in imitation of Fénelon's *Les Aventures de Télémaque;* some "idylls expressing situations, affections, historical adventures of my soul," that is, short poems on an autobiographical subject; a novel, *Eugenio,* in imitation of Johann Wolfgang von Goethe's *The Sorrows of Young Werther;* a series of philosophical odes modeled on William Collins; and so on.[2] The reader of today cannot help but be surprised by the dissonances created by certain combinations. It seems inconceivable to us that a novel in imitation of Diderot's *La Religieuse* can coexist with biographies written in imitation of Cornelius Nepos, Plutarch, and Tacitus; or that the project of a novel about an intellectual hero modeled on *The Sorrows of Young Werther* could be contemporary with the project of a prose epic modeled on *Les Aventures de Télémaque.* Two centuries later, we know that the works listed by Leopardi belong to two historical worlds, one modern and one—for want of a better expression—we will continue to call premodern. But Leopardi did not see it that way.

---

2. Ibid.

In only a few pages, this discordant list condenses in its dissonant brevity the effects of a great metamorphosis that European literature experienced between the late eighteenth and early nineteenth centuries, transmitting to us a vivid impression of the change and the image of its force. Like an artifact whose meaning is only decipherable centuries later, Leopardi's projects register the moment when a new literary space appears alongside an old one with a tradition lasting thousands of years. Leopardi thought it was still possible to move around in both, whereas those who read this assortment looking back from the present are surprised by the conflict between old and new, past and modernity that the writers of that period were unable to perceive. Like Leopardi, after writing *The Sorrows of Young Werther* Goethe could still imagine dedicating himself to *Iphigenia in Tauris* and *Hermann and Dorothea;* in the 1810s, Sir Walter Scott published both long narrative poems and historical novels; and Alessandro Manzoni, in the 1820s, worked at the same time on a tragedy in verse, *Adelchi,* and the first draft of *The Betrothed.* Today we recognize the protomodernity or modernity of *The Sorrows of Young Werther, Waverley,* and *The Betrothed,* but we view the idyll (*Hermann and Dorothea*), tragedies in regular verse (*Iphigenia in Tauris, Adelchi*), and poems in regular verse as extinct. In the first works we glimpse signs of the present, but we study *Iphigenia in Tauris, Hermann and Dorothea, The Lady of the Lake,* and *Adelchi* the way we study texts that no longer have a place on our historical horizon. The striking thing about "Literary Designs" is the absence of such a frontier. A few decades after the list was compiled, not many writers would have wanted to compose *novelle* in ottava rima or imitate Cornelius Nepos, Tacitus, Plutarch, Fénelon, or Pope, while some of the more recent genres that interested Leopardi during those same years, like short lyric poems or the artist's novel, would meet with huge success. Traditional literary histories often provide a fragmentary image of this unprecedented transformation of Western literature, perhaps the most sudden and profound it ever underwent; Leopardi's document, on the other hand, gives a confused but synoptic vision of this change, aptly capturing its sense.

Walter Benjamin likened the becoming of epic forms to the evolution of the earth's surface through the geological ages.[3] The comparison is worth

---

3. Walter Benjamin, "Der Erzähler: Betrachtungen zum Werk Nikolai Lesskows" (1936); English translation, "The Storyteller: Reflections on the Works of Nikolai Leskov," in Walter Benjamin, *Illuminations,* trans. Harry Zohn (New York: Schocken Books, 2007), 88.

developing, because if it is true that transformations are almost always gradual, it is also true that movements of long duration sometimes progress slowly for centuries and then bring on sudden earthquakes. Reading Leopardi's "Literary Designs" almost two centuries later, we immediately notice the fault line that splits this miscellaneous list of projects in two, and we understand that the works he talks about refer to two irreconcilable ideas of literature—almost as if the chronological distance gave us a snapshot of historical time condensed in these few pages, as the crystallized image of an epochal shift.

But Benjamin's geological simile has a hidden sense as well. It evokes another characteristic of aesthetic materials that traditional histories often end up concealing, because of their inclination toward describing small changes rather than reflecting on long continuities. Great artistic forms have longevity: it took centuries for the pictorial space inaugurated by perspective to dissolve, for European music to free itself of tonality, for the novel to achieve its hegemony over narrative, for Western literature to begin representing the everyday life of common people in a serious and problematic way. This may seem like a banal observation, but not much is needed to transform it into a philosophy of art. What Benjamin really wanted to show by talking about epic forms, and using the history of genres as a seismograph, was the changes in the way reality was experienced during the transition from the closed, community-based premodern world to the individualist, disintegrated modern world. From this perspective, his comparison with the times of the earth's surface acquires a philosophical significance: indeed, Benjamin seems to suggest that narrative structures—and, by synecdoche, aesthetic materials— evolve slowly because they express the deep transformations of human history, their long time. Thanks to its plastic force, art translates the conceptual continuity of an era into the visible continuity of a system of signs. It gives a sensible appearance to continuities and radical ruptures, exactly the way the earth's surface does with geological time. This is the philosophy of history to which Benjamin alludes in different forms: the same vision of history underpins his accounts of long durations, from his thesis on the baroque origin of German tragic drama[4] to *The Arcades Project*.[5] Aesthetic materials give us an

---

4. Walter Benjamin, *Ursprung des deutschen Trauerspiels* (1928); English translation, *The Origin of German Tragic Drama*, trans. John Osborne (London: Verso, 1998).

5. Walter Benjamin, *Das Passagen-Werk* (1927–1940); English translation, *The Arcades Project*, trans. Howard Eiland and Kevin McLaughlin (Cambridge, MA: The Belknap Press of Harvard University Press, 1999).

essential version of what takes place; their synthetizing, representational nature predisposes them to becoming "a philosophical sundial telling the time of history," as Adorno wrote when speaking about the art that I will be dealing with here: modern poetry.[6] Thus, the age-old persistence of a hierarchical scale of styles, genres, actions, and characters narrates in an admirably synoptic way the persistence of a hierarchical vision of life in European society;[7] the evolution of tragic drama in the nineteenth and twentieth centuries shows the impoverishment of human relations in an era when public action in the midst of others seemed less and less significant;[8] and the history of contemporary architecture, ahead of the history of mentality, announces the beginning of the postmodern condition[9] or the cultural contradictions of democracy.[10] The forms of art register the history of humanity with more justice than do historical documents.[11]

Models for a History of Culture

This way of understanding the becoming of art and culture has an illustrious genealogy. It grew out of a long tradition that began with Georg Wilhelm Friedrich Hegel's lectures on aesthetics and philosophy of history and was propagated in two different versions, one that was faithful to the original texts and another that broadened out. The first includes works that refer more or less directly to Hegel, such as those cited by Peter Szondi at the end of *Theory of the Modern Drama* when he makes explicit his own references: immediately after Hegel's *Aesthetics*, he names György Lukács's "The Sociology of Modern Drama" and Adorno's *Philosophy of New Music*. The second includes

---

6. Theodor W. Adorno, "Rede über Lyrik und Gesellschaft" (1957); English translation, "On Lyric Poetry and Society," in *Notes to Literature*, trans. Shierry Weber Nicholsen (New York: Columbia University Press, 1991), 46.

7. Erich Auerbach, *Mimesis: Dargestellte Wirklichkeit in der abendländischen Literatur* (1946); English translation, *Mimesis: The Representation of Reality in Western Literature*, trans. Willard R. Trask (Princeton, NJ: Princeton University Press, 2003).

8. Peter Szondi, *Theorie des modernen Dramas* (1956); English translation, *Theory of the Modern Drama*, trans. Michael Hays (Cambridge: Polity Press, 1987).

9. Fredric Jameson, *Postmodernism, or The Cultural Logic of Late Capitalism* (Durham, NC: Duke University Press, 1991).

10. Rem Koolhaas, "Junkspace," in *Harvard Design School Guide to Shopping* (Köln: Taschen, 2001) and *October*, vol. 100 (*Obsolescence*), 2002, 175–190.

11. Theodor W. Adorno, *Philosophie der neuen Musik* (1949); English translation, *Philosophy of New Music*, trans. Robert Hullot-Kentor (Minneapolis: University of Minnesota Press, 2006), 41.

Kulturgeschichte in all its variants, from Karl Lamprecht's history of mentalities to Wilhelm Dilthey's *Geistesgeschichte*.[12] Such diverse works are founded on a few shared assumptions that are easy to criticize today: faith in the *cultural unity* of an epoch; the conviction that there exist *significant discontinuities* between different historical periods; faith in the *representative value of works that have stood the test of time* by entering into our canons; the idea that *diverse works can be grouped* by origin, aim, and function into unified sets like styles, periods, and genres; and, finally, as far as the history of the arts is concerned, faith in the *representative value of aesthetic experiences*. Using the history of epic forms as a seismograph means taking for granted convictions that are anything but givens: for example, that works which have stood the test of time represent something broader than the particular interests that generated them and made them canonical; that it is possible to overlook differences between texts so as to talk about a singular literary genre, style, or epoch; that the forms of art tell the history of human beings in a profound and meaningful way; that it makes sense to distinguish a few unified stations in the flux of time or to think in terms of epochs. Today, all these assumptions have become questionable: positivist research, the sociology of culture, poststructuralism, feminist theory, new historicism, and cultural studies have contributed in various ways to undermining the apparatus of certainties on which they rested, destabilizing the "diluted Hegelianism" on which, according to Pierre Bourdieu, many philosophies of cultural history are based, from Hegel's to Michel Foucault's.[13]

Because the book I've written descends in part from this tradition, and since I agree with some of the criticisms that have been raised against them, I have preferred to avoid the sort of reticence that normally surrounds many intellectual constructions and make the assumptions of my discourse clear. I certainly cannot refound the critical tradition that the book draws from: I wouldn't be able to, and, in any case, I would have to write another book. However, I would like to at least explain which aspects of this tradition still

---

12. Ernst Gombrich, *In Search of Cultural History* (Oxford: Clarendon, 1967), 25–32. See also by Gombrich, "Hegel und die Kunstgeschichte" (1977); English translation, "Hegel and Art History," in *On the Methodology of Architectural History*, ed. Demetri Porphyrios (London: Architectural Design; New York: Saint Martin's Press, 1981), 3–9.

13. Pierre Bourdieu, *Les Règles de l'art* (1992, 1998); English translation, *The Rules of Art: Genesis and Structure of the Literary Field*, trans. Susan Emanuel (Stanford, CA: Stanford University Press, 1996), 199.

seem defendable to me so that my readers can know where they find themselves and what they are reading. I will therefore attempt to frame, apodictically, a few of this book's implicit assumptions.

1. Ernst Gombrich noted contentiously that it is mainly cultural historians who interpret epochs as unified entities. By doing so they end up assuming, in a more or less conscious form, a cohesiveness to historical periods and the existence of a spirit of the times that manifests in works of the same era. Political and economic historians serenely abandon any such idea:

> The cultural historian was much worse off than any other historian. His colleagues working on political or economic history had at least a . . . restricted subject-matter. They could trace the history of the reform of Parliament, of Anglo-Irish relations, without explicit reference to an all-embracing philosophy of history. But the history of culture as such . . . could never be undertaken without some ordering principle . . . , some hub on which the wheel of Hegel's diagram can be pivoted. Thus the subsequent history of historiography of culture can perhaps best be interpreted as a succession of attempts to salvage the Hegelian assumption without accepting Hegelian metaphysics.[14]

Certainly, the frequency with which cultural historians, especially art historians, have appealed to some sort of form to replace *Zeitgeist* is quite striking: in addition to the names mentioned by Gombrich (Jacob Burckhardt, Lamprecht, Dilthey, Max Dvořák, Erwin Panofsky, and Johan Huizinga), we could cite Erich Auerbach, Lukács, Benjamin, Adorno, Mikhail Bakhtin, Szondi, Arnold Gehlen (*Zeit-Bilder*), Foucault, Daniel Bell, Christopher Lasch, Fredric Jameson, and many others. But it would be reductive to show that all these thinkers remained imprisoned by what Gombrich represents as merely an error of perspective, unless we reflect on the reasons that led intellectuals so different in training, ideology, and interests to rediscover a unifying principle similar in every way to *Zeitgeist*—renaming it, for example, "mentality," *episteme,* or "the cultural logic of late capitalism."

The way Marcel Proust reflects on the concept of epoch in *In Search of Lost Time* is quite interesting. Few people have been able to show so ably that

---

14. Gombrich, *In Search of Cultural History*, 25–26.

the culture and social life of a particular historical period are torn apart by conflicts and differences; that values, tastes, and canons clash continuously; that contemporaries can inhabit very different mental worlds. In this respect, Benjamin's idea that one should examine history against the grain to rediscover the defeated traditions[15] and Bourdieu's idea that every epoch is above all a field of conflicting forces are anticipated in In Search of Lost Time—which, incidentally, both Benjamin and Bourdieu read attentively and Benjamin even translated. And, yet, in Proust's work we also find one of the strongest defenses of the concept of epoch:

> Better still now, the perfect conformity in appearance between a man of business from Combray of his generation and the Duc de Bouillon reminded me of what had already struck me so forcibly when I had seen Saint-Loup's maternal grandfather, the Duc de La Rochefoucauld, in a daguerreotype in which he was exactly similar, in dress, air and manner, to my great-uncle, that social, and even individual differences are merged when seen from a distance in the uniformity of an epoch. The truth is that the similarity of dress, and also the reflexion, from a person's face, of the spirit of his age [l'esprit de l'époque] occupy so much more space than his caste, which bulks largely only in his own self-esteem and the imagination of other people, that in order to discover that a great nobleman of the time of Louis Philippe differs less from a citizen of the time of Louis Philippe than from a great nobleman of the time of Louis XV, it is not necessary to visit all the galleries of the Louvre.[16]

Although Proust does talk about "the spirit of his age," the way he explains this continuity of signs, customs, and behaviors is purely mechanical, earthly, and contingent. Battles for hegemony, the succession of generations, and the tendency of human beings to simplify and to forget create a uniformity that

---

15. This idea is presented in "Theses on the Philosophy of History" (1940). In other pieces, Benjamin uses a more cohesive and unified notion of epoch: in his essay "The Storyteller," but also in some pages of his unfinished book, The Arcades Project, when, citing Jules Michelet, he writes that "Each epoch dreams the one to follow." Benjamin, The Arcades Project, 150.

16. Marcel Proust, Sodome et Gomorrhe (1921–1922); English translation, Sodom and Gomorrah, in In Search of Lost Time, vol. 4, trans. C. K. Scott Moncrieff and Terence Kilmartin, rev. D. J. Enright (New York: Modern Library, 1993), 110–111.

is revealed from the perspective of distance, as happens in some parts of *Time Regained*.[17] Perceiving the resemblance between contemporary phenomena does not in itself assume the existence of a unifying principle, an avatar of the *Zeitgeist*. This is what histories of the *longue durée* do, for example, by drawing on the synoptic *a posteriori* power of distance,[18] on its physical, almost optical evidence, just as, when taking off in an airplane, the fields that seem so different when seen from the ground become uniform, united by a single color, while the boundaries that divide them, invisible from the earth, suddenly become much clearer. This mechanical historicism with no subject, this history of spirit with no Spirit, which relies on the synoptic power of the long duration, trusts in the possibility of distinguishing fault lines and large aggregations in the continuous flux of events and local conflicts. When observed in the light of a different cultural logic, the representation of reality in ancient literature and in classicist literature of the early modern age reveals constants lasting hundreds or thousands of years.[19] Although every national literature possesses its own internal history, the major modern European literatures appear to be traversed by the same medium- and long-term phenomena, from the most extensive (the revolution of genres that took place

---

17. "Survivors of the older generation assured me that society had completely changed and now opened its doors to people who in their day would never have been received, and this comment was both true and untrue. On the one hand it was untrue, because those who made it failed to take into account the curve of time which caused the society of the present to see these newly received people at their point of arrival, whilst they, the older generation, remembered them at their point of departure. And this was nothing new, for in the same way, when they themselves had first entered society, there were people in it who had just arrived and whose lowly origins others remembered. In society as it exists today a single generation suffices for the change which formerly over a period of centuries transformed a middle-class name like Colbert into an aristocratic one. And yet, from another point of view there was a certain truth in the comments; for, if the social position of individuals is liable to change (like the fortunes and the alliances and the hatreds of nations), so too are the most deeply rooted ideas and customs." Marcel Proust, *Le Temps retrouvé* (1927); English translation, *Time Regained*, in *In Search of Lost Time*, vol. 6, trans. Andreas Mayor and Terence Kilmartin, rev. D. J. Enright (New York: Modern Library, 2003), 393–394.

18. See Fernand Braudel, "Histoire et sciences sociales: La longue durée" (1958); English translation, "History and the Social Sciences: The Longue Durée," trans. Immanuel Wallerstein, in *Review (Fernand Braudel Center)* 32, no. 2 (2009): 171–203. Among the three books that take a long-term view without presupposing an *a priori* unity of epochs, Braudel cites a work of literary history, *European Literature and the Latin Middle Ages* (1948) by Ernst Robert Curtius, along with *The Problem of Unbelief in the Sixteenth Century: The Religion of Rabelais* (1942) by Lucien Febvre, and *Peinture et Société: Naissance et destruction d'un espace plastique. De la Renaissance au cubisme* (1951) by Pierre Francastel.

19. Auerbach, *Mimesis*; and Ernst Robert Curtius, *Europäische Literatur und lateinisches Mittelalter* (1948); English translation, *European Literature and the Latin Middle Ages*, trans. Willard R. Trask (Princeton, NJ: Princeton University Press, 2013), 391–392.

between the eighteenth and nineteenth centuries) to the less extensive (the spread of new techniques between the late nineteenth century and the period of the historical avant-gardes that enriched narrative, poetry, and theater with previously unthinkable possibilities, such as interior monologue, free verse, and the montage principle). Similarly, although the genres of modern literature each evolve according to their own logic, the novel, poetry, and drama of recent centuries make up a relatively homogeneous system marked by common characteristics. For this reason, we can speak of a porous but visible fault line that divides modern poetry from previous poetry, with chronologies that differ depending on the national literature involved.

2. Cultural histories generally suffer from fetishism: even in the most meticulous books, even in studies that conform to rigid quantitative criteria, the texts that historians take into consideration amount to a very small percentage of the works composed in a certain place during a certain period, especially when the period and place in question are very spread out. Traditionally structured histories are based on a sort of synecdoche: an assumption that the few texts they discuss have the power to represent an entire epoch. Anyone with a more analytical attitude can easily demonstrate that the systematic reconstruction of a circumscribed literary space offers a much more layered panorama than those we are accustomed to reading.[20] Traditional histories often have an ingenuous approach to their subject matter: they presuppose an already-established canon and reflect the outcome of a battle over memory and oblivion, but without examining the genealogy of the victories. In their background hovers one of the most discredited ideologemes of our age, impossible to defend in theory but widely used in practice: the belief that the verdicts of history reflect some hypothetical, objective value of the works in question that is bound to emerge over the years thanks to the "judgment of

---

20. See Bourdieu, *The Rules of Art;* Gisèle Sapiro, *La Guerre des écrivains: 1940–1953* (1999); English translation, *The French Writers' War 1940–1953,* trans. Vanessa Doriott Anderson and Dorrit Cohn (Durham, NC: Duke University Press, 2014); Pascale Casanova, *La République mondiale des Lettres* (1999, 2008); English translation, *The World Republic of Letters,* trans. M. B. DeBevoise (Cambridge, MA: Harvard University Press, 2007); Anna Boschetti, *La Poésie partout: Apollinaire, homme-époque (1898–1918)* (Paris: Seuil, 2001). From a different point of view, literary history based on quantitative methods and analyzing big data underscores the gap that exists between the image of the literary past preserved by the monumental canons and the image that one arrives at from a statistical analysis of all published works. See Franco Moretti, *Distant Reading* (London: Verso, 2013), and Franco Moretti, ed., *Canon / Archive: Studies in Quantitative Formalism from the Stanford Literary Lab* (Brooklyn: n+1 Foundation, 2017).

time." Anyone who reconstructs the genealogy of the canons can easily demonstrate that the "judgment of time" is nothing but the posthumous sanctification of an arbitrary act, the attempt to attribute an unjustified universal value to texts, images of the world, and values that have triumphed at the end of a battle fought in the name of a pure will to power: a writer's struggle to outshine rival writers; the struggle of one literary circle to gain visibility at the expense of others; the struggle of one social group against competing groups to transform their tastes into everybody else's tastes. The results of this conflict between opposing wills are devoid of the objective value that traditional histories usually attribute to the consecrated works. From this perspective, the winner of the battle for memory does not embody the *Zeitgeist* but, rather, the triumph of one contingent interest over another contingent interest, of one egoism over another egoism. If an approach of this sort is accepted, then it becomes arbitrary to view canonical texts as representative of an epoch; rather, one should look for the network of proximate causes that lie behind the consecration of a writer, a movement, a fashion, or a genre, by scrutinizing history against the grain and reconstructing the battlefields as they appeared before the victors planted their insignias on them. In short, to recapture the authentic image of an epoch, one must liberate oneself from the synecdoche that legitimates the established canons, the accomplished facts, give up on the idea that a restricted number of writers can express the spirit of a time in its entirety, and concentrate instead on unearthing the ruptures, dispersions, and frictions that disturb the apparent unity of a historical period.

The myopic gaze of the genealogist, focused on proximate causes and human, all-too-human motives that underlie the formation of a culture, enriches and unravels our idea of the past. There are two versions of this approach—one ingenuous and one sentimental. The first is still more widespread than the second. It embodies the norm of studies that present themselves as "serious" or "scientific" and coincides with the philologically oriented criticism that continues the legacy of late nineteenth-century positivism and proliferates in traditional academic journals. By resorting to a mechanical idea of causality that modern common knowledge takes as natural, the critics who belong to this family ignore the existence of the whole and, with a good dose of conventional wisdom proportional to the myopia that they demonstrate, reconstruct the elementary genealogies that compose the raw material of any historical narrative: the influence of one writer on another, of a historical event on a cultural circle, of a particular milieu on a particular artistic form.[21] The sentimental version of genealogy is more recent, consisting in attempts to apply to historiography the consequences of philosophies that Paul Ricœur, borrowing from Friedrich Nietzsche, grouped together as "the school of suspicion."[22] The enormous success enjoyed by the thought of Karl Marx, Nietzsche, and Sigmund Freud in the twentieth century resulted in many cultural historians concentrating on the material interests underlying the invention of spiritual works—as neo-Marxist histories of art sought to do or poststructuralism, feminist theory, new historicism, cultural studies, and, from a different perspective, Bourdieu's sociology of culture and Pascale Casanova's sociology of world literature. Although they appear dissimilar, in reality these approaches share a more or less conscious rejection of the ideas that make an organic philosophy of history possible. By emphasizing difference at the expense of unity, and fragmentation at the expense of cohesiveness, their method ends up interpreting works in the light of proximate causes, as the result of particular interests and local struggles. Behind the cautious and impeccable myopia of the genealogist one detects a disenchanted metaphysics that understands reality as a web of clashes between opposing wills to power, whose outcome does not reflect a teleological design, a *Zeitgeist* or an *episteme*, but the contingent victory of one individual over another individual, one group over another group. This is how genealogical wisdom appears to destroy the foundations of a philosophy of history that presumes to think in terms of epochs by ignoring the enormous number of struggles, fault lines, and internal discontinuities of each epoch. But these same foundations reappear under a new light when small conflicts are placed in the perspective of the long duration. If individual victories are the effect of chance or contingent power relations, *extended, important, and long-lasting victories and defeats create a new cultural space, a new plane of reality, and, like it or not, actually mean something.* It is intriguing that Bourdieu himself, after criticizing the many disguised rewritings of Hegel, surreptitiously reintroduced a form of historicism when he argued that,

21. On mechanical causality, see Fredric Jameson, *The Political Unconscious: Narrative as a Socially Symbolic Act* (Ithaca, NY: Cornell University Press, 1981), chap. 1.

22. Paul Ricœur, *De l'interprétation: Essai sur Freud* (1965); English translation, *Freud and Philosophy: An Essay on Interpretation*, trans. Denis Savage (New Haven, CT: Yale University Press, 1970), 32–36.

although internal struggles within a cultural field follow their own independent rationale, the determining factor for establishing the success of a work or an idea is the correspondence between the winning positions and shifts in the relations of force that arise in the field of power:

> Internal struggles are somehow arbitrated by external sanctions. More generally, although largely independent of them *in principle,* the internal struggles always depend, *in outcome,* on the correspondence that they maintain with the external struggles—whether struggles at the core of the field of power or at the core of the social field as a whole.[23]

Nothing describes such an interweaving of contingent struggles and historical necessities as well as the concept of *hegemony* that Antonio Gramsci borrowed in part from linguistics and in part from the political writings of Lenin. He used it to describe the inextricable nexus of violence and consensus whereby a ruling class or a social group transforms their own ideas into everybody else's ideas. Criticizing the naive Machiavellianism of those who trace power back to violence alone, Gramsci argues that every stable governing force is based on a variable combination of "dominion" and "intellectual and moral direction," power and persuasion.[24] One can legitimately extend this concept to the sphere of culture and use it to explain the formation of canons: long-term memory, in other words, would not arise out of pure coercion or the "judgment of time" but from the capacity to transform the tastes of one group into shared tastes, by combining the power to impose certain ideas with the ability to interpret or shape the symbolic order of a society in a particular period. In the long run, the result of great battles internal to the cultural system always depends on the correspondence that these conflicts maintain with changes in "the social field as a whole":[25] an author may be included in school curricula thanks to contingent reasons and a genre can

---

23. Bourdieu, *The Rules of Art,* 127.

24. See Antonio Gramsci, *Quaderni dei carcere,* ed. Valentino Gerratana (Turin: Einaudi, 1975), Quaderno 19, § 24; vol. 3, 2010. See also Quaderno 13 § 37; vol. 3, 1638; partial English translation, *Selections from the Prison Notebooks,* ed. and trans. Quintin Hoare and Geoffrey Nowell Smith (New York: International Publishers, 1992), 57–59.

25. Bourdieu, *The Rules of Art,* 127.

never establish itself by chance. When the phenomena being talked about are very widespread, there is no need to resort to the mysticism of master-pieces to assert that, although canons arise from the pure will to power, they do not simply signify a random victory of one faction over another.

3. Cultural historians tend to think in terms of epochs because the terri-tory that we might call the field of expressive symbolism, borrowing from Ernst Cassirer, is the imaginary space where common knowledge and the collective unconscious of a social group best make themselves seen. More broadly, it is where common knowledge and the collective unconscious, having won the battle for hegemony, transform themselves into recognized cultural capital, into the spirit of the times. Among all the segments of this territory, which extends from the fine arts to religious rituals, the aesthetic is the most expressive, for three reasons.

In the first place, no other component of culture expresses with such im-mediacy the way a person, a social group, or an epoch interpret the great anthropological constants that form what Edmund Husserl calls the *Lebens-welt*, the lifeworld, namely, the inner and social life of human beings, the first stages of personal relations, our ways of perceiving space and time, and our relations with words, bodies, and things. If the forms of art register the history of humanity better than do historical documents, it is because they lend a plastic consistency to the primary anthropological structures of life, as we understand when we view their evolution from the perspective of the long duration. The capacity to express an image of the world is united with a representative force that other forms of knowledge do not possess. While the knowledge of philosophy, history, or the human sciences is always spe-cialized, aesthetic culture functions in principle as a system of signs that, the-oretically, everybody can understand. The representative power of artistic forms is augmented, at least in recent centuries, by their apparent *innocence*. The history of modern culture is a series of progressive neutralizations and depoliticizations, at the end of which a unified, theocratic, hierarchical, and censorious culture softens its tablets of law, relaxes its rigid framework of principles into a form of relativism, ideally leaving each individual the right to choose tastes, values, and lifestyles without having to justify them to anyone. Although the time when one could be put to death for a religious opinion, an immoral behavior, or a political idea is not that distant in the West, today a certain degree of relativistic tolerance is part of the written and unwritten laws that regulate life in our societies. Divergences that a few centuries ago led to physical confrontation or heated discussion have cleared out from the public sphere and become a matter of private choice. Hence, the first phase of cultural neutralization involves the aesthetic sphere and can be summed up in the saying *de gustibus non est disputandum,* "there is no disputing about tastes." Modern arts criticism has made its primary reason for existence to dispute tastes that are in principle indisputable. This primacy of the aesthetic sphere, for centuries the only partly depoliticized territory in a centripetal and intolerant culture, adds emblematic weight to the works that comprise it, since for a long time the major and minor arts permitted the representation of content that would have been rigorously suppressed in other cultural spheres.[26] Briefly stated, then, these are the foundations of my approach.

A Theory of Genres

As stylistic criticism and the "thick description" of the anthropologists teaches us, even a minimal sign can reveal a culture in its entirety; but if we look at the rule rather than the exception, it appears clear that the most complex and long-lasting structures are also the most significant. When Benjamin compared the morphology of narrative forms to the morphology of the earth's surface, he was thinking about groupings of works as complex as they are undefinable: *literary genres.* Taking his geological simile further, we would have to say that if the literary space of an epoch corresponds to the earth's surface, genres are the plates whose movements give form to the planet's crust.

But if literary histories of the *longue durée* often end up being genre histories, it is not at all clear what literary genres are. In the continuous semantic flux that characterizes discussions on this subject, it is easy to recognize a constant in any cultural debate. Owing to a primary process of semantic dissemination that is almost physical in origin, whenever a debate involves mass

---

26. See Francesco Orlando, *Per una teoria freudiana della letteratura* (1973); English translation, *Toward a Freudian Theory of Literature: With an Analysis of Racine's "Phèdre,"* trans. Charmaine Lee (Baltimore, MD: Johns Hopkins University Press, 1978).

participation, the topics under discussion end up with increasingly frayed senses and lose their specific meanings. There is nothing unusual about the fact that the topic we are talking about has succumbed to the same fate. What is meant by modern poetry? And, before that, what does it mean to talk about modern poetry as a literary genre? What are literary genres?

These questions, it seems to me, bring together three different uncertainties that demand separate responses: the first regards the criteria that allow the *boundaries* of genres to be marked out; the second concerns the *nature* of similarities between the texts gathered under the same name; the third is about the *meaning* of such families. The uncertainty regarding the boundaries of genre was formulated incisively by Goethe in one of the notes accompanying *West-East Divan* (1819). In his opinion, anyone who reflects on genres realizes immediately that the categories used to define these entities reflect diverse criteria:

> Allegory, ballad, cantata, didactic poem, drama, elegy, epigram, epistle, epic, fable, heroic poem, idyll, narrative, novel, ode, parody, romance, satire.
>
> If you wanted to classify methodically these poetical genres, which I have arranged in [German] alphabetical order, and more of the kind, you would encounter great difficulties, not easily put aside. If you look at the rubrics above more closely, you will find that they are labeled in some cases according to external criteria, in others according to the content, but only rarely according to an essential form. You will quickly notice that some of them can be coordinated, others subordinated one to another.[27]

In ordinary usage, the concept of genre indicates completely heterogeneous families of texts: allegory, ballad, cantata, didactic poem, drama, elegy, epigram, epistle, epic, fable, heroic poem, idyll, narrative, novel, ode, parody, romance, satire are in reality groups that cannot be compared with each other, that have arisen at various times out of similarities in content or form, or from a fluctuating combination of content and form. In common

---

27. Johann Wolfgang von Goethe, *West-östlicher Divan* (1819); English translation, *West-East Divan: The Poems, with "Notes and Essays": Goethe's Intercultural Dialogues,* trans. Martin Bidney and Peter Anton von Arnim (Albany: State University of New York Press, 2010), 226–227.

critical practice, these heteroclite categories lead us to use the same abstract noun "literary genre" to name completely different entities: the sonnet, medieval love poetry, or lyric poetry in general; the science-fiction novel, the romance, or the novel; Greek tragedy, tragedy without adjectives, or the corpus of texts written for the theater—and so forth. To avoid this kind of confusion, Goethe proposes to establish a hierarchy that would follow a more rational order. He suggests that a few ideal categories should be inferred from the logic of literature in order to regroup the congeries of historical categories, distinguishing the mass of *poetic genres* (*Dichtarten*) from the three great *natural forms* (*Naturformen*) of poetry—epic, lyric, and drama. These natural forms stand in the same relation to poetic genres as the particular does to the universal. The attempt met with success: a century and a half later, repeating Goethe's thought process, Szondi would oppose the empirical poetics of genres to speculative poetics. Similarly, Tzvetan Todorov would separate "historical genres," founded on observation of the literary reality, from "theoretical genres," born of inference; and Gérard Genette would divide historical "small forms" from archetypal large forms, which he would baptize *archigenres*.[28] This is a modern version of a dialectic already familiar to Plato, who in a passage of *Laws* names the categories that authors and the public used to classify melic poetry (hymns, threnodies, paeans, dithyrambs, and citharode chants); and in book three of *Republic* he deduces an ideal tripartition of all texts, placing "everything that's said by poets or storytellers" under the large forms that are either simple narrative (*aple diegesis*), imitation (*mimesis*), or a mix of the two, according to a purely philosophical taxonomy that unifies the small empirical genres into abstract categories.[29] Today we still use the same word to name both Goethe's natural forms, which are complex but substantially ahistoric, and the congeries of historical forms, which are concrete but limited. The first category includes, for example, the notions of narrative, drama, and lyric that organize the architecture of our literary histories; the second, the potentially infinite list of categories that

---

28. See Peter Szondi, "Von der normativen zur spekulativen Gattungspoetik," in *Poetik und Geschichtsphilosophie II* (1974), 7–183; Tzvetan Todorov, *Introduction à la littérature fantastique* (1970); English translation, *The Fantastic: A Structural Approach to a Literary Genre*, trans. Richard Howard (Ithaca, NY: Cornell University Press, 1975), 13–15; and Gérard Genette, *Introduction à l'architexte* (1979); English translation, *The Architext: An Introduction*, trans. Jane E. Lewin (Berkeley: University of California Press, 1992), 64–71. On this distinction, see also Jean-Marie Schaeffer, *Qu'est-ce qu un genre littéraire?* (Paris: Seuil, 1989), 64ff.

29. Plato, *Laws*, 3.700 a–d; *Republic*, 3.392 d.

various cultures have used to group their works: the hymns, threnodies, paeans, dithyrambs, and citharode chants of ancient Greek lyric; the chivalric, historical, realistic, fantastic, *Bildungsroman,* or family novels of modern narrative; the neoclassical, reformed, or *larmoyante* comedy of eighteenth-century theater—and so on. Once these boundaries are set, it is possible to arrange the various families according to a rational order, with a few large theoretical genres at the top that move downward by decreasing degrees of generality to empirical genres at the bottom. This is similar to the hierarchical chain that ties narrative in general to science-fiction novels in particular, passing by way of the intermediate forms of the novel and the romance. The confused congeries of names would thus find its own logic.

But even though some of these categories, those most closely tied to the empirical domain, seem to possess an irrefutable degree of reality, a skeptical nominalist might challenge the existence of the more abstract sets and the possibility of uniting the genres following coherent logical steps. Indeed, the *Naturformen,* the theoretical genres, the *archigenres,* only possess the value they claim to have if they truly descend by inference from the logic of literature itself. However, Genette has demonstrated with unassailable arguments that the only true *archigenres* are the notions of *diegesis, mimesis,* and mixed narrative already familiar to Plato and Aristotle, and that these three categories are in any case inadequate for establishing a well-structured system. To this is added the fact that the categories of narrative, drama, and lyric on which almost all modern systems are built have almost no absolute logical foundation but simply a relative, historical origin.[30] And yet the hierarchical distinction between the various forms seems to preserve a glaring obviousness, because it is undeniable that the families of texts we call genres lie on uneven planes of reality: some of them can be placed in an equal relationship with each other, as Goethe points out; others are in a relationship of subordination. For example, between the science-fiction novel, the romance, the novel, and narrative, there seems to be a relation of increasing generality, since the first is a subset of the second, the second is a subset of the third, and the third a subset of the fourth. Therefore, if we cannot defend *Naturformen* and the idea of a hierarchy inferred from the logic of literature, it seems reasonable to keep the sense of a progression from the particular to

---

30. See Genette, *The Architext.*

the universal, from the smallest and most contingent forms to the largest and most abstract: the epic, the romance, the novel, comedy, tragedy, and so forth. Modern poetry would be one of these large, expanded genres.

How can we give a solid foundation to a deductive chain of this sort? A rigorous examination of the genre categories reveals that it is very difficult to justify a move like the one Goethe attempts to legitimize, given that the difference between historical and theoretical genres, between small forms and large forms, has no solid foothold in thought. In fact, if we adhere strictly to the data of literary history, not only would we repudiate all foundations for theoretical genres such as narrative, lyric, and drama, but we would even have to challenge the existence of expanded genres such as the epic, the romance, the novel, the modern novel, modern drama, and modern poetry. More than anything, the status of these expanded sets changed after the crisis in European neoclassicism and the end of normative aesthetics: the ancient poetics recognized the existence of a few large synthetic forms (serious epic, comic epic, tragedy, and comedy), whereas modern literary aesthetics struggles to defend the value of such groupings from the attacks of a positivism that recognizes particulars but distrusts universals. Do we not perhaps do violence every time we talk about "modern poetry" in general, forgetting how many profound differences separate the lyric poems of English Romanticism from the texts of French Symbolism, Spanish or Spanish American Modernism, German Expressionism, or the Italian Neo-avant-garde? Furthermore, if we wanted to reflect on the underlying question, we would have to ask ourselves how much reality the data of literary history truly possess, and what marks the transition from a historical genre to a theoretical genre. The only certain distinction for establishing data and legitimizing difference would appear to be one that separates the endogenous categories, used by writers and the public, from the exogenous categories, used by literary theorists.[31] But when you try to bring this opposition into practice, you realize that the two groups get mixed up time and again. For writers and readers, the theoretical genres coexist with the historical genres in total confusion, something that becomes obvious when you look at bookstore shelves, where large abstract sets of "fiction," "theater," and "poetry" live alongside small concrete sets of "detective novels," "fantasy novels," or "romance novels," without any hierarchy

---

31. Schaeffer, *Qu'est-ce qu'un genre littéraire?*, 77.

taking shape. In reality, the hypothesis of a logical chain that makes it possible to pass from small forms to large expanded forms meets with so many difficulties because it relates to a more or less conscious comparison between literary families and plant or animal species—a comparison that fails to capture the overall logic of literary categories[32] and, more generally, the difference between cultural creations and organic forms. To truly understand the meaning of genres, we have to tackle the second problem implicit in the question on the status of modern poetry: its *nature.*

The Topography of Genres

What type of similarity is referred to in the groupings we are talking about? What are literary genres? In the first part of an essay on this topic, Hans Robert Jauss retrieves the vocabulary that medieval philosophy used for disputations on universals. He distinguishes three stances: for some theorists, genres embody *ante rem* essences, transcendental structures that precede the empirical existence of texts; for others, they represent *post rem* taxonomic grids, which readers apply to a confused and dispersed realty; for yet others, they are *in re* universals: they record the objective historical continuity between works of the same family and therefore represent the traces of an objective link between individual texts. Jauss defends this latter approach: in his view, anyone who wants to build a theory in keeping with our times must move between "the Scylla of nominalistic scepticism . . . and the Charybdis of regression into timeless typologies,"[33] between the myopia of those who see only the dispersion of small forms, and the naivety of those who too readily dissolve the particular into the universal. Genres do not reflect the essence of literature, as the theory of natural forms claims, nor do they allow themselves to be reduced to a pure *flatus vocis,* a mere name without a corresponding objective reality, as the skeptics would have it; rather, they designate sets of texts that are historically related to each other by some common traits. But who decides on the kinship relations? Who determines that a bunch

---

32. Ibid., chap. 4.

33. Hans Robert Jauss, "Theorie der Gattungen und Literatur des Mittelalters" (1972); English translation, "Theory of Genres and Medieval Literature," in *Modern Genre Theory,* ed. and with an introd. by David Duff (London: Routledge, 2016), 130.

of more or less obvious similarities are sufficient to aggregate a mass of texts into a common category?

To some measure, even when appealing to indisputable similarities, as in the case of genres based on an objective formal element, the perception of a similarity, and, above all, the idea that a certain similarity is relevant enough to justify the existence of a genre, is an issue at stake in conflicts internal to the literary space. Taxonomic activity is continuous and polycentric, so much so that in every epoch new offerings overlap and ignore or clash with each other due to their unpredictable nature and muddled origins: writing habits, proposals for new poetics, publishing categories, educational policies, literary criticism. Study of this restless field full of diverse taxonomies teaches us many things: for example, that the crude geography of literature proposed by publishers or school curricula counts much more than the sophisticated cartographies proposed by authoritative critics. Only a few of the proposed divisions become hegemonies and gain the right to a secure social existence. Today we can challenge the usefulness of theoretical categories like *Entwicklungsroman* or the "greater Romantic lyric," but no one can realistically dispute the existence of sets called the "modern novel" or "modern poetry," because a web of expectations rooted in the unconscious of writers and readers, thousands of critical works, and school curricula make these *in re* universals substantially unassailable.

No matter what degree of consensus they enjoy, genres are held together by two different factors: *an objective similarity of style and subject matter among the texts that comprise them,* and *a web of concepts that allow readers to perceive the similarity between the works.* The kinship arises out of an interweaving between things and words, between a real continuity of forms and content, and a set of categories, terms, and habits thanks to which a group of readers ends up giving the same name to works that, if judged on the basis of other categories, terms, and habits, would seem very different from one another.[34] These two factors of proximity appear together in almost all cases, albeit in varying quantities. When we refer to the sonnet as a genre, for example, we are alluding to a metric scheme that is objectively present; when we talk about the novel in the singular, we are pointing to a similarity rooted primarily in

---

34. On the importance of names in constructing genres, see Alastair Fowler, *Kinds of Literature: An Introduction to the Theory of Genres and Modes* (Oxford: Clarendon, 1982).

common knowledge, which now uses an all-encompassing word to indicate any modern narrative of a certain length that is realistic or fantastic, plausible or implausible, invented or testimonial, in prose but also in verse. A good theory of genres should explain this double genealogical link: a unified interpretation of the novel, for example, should reveal the aspects common to Heliodorus's *Aethiopica,* Mme de La Fayette's *La Princesse de Clèves,* Samuel Richardson's *Pamela,* Lev Tolstoy's *War and Peace,* and Virginia Woolf's *To the Lighthouse.* But it should also reconstruct the system of concepts that allow us to grasp the affinities and pass over the differences, perhaps by explaining that many of the works that now converge in the cultural artifact today called novel, *roman, Roman, novela,* or *romanzo* have long borne the names of different genres and, precisely for this reason, were not perceived as parts of the same set.[35]

In Adorno's lecture "On Lyric Poetry and Society," to describe the idea of poetry as sedimented in the collective unconscious of modern readers, he appeals to "the specifically lyric spirit familiar to us" and to "our primary conception of the lyric"[36]—to a perception of affinity among texts that does not arise from the mechanical sum of traits shared by all modern lyric poetry but to a concept that is synthetic, selective, and fluctuating. When we talk about modern poetry in the singular, we allude to two parallel and distinct continuities: the first arises out of similarities between works in verse written during the last two centuries; the second, from the idea of poetry that the Romantic culture passed down to us, from the unconscious expectations with which we browse through poetry collections, or from the very notion of modern poetry.

This transformation of the horizon also entails a change in the schemas we use to think about these issues. It rarely happens that cultural historians define the nature of their objects of study; but it is almost inevitable that when they do talk about their subject as something cohesive (Romanticism, Postmodernism, the Novel), they are referring more or less consciously to a model of unity: an essence that unfolds in phenomena, a body that maintains its own identity in all its parts, a mental construction of the interpreter that

---

35. I wrote about this in Guido Mazzoni, *Teoria del romanzo* (2011); English translation, *Theory of the Novel,* trans. Zakiya Hanafi (Cambridge, MA: Harvard University Press, 2017), 60–64.

36. Adorno, "On Lyric Poetry and Society," 47.

gathers and classifies *a posteriori* a myriad of scattered events. If the essentialist model presupposes *ante rem* universals, and if the taxonomic model presupposes *post rem* universals, then the only mental schema that fits *in re* universals is historical and topographic.

Perhaps the entities that come closest to the objects in question are *in re* universals that we encounter every day: cities. Our collective imagination does not represent them as natural organisms or as the abstract constructions of a geographer but as miscellaneous groups of buildings held together by spatial proximity, by architectural affinities, and by a proper name. In this case, too, the impression of cohesiveness arises out of structures similar to those that come into play in the formation of genres: the continuity of certain objective components (architecture, urban planning, administration) and a web of expectations, words, and discourses that blur differences, intensify similarities, and create a norm. Paris is not just its objective stylistic cohesion: Paris is also its idea, its name, its image imprinted in the collective imagination and arising out of the fusion of real and phantasmatic elements. This city with its cohesive features is made even more cohesive by our perceptual habits, which distinguish between Parisian stylistic elements and non-Parisian ones, even in areas where the latter are more numerous or significant than the former. This is why the idea of Paris remains unified even though some quarters have little to do with the Gothic, with Louis XIV's architects, or with Georges Haussmann's renovations. And Boulevard Raspail, as described in a guidebook, remains a "typical Parisian boulevard" even though one of its most beautiful buildings, Jean Nouvel's Fondation Cartier, does not reflect the ideas we are used to associating with the city.

If *in re* universals reflect a continuity that is partly immanent to the *res* and partly to the idea, this happens in some measure because ideas do not only emphasize norms: they also have the power to produce them. Just as the planning regulations of historical centers require new buildings to adapt to a certain image of the city, in the same way the expectations disseminated among readers and institutions influence writers, who end up adapting their works to the praxis of genres or asserting their identity by disobeying an implicit norm, which they allude to in any case by rejecting it. Simply put, genres relate to a double persistency: real and imagined, inscribed in the form of texts and sedimented in the expectations of writers, critics, institutions, and readers. Immaterial elements are no less important than material ones in forming the image of the whole. Sometimes it is enough to change the name to alter the entire perception of something: Saint Petersburg, Peter, Petrograd, and Leningrad are not the same city. All the major urban agglomerations extend well beyond the administrative boundaries of individual cities, but the perception of spatial unity is disturbed by the awareness of the changing names. The universals of criticism work the same way. Consider, for example, how our idea of the genre to which Ariosto's *Orlando Furioso* belongs changes depending on the name we give it: a "chivalric poem," a "chivalric romance," and a "chivalric novel" are not the same thing. Or consider a critical category like "twentieth-century novel," which describes objective phenomena and flattens out inconsistencies—because if it is true that our horizon of expectations is accustomed to narrative styles that did not exist in the nineteenth century, it is also true that it would be difficult to exclude certain works with a nineteenth-century structure that were published in the twentieth century, such as Thomas Mann's *Buddenbrooks*, Giuseppe Tomasi di Lampedusa's *The Leopard*, or Vasily Grossman's *Life and Fate*. The recording of an objective change coexists therefore with a shared simplification, and the "twentieth-century novel" refers to an idea in addition to a set of subject matters and techniques.

Like any space, literary genres also have a center and a periphery. The center is occupied by works that the readers' horizon of expectations views as close to the hypothetical ideal type; the periphery, by texts that are made to fit into the genre even though they lie outside a presumed norm. Once again, the criterion that distinguishes the positions taken in the field is a complex and variable interweaving of quantity and symbolic weight, dissemination and hegemony. We speak of the "twentieth-century novel" because it is likely that the number of novels presenting a variety of innovations objectively increased during the early decades of the twentieth century, but also because innovative novels had such a profound impact that they changed the topography of the genre. After the notion penetrates into common knowledge, some works end up embodying it better than others: at the center of the "twentieth-century novel" we find *In Search of Lost Time*, *Ulysses*, *To the Lighthouse*, and *The Man Without Qualities*, while *Buddenbrooks*, *The Leopard*, and *Life and Fate* occupy the periphery. The spatial categories have no aesthetic value: a work can have an eminent place in the literary canon and occupy a peripheral position in the territory of the genre to which it belongs;

The Waste Land is one of the indispensable works of the twentieth century, but it does not embody the most common form of modern poetry, and it continues to be perceived as a canonic but experimental work.

Symbolic Forms

Having clarified the boundaries and nature of genres, there still remains the essential question: What do these enduring entities refer to? What do literary genres *mean*? If the forms of art tell the history of humanity better than do historical documents, then genres are the signs of a deep cultural continuity. To really grasp the implications of such an idea, we could use a concept that Panofsky picked up from Cassirer and, by rising above differences between works, used to illustrate the essence of perspective in paintings.[37] According to Panofsky, perspective would be a *symbolic form* in which "'spiritual meaning is attached to a concrete, material sign." Although very different from one another, the works that use this technique remain united by a stylistic trait that puts a certain vision into plastic form, that is, the idea that space is infinite, obeys geometric laws, and exists independently from human beings. The way Cassirer and Panofsky use the concept of symbolic form reworks a fundamental Hegelian principle of aesthetics: "the sensuous aspect of art is spiritualized, since the spirit appears in art as made sensuous."[38] Rethinking this same idea, Adorno will say that the forms of art are sedimented content, and precisely for this reason they tell the history of humanity.[39] If this is the case, complex aesthetic constructions like perspective or literary genres represent images of the world condensed into a plastic form and intended for a certain public. Their birth, death, and transformations signify the birth, death,

---

37. Ernst Cassirer, *Philosophie der symbolischen Formen* (1923–1929); English translation, *The Philosophy of Symbolic Forms*, trans. Ralph Manheim (New Haven, CT: Yale University Press, 1996); Erwin Panofsky, *Die Perspektive als "symbolische Form"* (1927); English translation, *Perspective as Symbolic Form*, trans. Christopher S. Wood (New York: Zone Books, 1991), 41. Franco Moretti used the concept of symbolic form to interpret a literary genre in *Il romanzo di formazione* (1986); English translation, *The Way of the World* (London: Verso, 1987) 3–14. Curtius had already done so, but without explicitly mentioning Cassirer (Curtius, *European Literature*, 390).

38. Georg Wilhelm Friedrich Hegel, *Vorlesungen über die Ästhetik*; English translation, *Aesthetics: Lectures of Fine Art*, vol. 1, trans. T. M. Knox (Oxford: Clarendon, 1988), 39.

39. Adorno, *Philosophy of New Music*, 32. See also Theodor W. Adorno, *Ästhetische Theorie* (1970); English translation, *Aesthetic Theory*, trans. Robert Hullot-Kentor (London: Continuum, 2002), 144–145.

and transformations of a vision of reality and the social groups that identify with it.

To further refine the theory of symbolic form, we can reflect on genres from another point of view, that of the writer. Cassirer's and Panofsky's category actually arises from the gaze of the critic, who judges literary history once the history has been concluded, whereas the writer is always *preceded* by genres, which give form to the domain of literature even before it has arrived, by organizing the perception of reality *a priori,* like mobile but preexisting scaffolding. If we call literary space the set of works to which it is reasonable to dedicate oneself in a certain epoch, then genres are the transcendental structures that order this space. Choosing one instead of another (composing sonnets or madrigals, writing a novel or a romance) means adopting an image of the world and life, a relationship with the past, a position in the social space, and a readership. Therefore, the historian perceives our universals as symbolic forms, the writer as *a prioris:* in both cases, from different points of view, genres crystallize the long duration in literature.

What Is Modern Poetry?

The symbolic forms of modern literature emerged during a metamorphosis that lasted many centuries and culminated in a period of sudden changes between the late eighteenth and early nineteenth centuries. During this time, the genres that ancient and classicist poetics considered the most prestigious—the epic and tragedy—died or entered a phase of pure survival and were symbolically replaced by the novel and the *drame bourgeois,* two absolutely modern forms that tell or stage in a serious and problematic way the stories of ordinary people and the conflicts of everyday life. During the same years, poetry also changed completely. Reading "Literary Designs" and thinking about Leopardi's place in the history of Italian literature, one cannot help but be startled by how the territory of writing in verse was transformed in a matter of decades. It is surprising, for example, that between 1819 and 1821 the greatest modern Italian poet was still thinking about dedicating himself to a didactic poem on the woods—a genre from the past with no future, completely inconceivable for the modern horizon of expectations. The same can be said about the short satiric poem in ottava rima *Paralipomeni della Batracomiomachia* (*The War of the Mice and the Crabs*), on which Leopardi began to work in 1831. Today, the function and significance of poetry are different from what the author of the *Canti* seems to give it in parts of his "Literary Designs" and *Paralipomeni*. During the century that separates Voltaire's last verses from Mallarmé's "Sonnet en -ix," that divides Thomas Gray from Emily Dickinson, Friedrich Gottlieb Klopstock from Stefan George, Juan Meléndez Valdés from Rubén Darío, and Giuseppe Parini's last *Odes* from Giovanni Pascoli's *Myricae*, the art of poetry became something different.

We can start to define this transformation by reflecting on the astonishment that Leopardi's projects inspire at a distance of two centuries. Why is it that our horizon of expectations, unconsciously tied to a certain image of genres, is disoriented by the idea that, shortly after composing "The Infinite," Leopardi was thinking of writing a didactic poem about the woods? What surprises us about this? In the first place, we are taken aback by the purpose that Leopardi assigns to poetry when he proposes to write a poem illustrating the usefulness of the woods, by retelling stories that European literature had accumulated over centuries on a topic so conventional and so full of the past; in the second place, by the type of writing that the theme seems to presuppose, that is, an ornamental versification devised to be superimposed on a preexisting content. If we examine in detail what has been crystallized in our surprise, we discover a series of stylistic features and expectations that we normally associate with poetry referred to as modern. But what do we mean by this?

Our intellectual object should not be imagined as an organism or essence but as a complex and inhomogeneous space. The name associates a formal element to a historical epoch: "poetry" means, in the first place, a discourse written in verse; the "modern" epoch of writing in verse is usually said to begin at different times, but they all fall between the Romantic period and that of the first twentieth-century avant-gardes. Modern poetry has also come to encompass works in prose distinguished by their autobiographical content or formal density: prose poems. Like all *in re* universals, our genre has a periphery and a center, the latter occupied by short- or medium-length compositions, for the most part in verse, which talk about personal themes in a considered personal style—texts that in recent centuries have been called *lyric*. Today, when we approach a shelf in a bookstore where poetry books are stacked, we expect to find books containing versified, generally short pieces that describe experiences or reflections, voiced subjectively, in a style far from the degree zero of everyday communication. On closer inspection, the project of writing a poem on the woods astonishes us precisely because it contravenes these expectations. It seems premodern to us that Leopardi wants to use verse to speak about a conventional theme that is remote from his lived experience, or that he wants to dress up a prosaic subject matter with the ornaments of metrics and rhetoric. For at least two centuries, didactic poetry has ceased to exist, except in experimental or parodic forms, such as in the work of Wystan Hugh Auden or Raymond Queneau; for some time now the idea of style that poets and readers of poetry go back to is no longer ornamental.

The crisis in verse narrative was less sudden but equally clear. Until the mid-nineteenth century it was thought quite obvious to use verses to embellish a story or an argument. Epic and didactic poetry were part of the system of genres commonly used in classicist literature of the eighteenth century. The pre-Romantic and Romantic culture reinvigorated the tradition of the narrative poem, reinventing the narrative ballad and transforming *The Works of Ossian* and Byron's poetry into cult works.[40] Between 1800 and 1860 French epic poetry had an extraordinary explosion in terms of quantity.[41] In the last half of the nineteenth century some of the major English poets and novelists, such as Robert Browning, Elizabeth Barrett Browning, William Morris, George Meredith, and George Eliot, dedicated themselves to composing long narrative works in verse. Between 1785 and 1858 many epic poems celebrated the birth and development of a new world power, the United States,[42] and epic was widely practiced from 1790 to 1910 in Britain by Romantic and Victorian poets.[43] One of William Butler Yeats's first works was a legend in verse, *The Wanderings of Oisin* (1889). Nevertheless, despite these signs of resistance, the overall prestige of long narrative compositions would decline inexorably over the course of the nineteenth century, during the same period when lyric achieved its hegemony over verse writing.

---

40. Jean-Louis Backès, *Le Poème narratif dans l'Europe romantique* (Paris: Puf, 2003).

41. William Calin, *A Muse for Heroes: Nine Centuries of the Epic in France* (Toronto: University of Toronto Press, 1983), 298.

42. John P. McWilliams, *The American Epic: Transforming a Genre, 1770–1860* (Cambridge: Cambridge University Press, 1989).

43. Herbert F. Tucker, *Epic: Britain's Heroic Muse, 1790–1910* (Oxford: Oxford University Press, 2008).

Today the predominance of short, subjective pieces is so clear that it has become established in the language. Not by chance, the set of texts we call "poetry" is held together by two dissimilar taxonomic criteria: "poetry" is any text written in verse, regardless of its content; but "poetry" is also any brief prose piece with a lyrical orientation, according to a linguistic usage that takes for granted an idea that is anything but self-evident, namely, that the distance between a novel in verse and a novel in prose is greater than the distance between an epic in verse and a collection of prose poems. This idea was inconceivable before the crisis of the classicist literary system destroyed didactic poetry, before the development of the modern novel made prose the natural medium for narrative, and before lyric achieved its hegemony over writings in verse. In certain critical traditions, then, the centrality of subjective poetry is considered so tautological that it creates antonomasias. This is demonstrated by the habit of using words like "prose" and "poetry" as synonyms of "narrative" and "lyric," or the habit of superimposing the concepts of "modern poetry" and "modern lyric," according to a usage that Hugo Friedrich has tried to legitimize in a book as well known as it is questionable.[44] This predominance is further confirmed, unintentionally, by the arguments of those who defend an alternative idea of modern poetry but end up giving their essays a characteristically polemical tone, as if they were writing against a hegemonic opinion whose supremacy they acknowledge by the very act of contesting it. When Charles Bernstein attacked poetry founded on the centrality of "Sovereign Human Self (SHS) as the sole origin of authentic expression and meaning"[45] or when Bob Perelman attacked texts made of "first-person meditations | where the meaning of life becomes | visible after 30 lines,"[46] or when Jean-Marie Gleize derides *"repoésie,"* the "re-poetry" of contemporary lyrics,[47] their alternative poetics takes the form of a challenge to a mainstream idea. For the same reason, it often happens that someone commenting on a text

44. Hugo Friedrich, *Die Struktur der modernen Lyrik* (1956); English translation, *The Structure of Modern Poetry: From the Mid-nineteenth to the Mid-twentieth Century,* translated by Joachim Neugroschel (Evanston, IL: Northwestern University Press, 1974). On the superimposition of "poetry" and "lyric," see Meyer H. Abrams, *The Mirror and the Lamp: Romantic Theory and the Critical Tradition* (1953) (New York: Oxford University Press, 1971), 84–88; Giuseppe Bernardelli, *Il testo lirico: Logica e forma di un tipo letterario* (Milan: Vita e Pensiero, 2002), viii; Virginia Jackson, *Dickinson's Misery: A Theory of Lyric Reading* (Princeton, NJ: Princeton University Press, 2005), 6–8; and Lucy Alford, *Forms of Poetic Attention* (New York: Columbia University Press, 2020), 8–11.

45. Charles Bernstein, "Recantorium," *Critical Inquiry* 35 (Winter 2009): 341–350.

46. Bob Perelman, "The Marginalization of Poetry," in Bob Perelman, *The Marginalization of Poetry: Language Writing and Literary History* (Princeton, NJ: Princeton University Press, 1996), 9.

47. Jean-Marie Gleize, *Sorties* (Paris: Questions théoriques, 2009), 57ff.

that falls outside the lyric form feels obliged to explain to readers what the genre is—for instance, when we read that Ezra Pound sought to re-create the modern epic poem, or that Auden rediscovered premodern didactic poetry—whereas it seems quite unnecessary for someone to be concerned about describing the nature of texts written by Eugenio Montale, Jorge Guillén, René Char, Elizabeth Bishop, or Ingeborg Bachmann.

But subjective poetry does not exhaust the entire spectrum of modern poetry: in fact, on the periphery of the genre we find two extended families of texts that cannot be called lyrical. On the one hand, there are texts referred to as "long poems" in English-language criticism, which sometimes go beyond the limits of subjective poetry by taking on narrative or essay-type topics and eschew the generally short, opaque, and egocentric form of the modern lyric to pursue a clearer, more transparent public diction. On the other hand, there are texts that have the pretension of eliminating all subjective or prosaic content to shift attention onto pure form, according to a project first formulated by Stéphane Mallarmé. Naturally, just as in cities, the boundary between center and periphery is hazy: a book like Pier Paolo Pasolini's *Le ceneri di Gramsci* (1957, *The Ashes of Gramsci*), for example, can be read either as an attempt to revive narrative in verse on social subjects or as a series of long egocentric, confessional monologs, since, as it turns out, it is both; Anne Carson's "The Glass Essay" (1995) is at the same time a reflection on love written in verse, an essay on Emily Brontë, and an autobiographical text; *Citizen: An American Lyric* (2014) by Claudia Rankine alternates personal experiences with essaylike reflections. But although the genre of poetry does not coincide with the lyric, and some of its most canonical works (Mallarmé's *Un coup de dés,* or T. S. Eliot's *The Waste Land,* or Pound's *The Cantos,* and so forth) lie outside the sphere of subjective poetry, the centrality of the lyric nevertheless remains unscathed.

Moreover, the texts of recent centuries seem to have exasperated the egocentrism immanent in subjective poetry, exhibiting to the public eye personal experiences that in other eras would have been judged uninteresting or unsuitable for a serious work. They are also put in a form that seems governed, at least on the surface, by something T. S. Eliot would have called "the individual talent": a subjective difference from the collective norm of tradition.[48]

---

48. Thomas Stearns Eliot, "Tradition and the Individual Talent (1919)," in *The Sacred Wood: Essays on Poetry and Criticism* (1920) (Mineola, NY: Dover Publications, 1998), 27–33.

In principle, a modern poet can express any thought and any private passion in such an individualistic form that he or she need never paraphrase, almost as if over the last two centuries the Romantic idea of the lyric as a genre in which the self, by expressing itself, aspires to tell the truth to everyone and to "attain universality through unrestrained individuation" had truly been achieved:

> The lyric work hopes to attain universality through unrestrained in-
> dividuation. . . . To say that the concept of lyric poetry that is is in
> some sense second nature to us is a completely modern one is only
> to express this insight into the social nature of the lyric in different
> form. . . . I know that I exaggerate in saying this, that you could ad-
> duce many counterexamples. . . . But the manifestations in earlier pe-
> riods of the specifically lyric spirit familiar to us are only isolated
> flashes, just as the backgrounds in older painting occasionally antici-
> pate the idea of landscape painting. They do not establish it as a form.
> The great poets of the distant past—Pindar and Alcaeus, for instance,
> but the greater part of Walther von der Vogelweide's work as well—
> whom literary history classifies as lyric poets are uncommonly far
> from our primary conception of the lyric.[49]

This book proposes a unified reading of modern poetry in the Western tradition. It takes a comparative point of view but, inevitably, more space will be given to the national literatures I know best. This asymmetry has no explanation other than my limits. Comparative literature is faced today with an insurmountable task: the opening of horizons, the multiplication of data and research, the skepticism that our epoch nourishes toward master narratives, and the power relations between national literatures and languages[50] have made it impossible to take everything into account or to simplify unproblematically, as early twentieth-century literary theory did. In my opinion, this objective difficulty cannot be side-stepped by writing a grand encyclopedic treatise arranged to give every single thing some minimal diplomatic representation. Such a treatise would probably be an artificial work of

---

49. Adorno, "On Lyric Poetry and Society," 38 and 40.

50. On the power relations between national languages and literatures and their effects on the discipline of comparative literature, see Casanova, *The World Republic of Letters*, chap. 1, especially 17–21, and Gayatri Chakravorty Spivak, *Death of a Discipline* (New York: Columbia University Press, 2003), 9–15.

compilation, which makes little sense to write. It seems more reasonable to accept the inevitable partiality of all points of view, starting from the things we know, and to write an essay in the original sense of the word—a text that preserves the author's traces and particularity but seeks to transcend them as much as possible by broadening the gaze and entrusting the resulting work to the judgment of readers from other histories and traditions. They are the ones who will say if the essay speaks to them too.

I start by reconstructing the genesis of the modern conception of poetry: the idea that writing in verse during recent centuries is different from verse in the premodern period, that it has the genre of the lyric at its center, and that the lyric is what we understand today by this word. I start from concepts and not works, because in this case words change before things do. Although Western poetry experienced its most conspicuous metamorphosis between 1850 and the age of the historical avant-gardes, the modern conception of poetry began to emerge in the late sixteenth century and became prevalent between the late eighteenth and early nineteenth centuries. In the second chapter, I illustrate the novelties of modern poetry using as an example a text that many consider to be the first modern poem in Italian literature: Leopardi's "The Infinite." The third chapter is dedicated to the history of forms. In the fourth chapter, I construct a sort of map of the currents and tendencies that intersect and collide to make up the modern poetic space. In the final chapter, I reflect on the sedimented content of modern poetry as a symbolic form: what it means, what image of the world it transmits to us, what it allows us to understand, and what value it has for us today.

CHAPTER ONE

A History of Concepts

Lyric and Poetry in Modern Genre Theory

Between roughly 1550 and 1800, the concept of poetry underwent a profound metamorphosis, comparable in intensity to the transformation in the writing of poetry that took place between the time of Charles Baudelaire and the time of the historical avant-gardes. This change represents both the beginning of modern poetry and the necessary conditions for poetry's entrance into the modern epoch of its history. Five centuries ago, the ideas many people use today to describe this genre were literally inexpressible. Three centuries ago, they were endorsed by only a minority of specialist readers, starting with the most significant one: that poetry corresponds for the most part with the lyric, viewed as a genre in which a first person speaks about itself in a style intended to be personal. This conflation of attributes, a foregone conclusion in the eyes of many today, rests cn assumptions that are anything but to be taken for granted. The most important is a notion of the lyric that differs from the etymological meaning of the word.

In ancient culture, the lyric was a poem sung to the sound of a lyre. By metonymy, it was a poem intended to be read silently but whose subject matters and meters drew on the tradition of poetry accompanied by string instruments. In our culture, the lyric is one of the three major theoretical families into which literature is divided. It groups together texts in which a first-person speaker expresses content considered to be personal: individual passions, states of mind, reflections. This modern concept has an origin and a history: it is actually contemporary to the division of literature into three theoretical groupings that emerged around 1550 and became established between approximately 1750 and 1850. In only a few decades, it replaced the divisions that came into existence in classical antiquity but were still alive in eighteenth-century classicism, and it spread throughout Europe in countless variants that had different nuances but were similar in substance. The systematic version of this schema can be read in Hegel's *Aesthetics*. Literature is composed of three major genres: epic (or narrative), lyric, and drama. Epic "presents what is itself *objective* in its objectivity"; lyric gives voice to "the subject, the inner world, the mind that considers and feels, that instead of proceeding to action, remains alone with itself as inwardness, and that therefore can take as its sole form and final aim the self-expression (*das Sichaussprechen*) of the subjective life"; drama unites the characteristics of epic and lyric "into a new whole in which we see in front of us both an objective development and also its origin in the hearts of individuals."[1]

This three-part schema has become common knowledge. You understand this when you look at the categories found in twentieth-century criticism, categories coming out of critical writings as well as those crystallized in institutions.[2] Histories of literature organized by genre are often divided into three groupings: narrative, poetry, and theater, sometimes with the addition of a fourth, which collects forms that lie outside the literature of invention in its narrowest sense, what for some time has been referred to as nonfiction. In the public stacks of the largest library in the European Union, the Bibliothèque Nationale de France in Paris, literary criticism is divided into writings on poetry, the novel, and theater; on the shelves of many mainstream bookstores, the only theoretical genre that deserves to be broken down into subgenres is narrative, whereas writings in verse and for the stage are normally stacked on small shelves under signs saying "poetry" and "theater." In all these cases, the archetype to which these taxonomies refer unconsciously is the Romantic theory of literary genres. In lyric, an *I* speaks to itself in the first person, focusing the reader's interest not on the objective interest of the

---

1. Georg Wilhelm Friedrich Hegel, *Vorlesungen über die Ästhetik;* English translation, *Aesthetics: Lectures on Fine Art,* vol. 2, trans. T. M. Knox (Oxford: Clarendon, 1988), 1116.

2. See Gérard Genette, *Introduction à l'architexte* (1979); English translation, *The Architext: An Introduction,* trans. Jane E. Lewin (Berkeley: University of California Press, 1992).

experiences described but on the way of describing them and on the significance that these experiences have for the speaker. In drama, many first-person
voices speak and act within the public space of the stage. In narrative, the
narrator's persona recounts the words, thoughts, and actions of a number
of characters, or its own as a character, focusing the reader's attention on
the intrinsic interest of the things recounted rather than on the way they are
told. This schema does not change for a story told in the first person, because
there is usually a logical and chronological distance between the narrating *I*
and the narrated *I,* a distance comparable to that separating the narrator and
the hero in a third-person story. Obviously, as Goethe points out, theoretical
categories do not coincide perfectly with historical genres or real works:

> These three modes of poetry can work together or separately. They
> can often be found jointly even in the shortest poem, and precisely
> through this compression into the smallest space they engender the
> most admirable creations, as we can notice clearly in the ballads of
> all nations. In early Greek tragedy we see all three of them united
> as equals, and only after a certain period of time do they separate.
> So long as the chorus plays the primary role, lyricism ranks at the
> top. When the chorus becomes more of a spectator, the other two
> become more prominent. Finally, when the action is reduced to
> personal and domestic life, the chorus is felt to be unwieldy and
> burdensome.[3]

Following Goethe's reasoning, we might say that *The Cantos* by Pound, *Le
ceneri di Gramsci* by Pasolini, and "The Glass Essay" by Carson mix lyrical
and narrative elements, that Bertolt Brecht's theater superimposes epic forms
on top of dramatic forms, and that first-person novels based on style cast a
lyrical patina over the epic subject matter of the story. Although theoretical
categories do not correspond to historical genres, there do exist empirical
forms that almost match the ideal archetype: ones that are almost entirely
narrative, dramatic, or lyrical, as Goethe viewed the "purely epic" poetry of

---

3. Johann Wolfgang von Goethe, *West-östlicher Divan* (1819); English translation, *West-East Divan: The Poems, with "Notes and Essays": Goethe's Intercultural Dialogues,* trans. Martin Bidney and Peter Anton von Arnim (Albany: State University of New York Press, 2010), 227.

Homer.[4] A Greek *epos* is almost always narrative: the interest falls on the doings of the heroes and not on the bard's style, which transcends the personal; a fully dramatic text for the theater is one that succeeds in creating a perfect mimetic illusion according to the convention of the fourth wall; a lyric poem is one in which a first person speaks about itself in a strongly distinctive style.

Some consider this division to be immanent to the logic of literature, in part, perhaps, because this theory of the three genres appears to have deep linguistic roots. These are the same roots from which the system of personal pronouns arose, following the tripartite schema of *I-you-he / her / it* in every language, almost as if it mirrored the elementary anthropological structures of identity and otherness.[5] We find the same patterns again in the three major groupings of lyric, drama, and narrative, oriented respectively toward the first, second, and third persons.[6] The history of literature shows us instead that the modern triad actually has a specific genealogy: it did not exist before the Romantic age, and even when it began to exist in embryonic form, it had a minor status compared to another way of dividing up the literary space. This latter way was much more ancient, much more illustrious, and utterly impossible to reconcile with the genre of the lyric.[7]

---

4. Ibid.

5. Émile Benveniste, "La nature des pronoms (1956)"; English translation, "The Nature of Pronouns," in *Problems in General Linguistics*, trans. Mary Elizabeth Meek (Coral Gables, FL: University of Miami Press, 1971), 217–222.

6. See Peter Szondi, "Von der normativen zur spekulativen Gattungspoetik," in *Poetik und Geschichtsphilosophie II* (Frankfurt am Main: Suhrkamp, 1974), 7–183; Genette, *The Architext*, 39–49; Karl Viëtor, "L'Histoire des genres littéraires" (1931); French translation in Gérard Genette, Hans Robert Jauss, Jean-Marie Schaeffer, Robert Scholes, Wolf-Dieter Stempel, and Karl Viëtor, *Théorie des genres* (Paris: Seuil, 1986), 9–36; and William Elford Rogers, *The Three Genres and the Interpretation of Lyric* (Princeton, NJ: Princeton University Press, 1983), 53ff.

7. Irene Behrens, *Die Lehre von der Einteilung der Dichtkunst vornehmlich vom 16. bis 19. Jahrhundert: Studien zur Geschichte der poetischen Gattungen* (Halle / Saale: Niemeyer, 1940); Benedetto Croce, "La teoria della poesia lirica nella poetica del Cinquecento," in *Poeti e scrittori del pieno e del tardo Rinascimento* (1945), vol. 2 (Bari: Laterza, 1958), 108–117; Mario Fubini, "Genesi e storia dei generi letterari (1948–1951)," in *Critica e poesia* (Bari: Laterza, 1956), 143–274; Claudio Guillén, *Literature as System* (Princeton, NJ: Princeton University Press, 1971), 375–419; Teresa Michałowska, "The Notion of Lyrics and the Category of Genre in Ancient and Later Theory of Poetry," *Zagadnienia Rodzajów Literackich* 15, no. 1 (1972): 47–69; Antonio García Berrio, *Formación de la teoría literaria moderna: La tópica horaciana en Europa* (Madrid: Cupsa Editorial, 1977), 94–109; Genette, *The Architexte*; Walter Ralph Johnson, *The Idea of Lyric: Lyric Modes in Ancient and Modern Poetry* (Berkeley: University of California Press, 1982); Gustavo Guerrero, *Teorías de la lírica* (1998), French translation, *Poétique et poésie lyrique*, trans. Anne-Joëlle Stéphan and Gustavo Guerrero (Paris: Seuil, 2000); Giuseppe Bernardelli, *Il testo lirico: Logica e forma di un tipo letterario* (Milan: Vita e Pensiero, 2002); Jonathan Culler, *Theory of the Lyric* (Cambridge, MA: Harvard University Press, 2015), chaps. 2 and 3.

Lyric and Poetry in Ancient Poetics

There are three theoretical genres in the fundamental texts of ancient poetics too—Plato's *Republic* and Aristotle's *Poetics*—but the distinguishing criterion they use is completely different from the one employed by the Romantics. According to Plato, everything said by poets or storytellers is a story, and the story can be told using simple narrative (*aple diegesis*), imitation (*mimesis*), or both together. In pure narrative, poets speak in the first person; in the imitative form, they reproduce the characters' speeches; and in the mixed form, they alternate between their own speech and the speeches of the characters.[8] Tragedy and comedy are imitative, because the speeches are made directly by the characters without any mediation on the part of the narrator. Epic poetry is instead a mixed genre, because the narrator's speeches alternate with those of the characters. Only dithyrambs are pure story:

> One kind of poetry and story-telling employs only imitation— tragedy and comedy. . . . Another kind employs only narration by the poet himself—you find this most of all in dithyrambs. A third kind uses both—as in epic poetry and many other places.[9]

Thought on genres becomes more complex in Aristotle's *Poetics*, because he brings variables into play that Plato had not considered. Seeing that art is mimesis, there are three criteria for classifying works: the *media* used to imitate, the *objects* imitated, and the *mode* or manner of imitation.[10] The first distinguishes poetry from music and painting, and imitation in verse from imitation in prose; the second organizes works by subject matter, since imitators can represent the actions of people who are better than us, just like us, or worse than us; the third separates dramatic works from narrative and mixed works, because the poet can imitate by speaking directly, by giving voice to the characters, or by alternating the two techniques.[11] Aristotle basically picks up on Plato's groupings, divides the space of literary imitation into two big

---

8. Plato, *Republic*, 3.392d; English translation by G. M. A. Grube, rev. C. D. C. Reeve (Indianapolis: Hackett, 1992).

9. Plato, *Republic*, 3.394b–c.

10. Aristotle, *Poetics*, 1.1447a, 3.1448a.

11. Ibid., 3.1448a.19–23.

theoretical genres, and leaves a third possibility in the middle, which arises out of the intersection of the two ideal types. Both authors classify poetic works by looking at a formal difference, on the basis of a very simple question that can be answered only with objective responses: "Who is speaking in the text?" There are only three possible cases: either the narrator speaks alone, the characters speak alone, or both the narrator and the characters speak. The crucial difference seems to lie in how much imitative capacity each kind has: dramatic poetry has the most mimetic power, because it allows the characters to speak and act without mediation; the purely diegetic forms have the least, because they represent reality through the narrator's mediation; and the mixed kinds, which alternate the previous two, stand somewhere in between. Since public life and theater have the same nature—both consist of actions and speeches—stage art is able to arrive at a pure illusion of reality, whereas diegesis is forced to translate the characters' speeches and actions out of the original medium and into another, allowing the narrator's speech to intervene.

This schema, widely predominant in the poetics of antiquity[12] and the culture of the Latin Middle Ages,[13] precludes any concept of the lyric as we understand it now, after Romanticism. As a matter of fact, if we accept the mode of speech as the only distinctive feature, then epic and lyric poetry are virtually indistinguishable. Indeed, Plato's examples of pure narrative include a passage from the *Iliad* and dithyrambs,[14] while Diomedes, who reworked Plato's concepts more than seven centuries later, cites Lucretius's *De rerum natura* as an example of perfect diegesis and the poetry of Archilochus and Horace as examples of the mixed genre.[15] This wavering is justified, because if we look at the bare structure of the discourse—if we stick to the question "who is speaking?"—lyric and narrative as we understand them today are bound to be confused, since both in dithyrambs and in *De rerum natura* only a single voice speaks.

And yet modern literary perception picks up on a difference, one so deeply seated that it is difficult to define. It is a difference in content, but less obvious

---

12. See Hans Färber, *Die Lyrik in der Kunsttheorie der Antike* (Munich: Neuer Filser, 1936), 3ff.; Behrens, *Die Lehre von der Einteilung der Dichtkunst*, 17–32.

13. See Behrens, *Die Lehre von der Einteilung der Dichtkunst*, 33ff.; Ernst Robert Curtius, *Europäische Literatur und lateinisches Mittelalter* (Bern: Francke, 1948); English translation, *European Literature and the Latin Middle Ages*, trans. Willard R. Trask (Princeton, NJ: Princeton University Press, 2013), 438–443.

14. *Republic*, 3.394b–c, 3.392e–3.393b.

15. Diomedes, *Ars grammatica*, 3, *De poematibus* (1.482, 14ff. Keil).

than how it appears at first glance. Clearly, the story Virgil tells in the *Aeneid* is not autobiographical, and when Horace addresses Maecenas in the *Odes* he does so to talk about himself. But equally clearly, there are many examples of autobiographical poetry that take a narrative slant. The distinction seems to reside less in the choice of subject matter than in the intention of the speech: the voice in the *Aeneid*, we might say, is intended to raise interest in an event outside the speaker, whereas the voice in the *Odes* seeks to focus attention on a personal experience. In other words, narrative "presents what is itself *objective* in its objectivity," whereas lyric expresses "the inner world, the mind that considers and feels."[16] This reasoning is asymmetrical, though: the difference between epic and drama is irrefutable and rooted in the structure of the discourse, but the same can hardly be said for the difference between epic and lyric. The genre system from the Romantic and modern periods superimposes two different variables: in tracing out the boundary between dramatic and nondramatic texts it uses formal criteria inherent in the structure of discourse and implicit in the question "who is speaking?"; but in distinguishing between lyric and narrative, it follows a distinction based more on the content than on the form of the speech. For the core meaning of certain poems to be important to us, we must believe, first of all, that it does not lie in the story being told per se but in the relationship between the content and the inner life of the literary persona who says *I* in the text. The lyric is therefore a genre in which the narration of events about a first person (anecdotes, passions, thoughts, spontaneous reflections) is combined with a style constructed to focus attention on the speaker that expresses itself in the text. It is a genre in which a first person talks about itself in a personal way, so that the "core" of the work is not "the occurrence itself but the state of mind which is mirrored in it."[17] For modern aesthetics and for our reading habits, "autobiography," "self-expression," and "subjectivity" are everyday ideas. For ancient poetics, which revolved around the idea that poetry was a *mimesis* of actions performed according to a certain collective ritual, the speech of someone who narrates "what is itself *objective* in its objectivity"[18] and the speech of someone who talks about the external world but in reality wants to give voice to his or her inner world are practically

---

16. Hegel, *Aesthetics*, vol. 2, 1116.
17. Ibid.
18. Ibid., vol. 2, 1037.

indistinguishable. Indeed, ancient Greek and Latin culture had no knowledge of the modern notion of lyric poetry.

Alexandrian, Latin, and Medieval Categories

The word *lyrikoi* appears in Alexandrian times, between the third and second centuries BCE, to refer to the nine poets who make up the canon of ancient lyric poets: Alcman, Sappho, Alcaeus, Stesichorus, Ibycus, Anacreon, Simonides, Pindar, and Bacchylides. Initially used to define the authors of the corpus of works called *melike poiesis,* after the canon of the nine was established the term gradually replaced the more ancient *melopoios.* From the first century BCE on, the work of the *lyrikoi* began to be called *lyrike poiesis,* "poetry sung to the sound of the lyre."[19] Although the ancient poets never named their genre, Plato's dialogs contain many references to the *melopoioi* and to the class of texts called *melon poiesis,* or more often *melos* and *mele.*[20] In a passage of his *Laws,* we find a list of lyric subgenres: hymns, paeans, *threnoi,* dithyrambs, *nomoi.*[21] From the terms used, we understand that the feature shared by *melos* is an association with music, song, and dance; and that the division into subgenres follows very different boundaries from the current ones in our modern aesthetic vocabulary, seeing that they refer to public, social, and objective distinctions: the purpose of the discourse, the divinity to which the text was dedicated, the meter, the choreography, the dialect, and the type of music.[22]

The first to give a theoretical status to the ancient categories were the Hellenist grammarians and philologists of Alexandria, who established canons, consecrated models, and flattened out differences. A significant trace of this gigantic organizational effort has remained in a passage of Photios's *Bibliotheca* (855), which summarizes the taxonomies introduced in the *Chrestomathy* of Eutychius Proclus, a grammarian from the second century CE. Proclus, in his turn, refers to a more ancient theory, whose original source was

---

19. Färber, *Die Lyrik in der Kunsttheorie der Antike,* 11ff.; Rudolf Pfeiffer, *History of Classical Scholarship from the Beginnings to the End of the Hellenistic Age* (Oxford: Clarendon Press, 1968), 182–188.

20. Plato, *Gorgias,* 449d; *Republic,* 10.607a; *Laws,* 3.700a.

21. Plato, *Laws,* 3.700a–d; *Republic,* 3.392d.

22. See Färber, *Die Lyrik in der Kunsttheorie der Antike,* 4; Luigi Enrico Rossi, "I generi letterari e le loro leggi scritte e non scritte nelle letterature classiche," *Bulletin of the Institute of Classical Studies,* University of London 18 (1971), 74–75.

Didymus's treatise *Peri lyrikon poieton* (On Lyric Poets).[23] Taking up Plato's
and Aristotle's theoretical divisions, the *Chrestomathy* separates poetry into
diegetic (*diegematikon*) and imitative (*mimetikon*), placing theater types into
this latter group (tragedy, satiric drama, and comedy), and epic, iambic, elegiac, and melic poetry into the former. Within melic poetry, two families of
subgenres can be distinguished, sorted by subject matter: compositions dedicated to the gods and compositions dedicated to humans. Although this is a
uniform category, the poet's subjectivity is certainly not what holds it together: for Proclus, melic, iambic, and elegiac poetry are in any case three
different modes, based on the same distinction used in Hellenistic canons.

The work of the Alexandrian philologists, which was passed on to the
Latin, medieval, and Renaissance cultures, created a rigid separation between
poetic subgenres that, from Romanticism on, would become part of a single,
large, unified grouping. In time, other taxonomies would be added to the Alexandrian ones, but they would not change the structure of a system that remained in place until the second half of the eighteenth century. Today we see
no significant difference between letters in verse by John Donne, John Keats,
or Leopardi and their other subjective poetry: we perceive a fluctuation in
tone, in subgenre, but we do not view it as significant enough to shatter the
wider unity of the lyric genre understood in a broad, that is, modern sense.
Conversely, ancient poetics recognized no higher principle linking these texts,
which were almost always short and in verse, and in which a speaker expressed
content that today we would call private. In the literary system of antiquity, a
letter in verse and a lyric poem in the narrow sense are different types of compositions. While today we can interpret ancient Greek and Latin texts in light
of the modern concept of lyric and search for signs of self-expression in
the melic, elegiac, and iambic compositions of classical literature,[24] classical

---

23. See Proclus, *Chrestomathy*, fragment 11 Severyns (= Photios, *Bibliotheca*, 318b3–4).

24. See Odysseus Tsagarakis, *Self-Expression in Early Greek Lyric, Elegiac and Iambic Poetry* (Wiesbaden: Franz Steiner, 1977). The most interesting of these signs of self-expression involve lyric poetry in the narrow sense. In a well-known passage from *Ion*, in which Socrates explains poetic furor, the *melopoioi* are mentioned as inspired poets whose compositions are an example of *enthousiasmos* (533d–535a). Perhaps Plato was thinking of the ancient bond between lyric and religious ceremonies or of the transfiguring power of music and dance: the fact remains that the association between lyric poetry and the theory of furor runs throughout ancient poetics. It reappears in the way Horace describes the obsession of *lyricus vates*, and it becomes a *topos* of classicist poetics between the sixteenth and seventeenth centuries. There is no need to point out the asso- ciation between these commonplaces and the Romantic image of poets who lose themselves in the flow of passions, or the post-Romantic image of poets who, in allowing forces to speak through them, forget their

culture itself never arrived at the idea that a literary genre could hold to-gether on the basis of the subject's self-expression.[25]

Between the first century BCE and the first century CE, Latin literature gave new life to the forms of short poetry inherited from Greek culture, but the poetics remained faithful to the Hellenistic partitions:[26] Catullus, Tibullus, Horace, and Ovid organized their compositions to respect the divisions into subgenres. Without entering into the debate on Catullus's *Liber* (whether the collection was put together by him or assembled after his death), it is clear that its structure does not follow the story of a life or a love but, rather, an alternation of meters. Similarly, Horace's *Epodes, Odes, Satires,* and *Letters,* or Ovid's *Amores, Tristia,* and *Epistulae ex Ponto* belong to different genres. When it came to classifying texts, the differences in meter and subject matter counted for more than the identity of the authorial speaker.

At the end of the first century CE, in a representative, canonical work such as Quintilian's *Institutio oratoria* the architecture of literary forms was still identical to the Alexandrian system. In presenting literary genres to orators, Quintilian names epic, elegiac, and iambic poetry, lyric, satire, comedy, New Comedy, tragedy, history, oratory, and philosophy. He describes them as if they were separate forms, each with its own rules and models.[27] A passage from Tacitus's *Dialogus de oratoribus (A Dialogue on Oratory)* is helpful for un-derstanding how the different kinds of short poetry were perceived:

> For my part I hold all eloquence in its every variety something sa-cred and venerable, and I regard as preferable to all studies of other arts not merely your tragedian's buskin or the measures of heroic verse, but even the sweetness of the lyric ode, the lasciviousness of the elegy, the satire of the iambic, the wit of the epigram, and indeed any other form of eloquence.[28]

---

own identity and become the mouthpiece of an "other" language. In this regard, see Guerrero, *Poétique et poésie lyrique,* 24–26 and 49–50; and Bernardelli, *Il testo lirico,* 13–15.

25. See Paul Allen Miller, *Lyric Texts and Lyric Consciousness: The Birth of a Genre from Archaic Greece to Au-gustan Rome* (London: Routledge, 1994), 11–13.

26. See ibid.

27. Quintilian, *Institutio oratoria,* 10.1, 46–60.

28. Tacitus, *Dialogus de oratoribus,* 10.4; English translation, *A Dialogue on Oratory,* in *The Complete Works of Tacitus,* trans. Alfred John Church and William Jackson Brodribb (New York: Modern Library, 1942), 742.

Each kind corresponds to a specific attitude: lyric poetry is sweet, elegies are lascivious because they talk about love, iambic poets are sarcastic, and epigram writers are witty. In the first century CE, the idea that these subgenres might all be part of the same genre appears to be unthinkable.

A unified class of lyric poetry was missing from the taxonomies of the philologists and the philosophers. Moreover, the categories of the philologists were perfectly integrated with those of the philosophers: in his *Chrestomathy*, Proclus traces the swarm of small Hellenistic genres back to the large unifying schemas of Plato and Aristotle. This interweaving of differing but compatible criteria went on for a long time. We find it in a text that was crucial in transmitting the Platonic and Aristotelian taxonomy to medieval culture: Diomedes's *Ars grammatica*, written most likely in the second half of the fourth century. According to Diomedes, there are three major genres: the *genus activum* or *imitativum* (also called *dramaticon* or *mimeticon*), in which the poet allows the *dramatis personae* to speak in their own voices; the *genus enarrativum* or *enuntiativum* (*exegeticon* or *apangelticon*), in which only the poet talks; and the *genus commune* or *mixtum* (*koinon* or *mikton*), in which both the poet and the characters talk. The *genus imitativum* includes tragedies and comedies but also Virgil's first and ninth eclogues. The *genus enarrativum* includes book one, book three, and the first part of book four of Virgil's *Georgics*, and Lucretius's *De rerum natura*. There are two varieties of the *genus commune:* the *heroica species,* which includes the *Iliad* and the *Odyssey,* and the *lyrica species,* which includes the poetry of Archilochus and Horace.[29] Like Proclus, Diomedes also superimposes Plato's and Aristotle's theoretical frameworks onto the Alexandrian philological schema; and he too has no words for conceiving of something that approaches the idea of modern lyric poetry.

When the concepts of classical poetics diffused into medieval culture, they did so chaotically and in fragments. "The antique system of poetic genres had, in the millennium before Dante, disintegrated until it was unrecognizable and incomprehensible;"[30] medieval poetics and rhetoric used the classical groupings confusedly, making use of a mutable literary vocabulary.[31]

---

29. Diomedes, *Ars grammatica*, 3, *De poematibus* (1.482, 14ff. Keil).
30. Curtius, *European Literature and the Latin Middle Ages*, 358.
31. Paul Zumthor, *Essai de poétique médiévale* (Paris: Seuil, 1972), 157ff.

The Platonic and Aristotelian taxonomy managed to make it through the Middle Ages thanks to the mediation of Diomedes: the distinction between narrative, dramatic, and mixed forms appears in the Venerable Bede as well as in John of Garland.[32] The categories they commonly use to classify the poetry we today call lyric are based on meters (the ballad, sonnet, canzone) or subjects (the *aubade*, the *chanson d'ami*, the *chanson de croisade*)—categories that we are able to group into a logical typology only after the fact.[33] What remains unchanged with respect to the taxonomies of antiquity is the criterion used for classification, because medieval poetics and rhetoric also divide up writing in verse by examining variables that are public and objective (the topic, the kind of meter, the purpose of the discourse). As earlier in the Latin culture of the first century BCE, the renewal of lyric forms in the vernacular literatures of the Middle Ages did not give rise to a corresponding renewal in theoretical thought.

This disintegration continued long after Dante's time, for at least two centuries. If we look at the history of concepts, the rhetoric and poetics of the late Middle Ages and early Renaissance add little of substance to the ideas that European literature had inherited from classical antiquity.[34] The notion of lyric poetry remained tied to Horace, whom Petrarch, in one of his *Familiares*, crowns king of this genre,[35] and whose fame spread between the end of the fifteenth century and the beginning of the sixteenth century, thanks to the *edito princeps* of 1471–1472 and the Florentine edition of 1482, edited by Cristoforo Landino.[36] A coherent, philosophical, and innovative discussion would not resurge until the second half of the sixteenth century, when Francesco Robortello's commentary on Aristotle's *Poetics* (1548) ushered in a new age in the history of literary theory and discussion on poetic forms.

---

32. Behrens, *Die Lehre von der Einteilung der Dichtkunst*, 36–37, 53–57; Edgar de Bruyne, *Études d'esthétique médiévale* (Bruges: De Tempel, 1946), vol. 1, 156–157, vol. 2, 18ff.

33. See Pierre Bec, *La lyrique française au Moyen Âge (XIIe - XIIIe siècles): Contribution à une typologie des genres poétiques médiévaux* (Paris: Picard, 1977–1978), vol. 1, 35–39.

34. See Behrens, *Die Lehre von der Einteilung der Dichtkunst*.

35. Petrarch, *Familiares;* English translation, *Letters on Familiar Matters Vol. 3: Books XVII–XXIV*, trans. Aldo S. Bernardo (New York: Italica Press, 2005), 10, lines 1–2, 336.

36. See Guerrero, *Poétique et poésie lyrique*, 73ff.

The Renaissance Breakthrough

The integrated category of lyric poetry and the modern system of literary genres became established only around the mid-sixteenth century. The first writer to introduce them clearly was Antonio Minturno in his treatises *De poeta* (1559) and *L'arte poetica* (1563). Minturno proposes to divide what at the time was called poetry (and which, starting from the second half of the eighteenth century, would be called literature) into three major classes—*epic, scenic,* and *melic* (or *lyric*)—and to regard all other kinds as subgenres of these three main groups. The idea that compositions in verse on a subjective matter could belong to a large unified genre predated him by a few decades, but it had never been presented with such clarity.[37] In the second half of the sixteenth century, the idea quickly became a *topos:* it can be found in Giovan Battista Pigna's *Poetica horatiana* (1561), in "Lezioni intorno alla poesia" (Lectures on Poetry) by Angelo Segni (1573), in a lecture by Giulio Del Bene (1574), in a letter by Filippo Sassetti to Giovan Battista Strozzi (1574), and in *De poetica* by Giovanni Antonio Viperano (1579).[38] In 1594, Pomponio Torelli, a former pupil of Robortello, dedicated an entire treatise to lyric poetry and considered it a unified genre in which the odes of Pindar and Horace were able to coexist with Catullus's *Liber,* iambic poetry, and Petrarch's *Canzoniere.*[39] In 1599, forty years after Minturno's *De poeta,* this is how Alessandro Guarini summarized the system of literary genres that the Italian literary theorists of the late sixteenth century had created:

> There are three (leaving aside for now the other more subtle divisions, which have little relevance for our topic), as I was saying, three main kinds of poetry, to which all the others are reduced. Epic is one, Dramatic is another, which branches off into Tragic and Comic, and, finally, Lyric is the third, under which the ancient Greeks

---

37. See Behrens, *Die Lehre von der Einteilung der Dichtkunst,* 71ff. and 85ff.

38. See Bernard Weinberg, *A History of Literary Criticism in the Italian Renaissance* (Chicago: University of Chicago Press, 1961), vol. 1, 157–162, 209, 533–538, 541–542. Sassetti's letter was reported by Croce, "La teoria della poesia lirica nella poetica del Cinquecento," 109.

39. See Pomponio Torelli, *Trattato della poesia lirica* (1594), in *Trattati di poetica e retorica del Cinquecento,* ed. Bernard Weinberg (Bari: Laterza, 1974), vol. 4, 237–317, especially 263–266.

and Latins collected together Hymns, Encomiums, Elegies, Odes, Distiches, and Epigrams.[40]

The new category spread well beyond treatises on lyric poetry, as becomes evident when reading texts that take the tripartite division of literary genres for granted, only mentioning lyric poetry in passing. This occurs in Tasso's "Discorsi dell'arte poetica" ("Discourses on the Art of Poetry"), written in the early 1560s, and in one of the most important literary treatises of Renaissance culture, Lodovico Castelvetro's *Poetica d'Aristotele vulgarizzata e sposta* (1570, Aristotle's Poetics Translated in the Vulgar Language and Commented On). Tasso compares the style of the lyric poet to that of the heroic poet and the tragic poet;[41] Castelvetro first deduces an exceedingly complicated taxonomy of genres from Aristotle that leaves no place for lyric poetry, but he then observes that "generally speaking, we divide all poems into four parts: and under the first we place comedy, under the second, epic, under the third, tragedy, under the fourth, odes, epigrams, elegies, canzoni, and short poems of the like."[42]

Literary theory in the late sixteenth century is rigidly prescriptive: a text that fails to obey the rules is *ipso facto* considered imperfect and excluded from the canon; a genre that lacks precedents or legitimization is judged "minor poetry." Norms are inferred from the canonical texts of ancient poetics, especially Aristotle's *Poetics,* but also from Horace's letter on the art of poetry and, to a lesser extent, from Plato's *Republic.* Efforts are made to interpret Plato, Aristotle, and Horace as parts of a coherent system, blurring contradictions that appear blatant today.[43] Minturno's modern tripartite division arises out of a very liberal interpretation of an Aristotelian criterion, that is, his analysis of the means a poet uses to imitate. Epic poetry, writes Minturno,

---

40. Alessandro Guarini, "Lezione . . . sopra il sonetto 'Doglia, che vaga Donna . . .' di Monsignor Della Casa" (1599), in Giovanni Della Casa, *Opere,* vol. 1 (Venice: Angiolo Pasinello, 1728), 341.

41. Torquato Tasso, "Discorsi dell'arte poetica," in *Discorsi dell'arte poetica e del poema eroico,* ed. Luigi Poma (Bari: Laterza, 1964), 41ff.

42. Lodovico Castelvetro, *Poetica d'Aristotele vulgarizzata e sposta* (1570), ed. Werther Romani, vol. 1 (Bari: Laterza, 1978), 257.

43. Marvin T. Herrick, *The Fusion of Horatian and Aristotelian Literary Criticism, 1531–1555* (Urbana: University of Illinois Press, 1946). See also Weinberg, *A History of Literary Criticism in the Italian Renaissance,* chap. 4; Baxter Hathaway, *The Age of Criticism: The Late Renaissance in Italy* (Ithaca, NY: Cornell University Press, 1962); Antonio García Berrio, *Formación de la teoría literaria moderna;* Brigitte Kappl, *Die Poetik des Aristoteles in der Dichtungstheorie des Cinquecento* (Berlin: De Gruyter, 2006).

only requires speech, whereas scenic poetry uses theatrical representation, and lyric poetry uses speech accompanied by dance and song.[44] According to this schema, modern poetic forms like sonnets, ballads, canzoni, and madrigals represent the theoretical continuation of the ancient *melos* and are accordingly justified by the classic authorities.[45] The problem is that this reference to music did not take into account the concept of lyric poetry that Italian literati possessed in the mid-sixteenth century, when the majority of poems were written for silent reading, nor, most importantly, the work to which everyone looked to define the essence of this class of texts grouped together under the name of lyric poetry: Petrarch's *Canzoniere*.

Minturno mentions another characteristic shared by the texts collected under the name of melic or lyric, namely, the weight that the "affections of the soul"[46] have in these poems. This idea was well received and quickly became a commonplace, but it broke with some of the assumptions of classicist poetics. The canonical texts of ancient literary theory opposed three types of difficulties to the idea that lyric poetry gave voice to first-person affections. One is explicit: in a passage from Aristotle's *Poetics*, we read that whoever speaks in first person is not a true imitator: "the poet must speak as little as possible in his own name because otherwise he is not imitating."[47] In the second place, the literary system of antiquity insisted on differences, not similarities, between short poetic compositions: the ode, epigram, elegy, satire, iambic poetry, and epigram are different genres, and this made it difficult to think about the lyric as a unified genre. Finally, for Plato and Aristotle, the subject of mimesis is visible actions, acts that take place in the public space, not "affections of the soul." The sixth chapter of the *Poetics*, on tragedy, is quite clear on this point: the specific task of poetry is to represent what people do and say in the external world; true mimesis has as its object actions and not characters; the poet's purpose is to create a *mythos*, a plot, and not a static description of what we moderns would call the inner life. Why did the Italian theorists of the late sixteenth century, who were firm classicists and commentators of Aristotle, introduce a new and unprecedented system of genres by

---

44. Antonio Sebastiano Minturno, *De poeta* (Venice: F. Rampazetum, 1559), 27, and *L'arte poetica* (Venice: Giovanni Andrea Valvassori, 1564), 3.

45. Minturno, *L'arte poetica*, 169–170.

46. Ibid., 75.

47. Aristotle, *Poetics*, 14.1460a.7.

inventing a tripartite division of poetry into epic, lyric, and drama, conceiving of a large unified genre, and going against what was written in the theoretical works they admired?

The text that grasps and illustrates with lucidity the problem at the base of this tacit theoretical revolution is Segni's "Lezioni intorno alla poesia." The Florentine Academy regularly invited well-known men of letters to give lectures and during their series they were asked to comment on a few poems by Petrarch. Starting from the text of Canzone 127, "In quella parte ove Amor mi sprona" ("In that direction which love urges me"), Segni embarks on a reflection on the nature of poetry, recalling the principles of Aristotle and, above all, Plato. However, he soon finds himself up against a serious theoretical obstacle: in some passages of *Republic* and *Poetics* we read that "when a poet speaks in his own person, he is not an imitator"; in other words, authentic mimesis is irreconcilable with autobiographical discourse. If we took this as literally true, we would arrive at an untenable conclusion, namely, that Petrarch could not be a true poet:

> there would be many . . . from whom we would have to remove the title of poet held until now, and our Petrarch, the greatest to possess this name, would be chased out and driven from many, almost all parts, and would take refuge most wretchedly in a very cramped place, where on occasion he makes speak either Love or his lady's companions or certain birds he has caught and sent to be presented to I-don't-know-whom.[48]

Segni expertly grasps the problem that others also perceive but fail to express clearly. Italian literature written in the vernacular arose out of the unquestionable authority of Petrarch's *Canzoniere*, but the *Canzoniere* is hard put to stay inside the categories of poetics inherited from the ancients if these categories are interpreted literally. Petrarch's book contains texts that a literal interpretation of Plato and Aristotle would exclude from the roster of poetry and that had no precedents in ancient literature. The *Canzoniere* is not bound together by meter, because it uses different measures; it is not a simple collection of love poems, because it includes texts on political, moral, and

---

48. Angelo Segni," Lezioni intorno alla poesia," in *Trattati di poetica e retorica del Cinquecento* (Bari: Laterza, 1972), 21–22.

religious topics; it cannot be interpreted as a series of dramatic monologs spoken by a character or by a series of characters, because this is not the meaning of the work, as Segni states clearly. The core of the book and its unifying principle is the inner story of the character who says *I*.[49] There was the risk of a conflict between the theories and models inherited from the ancients and the cornerstone of Italian vernacular literature in the sixteenth century, the most canonic and imitated work of the time, which was changing the idea of subjective poetry in Europe thanks to the international success of Petrarchism.[50] Either Plato and Aristotle were wrong when they talked about the nature of poetry (and for a classicist of the time this was unacceptable) or Petrarch was not a true poet, because his work did not correspond to the idea of poetry established by the ancients (and this too was unacceptable).

The modern category of the lyric was born, therefore, as a compromise formation to resolve a conflict between *auctoritates* and canons. There had to be a way to reconcile two absolute models while staying faithful to the vocabulary of Plato, Aristotle, and Horace but diverging from some of their conclusions. If it had been a matter of a less important work, the Italian literati would certainly have expelled it from the canon, but Petrarch's authority was so unquestionable that it demanded a compromise, and that compromise was the invention of lyric poetry in the modern sense—as a unified genre at the same level as narrative and drama. This idea, completely foreign to Greek and Latin culture, owes its origin to the importance that Petrarch had in Italian vernacular literature.[51]

How could the *Canzoniere* be made to fit the rules? The first obstacle the ancients erected against the modern concept of lyric was easily surmounted: the passages in *Republic* and *Poetics* that deny the title of imitator to poets who speak in first person could simply be juxtaposed with other passages

49. See Marco Santagata, *Dal sonetto al canzoniere* (Padova: Liviana, 1989), 131ff., and *I frammenti dell'anima* (Bologna: Il Mulino, 1992).

50. See Croce, "La teoria della poesia lirica nella poetica del Cinquecento," 108; Hathaway, *The Age of Criticism*, 36–37; Giulio Ferroni, "La teoria della lirica. Difficoltà e tendenze," in *La 'Locuzione artificiosa': Teoria ed esperienza della lirica a Napoli nell'età del manierismo*, ed. Giulio Ferroni and Amedeo Quondam (Rome: Bulzoni, 1973), 13–32; Guerrero, *Poétique et poésie lyrique*, 101; Guglielmo Frezza, "Sul concetto di 'lirica' nelle teorie platoniche e aristoteliche del Cinquecento," *Lettere italiane* 53, no. 2 (2001): 278–294; and Bernardelli, *Il testo lirico*, 41 and 48–54.

51. Croce, "La teoria della poesia lirica nella poetica del Cinquecento," 111–112; Fubini, "Genesi e storia dei generi letterari," 159ff.

from the same texts that argue the opposite.[52] It was more difficult to counter the classical theory of genres, which is decidedly hostile to a work that allows different meters and subjects to coexist and whose overall unity is enforced purely by the unity of a first person that says *I*. The Renaissance men of letters tried to give completely new meanings to the ancient categories, almost to the point of distorting the evidence. When Guarini writes that the Greeks and Latins put hymns, encomiums, elegies, odes, distiches, and epigrams into the category of lyric poetry, he is unaware of the fact, or pretends not to know, that ancient poetics never included elegies and epigrams in the same class as the ode, which was the genre of lyric poetry in the strictest sense.[53] The third was the most difficult obstacle though. While it may have sufficed to appeal to the spirit of the theory to argue that one can imitate even while speaking in the first person, it was hardly so easy to reconcile the modern idea of the lyric with the theory of poetry as mimesis of actions, which was the architrave of the system of concepts inherited from Greek and Latin culture:

> This is where the doubt arises. Whether the Sonnet and other lyric compositions are worthy of the name of Poetry, and whether the Composer of lyrical things can rightly be called a Poet. Nor should our doubting appear strange to you, because it is a matter of men of letters, with solid reputations, who having made themselves the judges in this quarrel, have pronounced their judgments against lyric poets. First of all, then, it would seem that this could be denied, namely, that the composer of things lyrical deserves the name of Poet, because of two fundamentals, taken from Aristotle's doctrine in *Poetics*. The first is that every poem is a likeness (*rassomiglianza*), or imitation, we mean. The second, that a Poet is a poet because of the plot (*favola*). These principles have such force that anything that does not create a likeness and does not imitate will not be poetry, and

---

52. "Let them see what an opinion and judgment they attribute to Aristotle, and if it is worthy of him, but let them see rather that he cannot intend it in this way, because if poetry is imitation and if imitation is what has been said, that is, speaking in the person of others, then dithyrambs, which are not lyrical verses, will not be poetry because Plato says manifestly that in dithyrambs the poet does not speak in the person of others but always as himself; and nevertheless Aristotle establishes dithyrambs as one of the main kinds of poetry and consequently for imitation, but never speaking in the person of others." Segni, *Lezioni intorno alla poesia*, 22–23.

53. Guarini, "Lezione . . . sopra il sonetto 'Doglia, che vaga Donna . . .' di Monsignor Della Casa," 341.

anyone who is not a composer of plots will not be called a poet. . . .
Now, if imitation makes the poetry, and plot makes the poet, how
can lyrical composers and compositions be poetry and poets, since
poets do not fashion a plot, nor is imitation to be found in poetry?[54]

Although Aristotle's *Poetics* states clearly that poetry is mimesis by virtue
of what Guarini calls *favola,* Aristotle calls *mythos,* and moderns call "plot,"
lyric poems that narrate a plot are few and far between—hence the doubt
about whether the new genre is "worthy of the name of Poetry" and deserves
a place alongside epic and tragedy as a canonic and perfect form.

The most common way of getting around a literal interpretation of Aristotle was to argue that the narration of actions is the species of a broader
genre that encompasses the mimesis of affections, deeds, speeches, and things
of the senses.[55] Epic poetry, tragedy, and comedy would represent human actions, and lyric poetry their passions, but the mimetic logic would be the same
in each of the genres. Once this foothold is gained, it can be argued that the
narration of a passion is organized in the form of *mythos,* as Minturno, Segni,
Viperano, Torelli, and Guarini do.[56] Nevertheless, some lyric poems were so
devoid of plot that, for some, the idea of "imitation of the passions" was not
sufficient to reconcile the authority of the classics with that of Petrarch. To
truly respond to the objections it was necessary to change the concepts and
the words. This is what Tasso sought to do:[57]

if we want to find some part in the lyric that corresponds propor-
tionately to the plot in epics and tragedies, we cannot say there is anything apart from the concepts: because, just as affections and customs are based on plot, so the lyric is based on concepts.[58]

54. Ibid., 346–347.

55. See Hathaway, *The Age of Criticism,* 81–87; Frezza, "Sul concetto di 'lirica' nelle teorie platoniche e aristoteliche del Cinquecento," 281.

56. Minturno, *L'Arte poetica,* 175; Segni, *Lezioni intorno alla poesia,* 35; Giovanni Antonio Viperano, *De poetica
libri tres* (Antwerp: Christophori Plantini, 1579), 149; Torelli, *Trattato della poesia lirica,* 265; Guarini, "Lezione . . .
sopra il sonetto 'Doglia, che vaga Donna . . .' di Monsignor Della Casa," 347–349.

57. See Hathaway, *The Age of Criticism,* 15, 35, 43–45, 84–88; Frezza, "Sul concetto di 'lirica' nelle teorie platoniche e aristoteliche del Cinquecento," 285–287.

58. Tasso, "Discorsi dell'arte poetica," 49.

For Tasso, the prime mover of the lyric is not the plot (*favola*) but the concepts (*concetti*), by which he means matters of the inner life.[59] A few years before Tasso, Giulio Cesare Scaligero had also defended a similar theory. In his opinion,

> There are many kinds of odes and poems . . . lyrical, melic, paeans, elegies, epigrams, satires, *silvae,* epithalamiums, hymns, and others— in which there is no *imitatio* but just the bare narration (*enarratio*) or explanation (*explicatio*) of those affections that come from the mind (*ingenium*) itself of the person who sings, and not from the poetic character who is represented.[60]

Filippo Sassetti also arrives at a similar conclusion in a letter he wrote in reply to Giovan Battista Strozzi. Strozzi had given a lecture at the Florentine Academy on the genre in which he excelled, the madrigal. He wanted to find titles of nobility for a poetic form that court audiences enjoyed but which orthodox classicists regarded as minor. Sassetti provides Strozzi with new arguments, following an original line of thought that was destined to become a *topos*. First of all, he considers the madrigal to be a wider species than the genre of lyric. Then, he criticizes the opinion of those who, when interpreting subjective poems according to the logic of mimesis, try to read them as stories or dramatic representations and consequently end up confusing particular cases with universal law. Madrigals do not imitate any discourse or action but, rather, present "the concepts of the person who composes them":

> [For some] it is enough that some madrigals imitate human actions and are dramatic and dramatized, but I reckon that they make up a small number. Consequently, saying that madrigals are an imitation of action would make as much sense as saying that wintertime is hot, just because there was nice weather one day. Now, if for this reason we cannot call them an imitation of actions—because for the most part they contain the concepts (*concetti*) of the person who composes them, sparked by matters of love or whatever other reason,

---

59. See Guerrero, *Poétique et poésie lyrique,* 177–183.

60. Giulio Cesare Scaligero, *Poetices libri septem* ([Lugduni]: Antonium Vincentium, 1561), book 7, 347.

or a description of a time and a land, which are also concepts we have in our mind of that thing—let us see if we can call them an imitation of concepts, which is what our imagination is.[61]

But even the expression "imitation of concepts" was not entirely convincing. The idea of imitation, writes Sassetti, presupposes a prior content to which the poet's speech must adapt, while in the case of the lyric, this model does not exist—or, rather, it exists in the way that someone who writes or speaks about philosophy puts the concepts they have in their mind onto paper. Under such circumstances, Sassetti would not speak of imitation but of expression:

> But saying what is true in this manner is to express the concepts of the mind and not to imitate them: . . . I would resolve this Platonic imitation in the peripatetic meaning or expression.[62]

Whereas epic and dramatic poets represent an external event that exists before the representation, like an object that stands before a painter, the lyric poet expresses a content that is entirely within. The reflections of Scaligero, Tasso, and Sassetti contain the first traces of an idea that would become central in the Romantic age.

Classicist Resistance and National Differences

Between the end of the sixteenth and the beginning of the eighteenth centuries, the division of poetry into epic, lyric, and dramatic spread throughout all the major European literatures. It was reintroduced, among others, by John Milton in his treatise *Of Education* (1644), by John Dryden in his *Essay of Dramatic Poesy* (1668), by Giovanni Mario Crescimbeni in his *Istoria della volgar poesia* (1698, History of Vernacular Poetry), by Gian Vincenzo Gravina in his *Della ragion poetica* (1708, On Poetical Reason), by Antoine Houdar de La Motte in his *Réflexions sur la critique* (1716, Reflections on Criticism), and by

---

61. Filippo Sassetti, *Lettere edite e inedite,* ed. Ettore Marcucci (Florence: Le Monnier, 1855), 65.
62. Ibid., 66–67.

Alexander Baumgarten in his *Meditationes philosophicae de nonnullis ad poema pertinentibus* (1735, *Reflections on Poetry*). This theory of lyric poetry as the expression of concepts was taken up and expanded by Francisco Cascales in his *Tablas poéticas* (1617, Poetic Tables) and in *Cartas filológicas* (1634, Philological Letters).[63] Nevertheless, the modern triad never entered common usage and for almost two centuries continued to clash with the more widespread and considerably more authoritative taxonomies of antiquity, which denied lyric the rank of major theoretical genre and continued to segment it into subgenres based on meter and subject matter. The only composition with undisputed prestige in this congeries of scattered forms, the only one considered worthy of being called lyric, was the Pindaric and Horatian ode. The other subgenres were treated separately, relegated to the lower ranks of the literary hierarchy and viewed as minor poetry.[64]

The national culture of the interpreter also influenced which system predominated. Italians, for example, were inclined to put the lyric at the same level as the *epos,* tragedy, and comedy, whereas the French tended to separate the ode off from the other forms, which they grouped together under the vaguely disdainful category of *petite poésie.*[65] At the beginning of the eighteenth century, Eustachio Manfredi, a professor of mathematics at the University of Bologna, member of the Accademia della Crusca, and an Arcadian, lucidly formulated the terms of the problem in a letter to Marquis Giovan Gioseffo Orsi, author of *Considerazioni sopra un famoso Libro Franzese intitolato: La Manière de bien penser dans les ouvrages d'esprit* (1703, Considerations on a Famous French Book Titled: How to Think Clearly in Works of the Mind). The book was written to rebut Dominique Bouhours's thesis that the only modern authors capable of rivaling the ancients were French.[66] Orsi's *Considerazioni* sparked an enormous controversy; its traces remained in the second edition of the work (1706), which collected letters sent to Orsi from several authoritative readers, including Eustachio Manfredi. Bouhours shows that he

63. Behrens, *Die Lehre von der Einteilung der Dichtkunst,* 125–127, 158–160, 165–167; Genette, *The Architexte,* 28.

64. Behrens, *Die Lehre von der Einteilung der Dichtkunst,* 134ff. and 206ff.; Meyer H. Abrams, *The Mirror and the Lamp: Romantic Theory and the Critical Tradition* (1953) (New York: Oxford University Press, 1971), 84–88; Genette, *The Architexte,* 28–31.

65. See Behrens, *Die Lehre von der Einteilung der Dichtkunst,* 134–147; René Bray, *La Formation de la doctrine classique en France* (Paris: Nizet, 1945), 350–354.

66. See Dominique Bouhours, *La Manière de bien penser dans les ouvrages d'esprit* (Paris: Veuve de Sébastien Mabre-Cramoisy, 1687).

does not know true Italian poetry, writes Manfredi: he gets steamed up about a group of minor poets but fails to cite Petrarch.[67] Bouhours's attitude is actually typical, Manfredi continues: much of the French aversion to Italian poetry comes from the fact that literature beyond the Alps does not have an illustrious tradition of "serious lyrical compositions" (for Manfredi, Pierre de Ronsard is nothing but an imitator of Petrarch and Pietro Bembo).[68] It associates short poems with the comic-playful register; and it does not understand the greatness of serious lyric poetry written in the vernacular.[69] Italians, on the other hand, excel in lyrical love poems and heroic poems written in the high style, thanks to Petrarch and Gabriello Chiabrera, whereas the French language is better suited to the *petite poésie* of madrigals, canzonets, and epigrams.[70] Manfredi understood that some judgments depend on the role of the literary genres in their respective national canons: in Italy, the *Canzoniere* legitimated lyric poetry because, after Petrarch, Italians could have no doubt that subjective poetry in a serious style possessed a dignity equal to that of the great classicist genres; in France there had been no poet capable of giving the lyric the same prestige enjoyed by the epic, tragedy, and comedy.

The New Romantic Theory

The modern category of the lyric and the tripartite division into epic, lyric, and dramatic became established definitively in the second half of the eighteenth

---

67. Eustachio Manfredi, "Lettera al signor marchese Giovan Gioseffo Orsi," in Giovan Gioseffo Orsi, *Considerazioni sopra la Maniera di Ben Pensare ne'componimenti* (Modena: Bartolomeo Soliani, 1735), 684 and 700. On the Franco-Italian controversy in the early eighteenth century, see Corrado Viola, *Tradizioni letterarie a confronto: Italia e Francia nella polemica Orsi-Bonhours* (Verona: Fiorini, 2001).

68. Manfredi, "Lettera al signor marchese Giovan Gioseffo Orsi," 686.

69. "And to reveal this secret in brief, I believe that the aversion of the French to the Tuscan Poets arises from them having given themselves over almost entirely to certain familiar and playful kinds of compositions, for which, to perfect them, they seem to pursue nothing more than what a written Oration would require, other than the poetic meter and rhyme. As a consequence, it then followed that even in serious Lyrical Compositions they necessarily kept the use of largely the same domestic manners of telling tales, without putting much care into investing in their style so that it may be raised above prose and be distinct from it. . . . That the French have reduced almost all their Poetry to a playful and domestic style requires no proof at all, methinks. For starting from *Villon*, and *Marot*, who are the oldest among those they recognize as their Poets, and finishing with the times of today, including the most select Compositions, I believe that three-quarters at least are written in this playful and risible style." Ibid., 687.

70. Ibid., 688–689.

century along with the crisis in European classicism. We glimpse the first signs of the change in a chapter Charles Batteux dedicated to lyric poetry in *Les Beaux-Arts réduits à un même principe* (1746, *The Fine Arts Reduced to a Single Principle*), one of the last great defenses of classicist poetry in the age of its decline.[71] To demonstrate that every fine art is imitative, Batteux must refute several objections, one of which concerns the genre that many find to be incompatible with the principle of mimesis.[72] In citing the opinion that he intends to criticize, Batteux sets out clearly the idea of poetry that was becoming established in the mid-eighteenth century and which Romanticism would lay claim to:

> What! someone could immediately object: are the Songs of the Prophets, the Psalms of David, the Odes of Pindar and Horace not real poems? On the contrary, they are the most perfect. Let us go back to the origins of poetry. Isn't poetry a song that arouses joy, appreciation, and gratitude? Isn't it a *cri du cœur* or an expostulation, where nature does everything and art nothing? We see no pictures or depictions. In the beginning, lyric poetry amounted to passion, feeling, and intoxication. Two conclusions seem to follow from this: first, that lyric poems are real poems and, second, that these poems are not imitative.[73]

According to this theory, which Abrams calls "expressive" and which he opposes to the aesthetic of mimesis, poetry is an "outpouring from the heart," an immediate voice of feeling, and its original form is lyric poetry.[74] A few decades later, certain statements would become conventional wisdom; Batteux was still trying to refute them with Aristotelian arguments. If lyric poetry was the authentic expression of the poet rapt in an instant of enthusiasm, he writes, the feelings that we read in it would be real, but they would not necessarily be verisimilar. Consequently, they may be so narrowly tied to a particular circumstance that they would not be meaningful to everyone. The

---

71. Charles Batteux, *Les Beaux-Arts réduits à un même principe* (1746); English translation, *The Fine Arts Reduced to a Single Principle*, trans. James O. Young (Oxford: Oxford University Press, 2015).

72. Ibid., chap. 10 ("On Lyric Poetry").

73. Ibid., 119.

74. Abrams, *The Mirror and the Lamp*, 21–26.

reason sacred poetry appears so beautiful to us is not because it records the real voice of the prophets, but because "we find perfectly expressed in them the feelings that it seems we would have experienced were we in the position of the prophets."[75] These are verisimilar, typical, universally human feelings, which are therefore different from real ones, and this is exactly what goes on in tragedy, the archetypal genre of classicist aesthetics. In other words, Batteux is not ready to accept that lyric poetry is the self-expression of a real individual. This is why, resurrecting a two-hundred-year-old argument, he corrects Aristotle and falls back on the "imitation of the passions" idea, as had Minturno, Segni, Viperano, Torelli, and Guarini before him:

> Therefore, just as actions and customs are imitated in epic and dramatic poetry, in lyric poetry we sing of imitated feelings or emotions. If it contains something real, this is mixed with something fictional in order to make a composite whole. The fictional embellishes the truth and the truth lends credibility to the fictional.[76]

In the years to come, the expressive theory of poetry that Batteux sought unsuccessfully to reconcile with the principle of imitation would become a commonplace. Two decades later, when William Jones posed the same problems in his *Essay on the Arts Commonly Called Imitative* (1772), he arrived at a completely different result:

> It is the fate of those maxims, which have been thrown out by very eminent writers, to be received implicitly by most of their followers, and to be repeated a thousand times, for no other reason, than because they once dropped from the pen of a superior genius: one of these is the assertion of *Aristotle*, that *all poetry consists in imitation*, which has been so frequently echoed from author to author, that it would seem a kind of arrogance to controvert it; for almost all the philosophers and cricks, who have written upon the subject of *poetry, musick,* and *painting*, how little forever they may agree in some points, seem of one mind in considering them as arts merely imitative: yet

---

75. Batteux, *The Fine Arts Reduced to a Single Principle*, 120.
76. Ibid., 123.

it must be clear to any one, who examines what passes in his own mind, that he is affected by the finest poems, pieces of musick, and pictures, upon a principle, which, whatever it be, is entirely distinct from imitation. *M. le Batteux* has attempted to prove that all the fine arts have a relation to this common principle of imitating: But, whatever be said of painting, it is probable, that poetry and musick had a nobler origin.[77]

Music and poetry cannot be explained by imitation. In its original form, poetry is "a strong, and animated expression of the human passions." Poetic meter and style are born from the passions: "if we observe the voice and accents of a person affected by any of the violent passions, we shall perceive something in them very nearly approaching to *cadence* and *measure*."[78]

Poetry does not imitate fictional affections but, rather, gives voice immediately to real feelings. It is "the language of the violent passions, expressed in exact measure, with strong accents and significant words."[79] Jones arrives at these conclusions because, when he reflects on the essence of poetry in general, what comes to mind is almost always the lyric: the Psalms, the Greek, Arab, or Persian lyric poets, Petrarch. The *Essay on the Arts Commonly Called Imitative* overturns Aristotle's theory, explicitly refutes Batteux, once more adopts the premises of expressive poetics, and shows the effects on literary criticism of primitivist theories on the origins of poetry, which Giambattista Vico and others had helped to popularize during the previous fifty years.[80]

The corollaries of this theory form a constellation of ideas on which the most widespread version of Romanticism rests: originality, genius, the glorification of immediacy at the expense of rules, of individual talent at the expense of tradition, authenticity as the origin of art and as the criterion of judgment. In the late eighteenth century, these ideas and the tripartite division of literature into epic, lyric, and drama became *topoi*. Many began to invert the traditional hierarchy and put lyric in first place, inasmuch as it was the form of original poetry from which all the others were thought to

---

77. William Jones, *Essay on the Arts Commonly Called Imitative,* in *The Collected Works of Sir William Jones* (New York: New York University Press, 1993), vol. 10, 363.

78. Ibid.

79. Ibid., 371.

80. Abrams, *The Mirror and the Lamp,* 87–88.

derive, according to an idea that began to spread in the first half of the eighteenth century.[81] While classicist poetics are suspicious of subjective poetry, Romanticism views it rather as the foundation of writing in verse. When Leopardi, half a century after William Jones, wrote that lyric is the "only primitive and true genre,"[82] and that epic and drama are derivative forms, he was repeating a commonplace.

The Romantic paradigm consists of four essential elements.[83] In the first place, lyric poetry is no longer defined in relation to the principle of imitation practiced according to the rules but is instead the genre of self-expression and confession:

> *Petrarch* was, certainly, too deeply affected with real *grief . . . to imitate* the passions of others.[84]

> The more he is a man of genius, the more he is a poet, the more he will have his own personal feelings to express, the more he will be averse to clothing another character, to speaking in the voice of another person, to imitating. The more he portrays himself and feels the need to do so, the more lyrical he is.[85]

In the second place, the concept of the lyric spills out from its own sphere of relevance and becomes a general aesthetic category that can be applied to other forms as well. This is demonstrated from the late eighteenth century on by the dissemination of the neologism "lyricism" in English criticism, first appearing in 1760, and of "lyrisme" in French criticism, first appearing in 1829.[86] From that moment on, "lyric" can be anything that has to do with

---

81. Guerrero cites *Lectures on Poetry* (1711) by Joseph Trapp, in which the lyric is presented as the most poetic of all kinds of poetry (Guerrero, *Poétique et poésie lyrique*, 191). It should be noted that *Lectures on Poetry* is the English translation of the Latin *Praelectiones poeticae*, and that Trapp is referring to lyric in the narrow sense, as defined by the criteria of classicist poetics and rigorously separated off from the other genres of short poetry. See Joseph Trapp, *Praelectiones poeticae* (Oxford: Lintott, 1711).

82. Giacomo Leopardi, *Zibaldone di pensieri* (1817–1832); English translation *Zibaldone*, trans. by Michael Caesar and Franco D'Intino (New York: Farrar, Straus and Giroux, 2013), 4357–4358, August 29, 1828.

83. See Bernardelli, *Il testo lirico*, 76–91.

84. Jones, *Essay on the Arts Commonly Called Imitative*, 374.

85. Leopardi, *Zibaldone*, 4357–4358, August 29, 1828.

86. See Bernardelli, *Il testo lirico*, 3 and 79.

the expression of subjectivity: a lyrical novel, a lyrical drama, or a lyrical state of mind.

In the third place, lyric poetry eventually came to coincide with the idea of poetry itself. William Jones's essay is very clear in this regard. Equally explicit is the entry for *Lyrisch* in the *Allgemeine Theorie der schönen Künste* (1771–1774, General Theory of Fine Arts), which Johann Georg Sulzer published in the same period as Jones's *Essay on the Arts Commonly Called Imitative*.[87] In general, the Romantic theory of poetry favored a division of literary work that the novel was also pursuing, completely independently, during the same period. Prose was gradually becoming the natural medium of storytelling: in the long run, the tradition of the narrative poem, which was still very much alive during the nineteenth century, would not stand up to the challenge; at the same time, verse writing would become more and more specialized toward the lyrical. A corollary of this progressive differentiation was the idea that there exists a necessary relationship between poetry and brevity. In the Romantic era a *topos* began to circulate that poetry is by nature short, just as the rush of inspiration is brief, whereas long poetry written on the basis of an ordered plan is cold and artificial. Leopardi expresses it this way in his *Zibaldone:*

> And in fact the epic poem is contrary to the nature of poetry. (1) It requires a plan which is conceived and arranged completely coldly. (2) How can a task requiring very many years of work have anything to with poetry? Poetry consists essentially in an impetus. It is also against nature absolutely. Impossible that imagination, the poetic vein, poetic spirits should endure, be sufficient, not diminish in so long a work on the same argument. . . . Virgil's tiredness and strain in the last 6 books of the *Aeneid* is well known as well as apparent; they were written for a purpose, and not from an inner impulse or desire. . . . Works of poetry should by nature be short, as were all primitive poems (that is, the most poetic and true), of whatever kind, among all peoples.[88]

---

87. Johann Georg Sulzer, *Allgemeine Theorie der schönen Künste* (1771–1774), vol. 3 (Hildesheim: Georg Olms, 1994), 299–305.

88. Leopardi, *Zibaldone,* 4356, August 29, 1828.

A few decades later, in a peremptory and normative fashion, Edgar Allan Poe formulated this principle in two of his most famous essays, "The Philosophy of Composition" (1846) and "The Poetic Principle" (1850):

> What we term a long poem is, in fact, merely a succession of brief ones—that is to say, of brief poetical effects. It is needless to demonstrate that a poem is such. only inasmuch as it intensely excites, by elevating, the soul; and all intense excitements are, through a psychal necessity, brief. For this reason, at least one half of the "Paradise Lost" is essentially prose—a succession of poetical depressions.[89]

> In regard to the *Iliad,* we have, if not positive proof, at least very good reason for believing it was intended as a series of lyrics; but, granting the epic intention, I can say only that the work is based on an imperfect sense of art. The modern epic is, of the supposititious ancient model, but an inconsiderate and blindfold imitation. But the day of these artistic anomalies is over. If, at any time, any very long poem *were* popular in reality, which I doubt, it is at least clear that no very long poem will ever be popular again.[90]

"No very long poem will ever be popular again." Poe is ahead of his times: in English literature, narrative poetry would be popular throughout the nineteenth century and remain so until the beginning of the twentieth. In the late 1920s, for example, Edwin Arlington Robinson and Stephen Vincent Benét would win the Pulitzer Prize with two long narrative poems, *Tristram* (1927) and *John Brown's Body* (1928). And yet, in the long run, Poe was right: almost all long narrative poems have exited our canons. Narrative poems and didactic poetry have moved out to the periphery of the Western literary system, like a subterranean current that someone tries periodically, endemically, to bring back to light in order to counter the mainstream lyric.

In the fourth place, the Romantic theory reestablishes the relationship between poetry and style on new bases. It interprets the gap between the

---

89. Edgar Allan Poe, "The Philosophy of Composition" (1846), in *Essays and Reviews*, ed. Gary Richard Thompson (New York: Library of America. 1984), 15.

90. Edgar Allan Poe, "The Poetic Principle" (1850), in *Essays and Reviews*, 72.

poetic text and degree-zero discourse not as the sign of a collective convention but as the effect of self-expression on form: the style of the poem expresses the inner world of the poet rather than faithfulness to a passed-down ritual. This always holds true, even when it is a matter of justifying the most artificial of poetry's stylistic traits: meter. Here is how Hegel explains the difference between the meter of a kind of poetry that belongs to the communitarian past, such as epic, and the meter of lyric:

> It is easy to see that the finest measure for the syllables in epic is the hexameter as it streams ahead uniformly, firmly, and yet also vividly. But for lyric we have to require at once the greatest variety of different meters and their more many-sided inner structure. The material of a lyric poem is not an object in its own appropriate objective development but the subjective movement of the poet's own heart; and the uniformity or alteration of this movement, its restlessness or rest, its tranquil flow or foaming flood and fountains, must also be expressed as a temporal movement of word-sounds in which the poet's inner life is made manifest.[91]

Meter is not a convention perpetuated out of habit or out of faithfulness to an ancient ritual; rather, like any other element of style, it expresses "the subjective movement of the poet's own heart."

The Modern Idea of Lyric Poetry

The idea of lyric that took root during the Romantic age is very different from the idea of lyric commonly held in ancient and classicist literature. The fundamental assumptions of the Romantic paradigm would have been questionable or incomprehensible before the long transformation that prevailed definitively only between the second half of the eighteenth century and the first half of the nineteenth.

The most questionable premise is the close association between poetry and the author's personal life. The Romantic *doxa* took it for granted that

---

91. Hegel, *Aesthetics*, vol. 2, 1136.

poets had to speak about their own experience and inner life; at the beginning of the nineteenth century an association of this sort was not yet obvious. There is a vast tradition of lyric poetry in the broadest sense in which
a first person occupies the center of the discourse but as pure speaker, without
talking about his or her own life, or without expressing thoughts and passions that bear any trace of a precise individuality. And there is a vast tradition of lyric poetry based on a generic speaker, "not a voice but voicing," to
use an expression from Jonathan Culler.[92] A quick look through the most
canonic and imitated lyrical text of the premodern period, Horace's *Odes*, suffices to understand that expression of the self or of private anecdotes are
not the only subjects of traditional lyric discourse, and perhaps not even its
main themes. Similarly, when reading the *Crestomazia poetica*, the anthology
that Leopardi put together with the aim of creating a collection of the best
Italian poetry (excluding the great classics and contemporary living authors),
one is struck by the number of lyric texts that are not autobiographical: little
narrative scenes, descriptions of landscapes and cities, vocative poems, gnomic
compositions, texts on political, philosophical, and moral issues framed from
an almost impersonal point of view. Leopardi's chrestomathy seems to con-
tradict the Romantic poetics he was developing at that very time—or, rather,
helps to historicize it. The association with subjectivity and brevity that Leopardi attributes to the nature of true poetry is in reality the result of a historical
process, a long mutation.

In ancient poetics, when it came to identifying a text, the connection between subjectivity and lyric was less important than the public function of
the work, its objective content, its meter, and, originally, the type of musical
accompaniment. A song in honor of Dionysus and a song in honor of Apollo,
a song dedicated to the winners of races and a song that celebrates weddings,
a poem accompanied by the lyre and a poem accompanied by the flute, a
poem written in iambics and a poem written in hexameters did not have the
same name; nor did there exist a higher category under which to group the
small, scattered forms into a large unified genre. The normative passages in
Aristotle's *Poetics*, which state that true imitation is the mimesis of actions
and that the true poet should speak as little as possible in first person, are
a sign of the difficulty inherent in classical antiquity of including in public

---

92. Culler, *Theory of the Lyric*, 31.

discourse any ordinary person's private life, considered too obscure, irrelevant, or incommunicable to be worthy of collective attention.

The history of genre categories provides the clearest demonstration of this lacuna. Even in epochs in which short forms developed with a first person that had an individual voice and talked about an individual matter, ancient poetics maintained unaltered the schemes serving to describe archaic Greek poetry. Short texts told by a first person fell under determinate subgenres because they versified a publicly recognizable subject matter (praise, satire, the pangs of love) in an appropriately corresponding form (sapphic stanza, iambics, hexameters, elegiac couplet). In other words, the text's identity was not defined by its reference to a particular person's story but by criteria that bore signs of the social function performed, in the present or past, by certain types of poetry. What matters was not "the self-expression of the subjective life," as Hegel says, but the trace of its ritual function.

This schema, born to describe archaic Greek poetry, resisted the slide toward the private that poetry underwent during the Alexandrian age and later centuries. Even when compositions were no longer performed in public and accompanied by music, even when they left the realm of performance altogether, even when the speaker gave itself and the people it named an individual identity, even when it shifted the reader's attention from the objective content of the discourse to the author's private life, the categories inherited from the age when poetry was truly a social discourse lived on. It was not until the sixteenth century that the terms from the ancient taxonomy, by then inadequate for describing its objects, acquired other meanings. Two centuries after the appearance of Petrarch's *Canzoniere,* Italian theorists acknowledged that the ancient categories did not explain the text that, for them, was the most important work of Italy's vernacular literature and the most important book of lyric poetry that had been written since Horace's *Odes.* What gives cohesiveness to such a work is the expanded space granted to the first person, or, in the language of the sixteenth-century theorists, to the imitation of the affections. Taking the *Canzoniere* as a model for the entire genre, it is possible to transform its egocentrism into a norm and find the same characteristics in every short composition scaffolded by an *I.* This was how a system of genres was born that shifted the axis of criteria from the public to the private, from the external to the internal, from objective content to subjective perception, and from ritual mimesis to self-expression.

The Concept of Modern Poetry

Along with the modern idea of the lyric, in the Romantic age a schema of literary history became popular that rediscovered two or three momentous fractures in the emergence of verse writing. Some literary historians settled for opposing ancient and classicist poetry to Romantic poetry; others turned to a three-part schema: a primitive age, when lyric was the spontaneous voice of the passions, was followed by a premodern age dominated by artifice, which lasted until the modern (that is, Romantic) writers recaptured the original spirit of lyric poetry. Although the idea of primitive poetry implicit in this arrangement would not have stood up to philological examination, almost all the national literary histories continued to accept the second part of this narrative. They dwelt at length on the metamorphosis of poetry between the second half of the eighteenth and early nineteenth centuries and reflected on the differences separating the earlier from the later: Thomas Gray from William Wordsworth, Albrecht von Haller from Friedrich Hölderlin, Voltaire from Victor Hugo, Giuseppe Parini from Giacomo Leopardi.

In English literature, one of the crucial texts that articulated and at the same time created this threshold was the preface Wordsworth wrote for the second edition of *Lyrical Ballads,* published for the first time in the 1800 edition and again, revised and expanded, in 1802. "All good poetry is the spontaneous overflow of powerful feelings," writes Wordsworth.[93] Although poetic discourse is tempered by contemplation, which reconstructs the emotion in a state of tranquility, it allows the rhythm of passion to come through and makes poetic style completely different from prose style. But verse writing had not always possessed these traits. The return to immediacy preached by *Lyrical Ballads* was in reality a revolution:

> The earliest Poets of all nations generally wrote from passion excited by real events; they wrote naturally, and as men: feeling powerfully as they did, their language was daring and figurative. In succeeding times, Poets, and men ambitious of the fame of Poets, perceiving the influence of such language, and desirous of producing the same effect,

---

93. William Wordsworth and Samuel Taylor Coleridge, *Lyrical Ballads,* 2nd ed., ed. R. L. Brett and A. R. Jones (London: Routledge, 1991), 291.

without having the same animating passion, set themselves to a mechanical adoption of those figures of speech, and made use of them.[94]

The spontaneous language of feeling was opposed in times of decadence to what Wordsworth calls *poetic diction*. These two codes differ from the prose of everyday language, but for opposite reasons: while primitive lyric poetry and the kind of lyric poetry Wordsworth would like to write both speak the language of "passion excited by real events," poetic diction generates an artificial and mechanical style, an "adulterated phraseology," chosen coldly and lacking any relation to true passions or to the natural way of saying things. This is the case for the classicist lyric poetry of the eighteenth century, which Wordsworth holds up as representative of premodern lyric poetry that came from imitating preexisting models, and which he criticizes roundly in a few passages of textual analysis.[95] When Wordsworth opposes the "spontaneous overflow of powerful feelings" of new Romantic poetry to classicist poetic diction, he defines a decisive transition in an marvelously succinct way and also sets out a philosophy of literary history.

No text in the history of Italian literature had an influence and symbolic force comparable to that of Wordsworth's preface to *Lyrical Ballads*. Only slowly, over the course of the nineteenth century, did an awareness grow that Ugo Foscolo and Giacomo Leopardi were a new kind of lyric poet and that their work marked a historical discontinuity. Francesco De Sanctis's *Storia della letteratura italiana* (1870–1871) was a pivotal work.[96] In chapter 20, he talks about the passage from the "old literature," superficial and stereotyped in content, decorative and conventional in form, servile and antipolitical in public life, to the "new literature," announced by Melchiorre Cesarotti, Carlo Goldoni, Parini, and Vittorio Alfieri, and brought to perfection by Foscolo, Manzoni, and Leopardi.[97] For De Sanctis, the first great lyric voice of the new kind is Foscolo: in his *Sonnets* there reappears "that intimacy, sweet and melancholy, of which Italy had lost, as it seemed, the memory," a prelude to the lyrical tone of Leopardi; Foscolo's *Dei sepolcri* (1807, *On Sepulchres*) is the triumph

---

94. Ibid., 365–366.

95. Ibid., 367–370.

96. Francesco De Sanctis, *Storia della letteratura italiana* (1870–1871); English translation, *History of Italian Literature*, trans. Joan Redfern (New York: Harcourt, Brace and Company, 1931).

97. Ibid., vol. 2, chap. 20 ("The New Literature").

of the spirit of the new poetry, the "affirmation of the new consciousness, the birth of the new man."[98] Foscolo is the harbinger of new times for two reasons, says De Sanctis. The first is the content of his work: the speaker is "a real person," not the conventional mask of Arcadian poetry but "a man in his integrity—in the active life as a patriot and citizen and in the intimacy of his private affections."[99] The poetic subject and the biographical persona coincide, as if the distance between the speaker and the person who puts his name on the book were obliterated.

The second reason is the novelty of the style. Between Tasso and Metastasio, writes De Sanctis, poetry experienced a period of decadence. An eloquent sign of this crisis was the subordination of words to sounds in melodrama and poetry accompanied by music. For De Sanctis, when the word is subservient to sound it loses its importance; it ceases "to have a message, but acquires a value in its trills."[100] Foscolo, on the contrary, removes all residue of eighteenth-century musicality and invents a new style that is assertive, because it says "things and not words," and at the same time personal, because it avoids artifice and, with immediacy, expresses the "inner world of consciousness."[101] This is why he gradually abandons overly closed forms like the sonnet and the canzone, leaves off fixed rhyme, and chooses freer rhyme that is able to follow the "natural voice of the soul."[102]

Fifty years before De Sanctis, Leopardi had already provided an Italian version of the Romantic paradigm in his thoughts on literary genres, scattered throughout his Zibaldone. His theory of poetic forms changed radically between 1817 and 1826, following a path that, in retrospect, assumes an emblematic value. Until the mid-1820s, he did not view short poems on autobiographical subjects as a unified genre. Leopardi continued to use categories of classicist origin and distinguished between subgenres based on meter and theme, each different according to style and subject: canzoni, idylls, elegies, odes, epistles, and hymns.[103] The titles of his works faithfully reflect this sort of taxonomy: in 1824, his series Canzoni was published; between December 1825

98. Ibid., 905–906.

99. Ibid., 909.

100. Ibid., 853.

101. Ibid., 908.

102. Ibid.

103. See Karl Maurer, Giacomo Leopardis 'Canti' und die Auflösung der lyrischen Genera (Frankfurt: Klostermann, 1957), 15–193.

and January 1826, his "Idilli" appeared serially in a literary magazine. In this phase, he used the category of lyric poetry in a narrow sense, to indicate the genre originated by Greek lyric poets and continued by Horace, Petrarch's civil poems, and anyone who had written odes and canzoni about public issues.

Leopardi's conversion to the Romantic theory of genres appears on a famous page of the *Zibaldone*, dated December 15, 1826:

> Poetry can be divided, in substance, into only three real, principal kinds: lyric, epic, and dramatic. Lyric poetry is the firstborn of all; it is to be found in every nation, including savage ones; it is more noble and more *poetic* than every other kind; it is true and pure poetry in its every form; it is to be found in anyone, whether cultured or not, who seeks recreation or consolation in song and with words measured in whatsoever way, and with harmony; it is a free and straightforward expression of any living and deeply held human feeling. The epic was created after this, and from it. In a certain way, it is no more than an extension of lyric poetry or, shall we say, it is the lyric genre which, among its other means and subjects, has principally assumed and chosen narration, and modified it poetically. . . . Dramatic poetry is the last of the three kinds of poetry, in time and in nobility. It is not an inspiration, but an invention; it is the child of civilization, not of nature; it is poetry by convention and by the wishes of its authors, rather than by reason of its essence.[104]

Poetry is divided into three kinds, but the first in order of time and rank is lyric. "True and pure poetry in its every form," the lyric appears to have spread to all peoples, for it is the primitive form of verbal art, the "free and straightforward expression of any living and deeply held human feeling"; and it is distinguished from the other kinds just as an original is opposed to a derivative, or the natural is opposed to the artificial. The categories that Leopardi uses to define theater in verse trace out a negative outline of the qualities of lyric poetry: drama is "the child of civilization," that is, "poetry by convention and by the wishes of its authors"; by contrast, lyric is the child of nature, that is, poetry "by reason of its essence" and by "inspiration."

---

104. Leopardi, *Zibaldone*, 4234–4235, December 15, 1826.

A year and a half after his reflections from December 1826, Leopardi returns to his theory of genres in order to refine it. He writes that because *epos* requires a plan, arranged coldly in advance, it goes against the nature of poetry; that authentic inspiration cannot be prolonged; and that works of poetry are necessarily short.[105] He adds that primitive poems are the most poetic and true, and he distinguishes between the conventional verses typical of drama and the natural verses suited to lyric. He writes that the more of a genius the writer is, the greater desire he or she will have for self-expression.[106] A few days later, in an entry dated September 10, 1828, Leopardi's theory of genres arrives at its ultimate achievement:

> The poet does not imitate nature: rather is it true that nature speaks within him and through his mouth. *I' mi son un che quando Natura parla* [I am one who when Nature speaks], etc., a true definition of the poet. Thus the poet is not an imitator except of himself. When through imitation he truly takes leave of himself, that really is no longer poetry, a divine faculty; that is a human art, it is prose, despite the verse and the language.[107]

This is perhaps the most markedly Romantic passage, the one in which some ideas that had circulated since the second half of the eighteenth century assume a radical form. Authentic poetry is foreign to artifice, convention, and imitation; the poet imitates only himself. From that moment on, for the sake of the idea that poetry is identical to lyric, understood in the Romantic and modern sense, Leopardi abandoned classicist subgenres. Titles like *Canzoni* or "Idilli" disappeared. The Florentine edition of his poetry (1831) would be titled simply *Canti,* a word that belongs neither to the categories used by ancient poetics to classify short poetic forms, nor to the categories based on meter originating in medieval times. Although it derives from the epic tradition, it is used in a markedly lyrical sense.[108]

Purified of a few outdated associations, the Romantic theory of lyric poetry continues to have a place in modern common knowledge: the words

---

105. Ibid., 4357–4358, August 9, 1828. See also 4413, October 20, 1828; 4417, November 3, 1828; and 4461, February 16, 1829.

106. Ibid., 4357–4358, August 29, 1828.

107. Ibid., 4372–4373, September 10, 1828.

108. See Maurer, *Giacomo Leopardis 'Canti,'* 197ff.

have changed but the reasoning of the discourse has remained the same. Nobody today would use the vocabulary of Wordsworth or Leopardi, but it is very common to come across the same idea in its twentieth-century version and read that the poet is spoken by the unconscious, by language, by rhythm, or by pure signifier. The Romantic paradigm appears to describe well the mainstream current of modern poetry. For this reason, anyone who chooses to challenge this idea of poetry moves around a hegemonic tradition without ever managing to take away its primacy, like a satellite around a planet. Today, despite the power of alternative models, the poetry collections we leaf through in bookstores contain for the most part short texts in which the poet speaks about himself or herself in a style interpreted as personal.

The lyric spirit we are familiar with is thus formed at the confluence of two theories or, better yet, two discourses. The first describes the overall structure of literature; the second recounts the metamorphosis that poetry is said to have experienced beginning in the late eighteenth century, crossing a historical threshold that varies depending on the national culture. These discourses form a narrative with a simple plot: literature is divided into three genres, two of which are defined by unquestionable formal traits, whereas the third, lyric, owes its identity to the combination of a thematic element (the poet talks about himself or herself) and a formal element (the poet expresses himself or herself through style). This conceptual change was accompanied by an extraordinary transformation in the practice of writing. It was a slow metamorphosis whose effects unfolded for almost a century, in different stages from one literature to another, but which all essentially obeyed the same underlying logic. I will tell this story on two levels: an analysis of an emblematic poem and a history of literary forms in the *longue durée*. I have chosen to start with an exemplary text, a work that many believe to be the first modern poem of Italian literature.

CHAPTER TWO

A New Paradigm

An Exemplary Text

L'infinito

Sempre caro mi fu quest'ermo colle,
E questa siepe, che da tanta parte
Dell'ultimo orizzonte il guardo esclude.
Ma sedendo e mirando, interminati
Spazi di là da quella, e sovrumani   5
Silenzi, e profondissima quiete
Io nel pensier mi fingo; ove per poco
Il cor non si spaura. E come il vento
Odo stormir tra queste piante, io quello
Infinito silenzio a questa voce   10
Vo comparando: e mi sovvien l'eterno,
E le morte stagioni, e la presente
E viva, e il suon di lei. Così tra questa
Immensità s'annega il pensier mio:
E il naufragar m'è dolce in questo mare.[1]   15

---

1. Giacomo Leopardi, *Canti,* critical edition by Emilio Peruzzi (Milan: Rizzoli, 1981), 271. All translations of poems in this chapter are by Zakiya Hanafi, unless otherwise noted.

The Infinite

Always dear to me was this solitary hill,
And this hedge, which such a large part
Of the farthest horizon from my view excludes.
But sitting and gazing, interminable
Spaces beyond that, and superhuman   5
Silences, and the most profound quiet
I, in my thought, imagine; where nearly
My heart takes fright. And as the wind
I hear rustling among these plants, that
Infinite silence with this sound   10
I begin to compare: and what comes to me is the eternal,
And the seasons dead, and the present
And alive one, and the sound of it. Thus amidst this
Immensity my thought drowns:
And being shipwrecked is sweet to me in this sea.   15

Leopardi wrote "The Infinite" between the spring and fall of 1819 and published it for the first time, with a few variations, in the literary magazine *Nuovo Ricoglitore,* between December 1825 and January 1826, in a series of pieces titled "Idilli." The poem was later included in the collection *Versi,* which came out in 1826, and finally in the first edition of *Canti,* published in 1831. For anyone familiar with Italian literary language who knows the meaning of words outside contemporary usage, such as *ermo* ("solitary"), *il guardo* ("gaze"), and *mi fingo* ("I imagine to myself"), the literal meaning is not hard to understand.[2]

The meter of this poem, free hendecasyllable,[3] proliferated starting in the second half of the sixteenth century and was very popular from the second half of the eighteenth century on, in texts very different from one another

---

2. The only confusion regards *quella* ("that," feminine singular) in line 5: some critics believe it refers to *tanta parte* ("such a large part"); according to the traditional interpretation, however, which remains the most probable, it indicates the *siepe* ("hedge") mentioned in line 2. See Antonio Baldini, "Questa e quella . . . ," *Corriere della Sera,* February 7, 1950; Riccardo Bacchelli, "Sugli aggettivi determinativi dell' 'Infinito,'" *Letterature moderne* 1, no. 2 (1950): 56–57.

3. In Italian, free hendecasyllable refers to a series of verses with eleven syllables that are not connected by a fixed rhyme scheme.

in tone and topic. We find it in Giuseppe Parini's *Il giorno* (1763–1765 and 1801, *The Day*), in some lyrical introspective poems by Vincenzo Monti, "Pensieri d'amore" (1783, "Love Thoughts") and "Al Principe Don Sigismondo Chigi" (1783, "To Prince Don Sigismondo Chigi"), and in Foscolo's *On Sepulchres* (1807). Given that Leopardi had only written one sonnet in a serious style,[4] preferring less fixed and less rhymed poetic forms, it is likely that the fifteen verses of "The Infinite" and the sixteen of another one of the "Idylls," "Alla Luna" ("To the Moon"),[5] represent a challenge to the traditional meter of short Italian lyric poetry. It seems as if he sought to condense content suited to a sonnet into a form freed from the constriction of rhyme.[6]

The poem is composed of four sentences, but it can be divided into three parts. Lines 1–3:

> Always dear to me was this solitary hill,
> And this hedge, which such a large part
> Of the farthest horizon from my view excludes.

The main body (lines 4–13):

> But sitting and gazing, interminable
> Spaces beyond that, and superhuman   5
> Silences, and the most profound quiet
> I, in my thought, imagine; where nearly
> My heart takes fright. And as the wind
> I hear rustling among these plants, that

---

4. This refers to "Letta la vita dell'Alfieri scritta da esso" ("Reading the Life of Vittorio Alfieri Written by Himself"), composed in 1817 and accompanied by a significant comment: "First sonnet composed all through the night before November 27, 1817, staying in bed, before falling asleep. A few hours earlier, I finished reading the life of Alfieri, and a few minutes earlier still in bed, I had criticized his facile rhyming, telling myself that no sonnet would ever come out of my pen." Giacomo Leopardi, *Poesie e prose,* vol. 1, *Poesie,* ed. Rolando Damiani (Milan: Mondadori, 1988), 381.

5. Initially, "La ricordanza" (later, "Alla luna") had fourteen lines. They would be changed to sixteen in the posthumous edition of the *Canti* (1845), edited by Antonio Ranieri.

6. See the introduction by Ugo Dotti to the edition of the *Canti* that he also edited (Milan: Feltrinelli, 1993), 54.

Infinite silence with this sound   10
I begin to compare: and what comes to me is the eternal,
And the seasons dead, and the present
And alive one, and the sound of it.

And the closing (lines 13–15):

> Thus amidst this
> Immensity my thought drowns:
> And being shipwrecked is sweet to me in this sea.

At the beginning, the speaker says that he has always cherished a particular landscape, and he describes it briefly in a few words. The number of
deictics (eight in fifteen verses) is surprising, as is the fact that the background is almost completely suppressed, because it is already known to
the speaker, who refers to it using the deictics of familiarity ("this hill,"
"this hedge"). The anecdote is not a *topos*. Leopardi describes similar things
in two prose passages that refer to a lived experience, either imaginary or
real. The first dates back to the spring of 1819, from the same period as the
poem, and appears in notes for his future autobiographical novel. What
remains of the work are only a few pages, rough sketches of some scenes,
including this one:

> my observations on the plurality of worlds and the nothingness of
> us and this earth and on the greatness and force of nature that we
> measure by torrents, etc., which are nothing on this globe, which is
> nothing in the world, *and awakened by a voice calling me to dinner so
> that our lives seem like a nothingness to me and time and famous names
> and all of history, etc.,* on the biggest and most admirable buildings
> that do no more than roughen up this little globe the rough things
> that can't be seen from slightly above and slightly far away, but from
> slightly above our globe appears to be smooth . . . [7]

---

7. Giacomo Leopardi, "Ricordi d'infanzia e d'adolescenza," in *Poesie e prose*, vol. 2, *Prose*, ed. Rolando Damiani (Milan: Mondadori, 1988), 1190 (emphasis added).

The second, written after he composed the idyll, comes from the *Zibaldone:*

> Besides, sometimes the soul might desire, and actually does desire, a view that is restricted or confined in some way, as in Romantic situations. The reason is the same, a desire for the infinite, because then, instead of sight, the imagination is at work and the fantastic takes over from the real. *The soul imagines what it cannot see, whatever is hidden by that tree, that hedge, that tower, and wanders in an imaginary space and pictures things in a way that would be impossible if its view could extend in all directions, because the real would exclude the imaginary.*[8]

In the first lines of "The Infinite," the speaker describes once something that can be assumed to have happened several times in reality.[9] An interval of time separates the experience from the writing about the experience, as suggested by the past simple used in the first line ("Always dear to me *was* this solitary hill").[10] In line 4, the static, declarative rhythm of the opening sentence is interrupted by a visual sensation: the interminable open spaces beyond the hedge summon up the first perception of the infinite—a spatial perception—to which the speaker reacts with fear (lines 4–8). Then, when the wind rustles among the plants, the sound summons up a second perception of the infinite, this time of a temporal nature (lines 8–13). The second segment of the text is stirred up by the conflict between meter and syntax. Compared to lines 1–3, the chronological distance between the event and the writing seems to have changed in lines 4–13: it seems as if the poem no longer describes a habit, as in the first lines, but an experience happening here and now. In line 1 the simple past was used ("mi *fu,*" "to me *was*"); in line 8 the simple present is used ("E come il vento | *Odo* stormir fra queste piante," "And as the wind | *I hear* rustling among these plants"), as if to record an unexpected, specific event.[11] In lines 13–15 the speech seems to calm down:

---

8. Giacomo Leopardi, *Zibaldone di pensieri* (1817–1832); English translation, *Zibaldone,* trans. Michael Caesar and Franco D'Intino (New York: Farrar, Straus and Giroux, 2013), 171, July 12–23, 1820 (emphasis added).

9. Luigi Blasucci, "Paragrafi sull' 'Infinito,'" in *Leopardi e i segnali dell'infinito* (Bologna: Il Mulino, 1985), 97.

10. Ibid.

11. The same technique is used two other times in the *Canti:* in the passage of "La sera del dì di festa" ("The Evening of the Holiday") where Leopardi describes the solitary song of a workman returning home

the meaning of the experience is summarized by the speaker in the form of a declarative statement; the fear in line 8 is replaced by the sweetness of the final shipwreck, and the distance seems to grow between the event and the telling of the event.

This division into parts based on content is mirrored in a division into parts based on form. In the first three lines the conflict between meter and syntax is minimal, the verses end with a uniform cadence,[12] the vocabulary derives from Petrarch or from the bucolic tradition,[13] and the syntax is less impressionistic, giving an assertive order to the experience. There are two anastrophes, but the second one is not particularly striking in a poetic text, while the first one (line 1) is more the product of structural constraints than an aesthetic choice. While the syntax of the first segment follows the standards of rational ordering, the second opens with an adversative conjunction that is difficult to interpret. Why does it say *"But* sitting and gazing"? How are we to explain this sudden "But," which would be only partially justified by a purely rational arrangement of the words? According to Franco Ferrucci, the adversative would be the remains of an aborted speech, almost as if the lyric speaker intended to say "I can't go on the way I began—I wanted to express something in particular, but here instead is what came to me later." What ends up on the page would thus be the elliptical remains of his original intention: a sort of amputated grammatical stump that does not fit into a purely explicative sentence.[14] According to Luigi Blasucci, the opposition set up by "But" refers only to the second part of the preceding sentence ("this hedge, which such a large part | Of the farthest horizon from my view excludes"), and the logic it obeys is more poetic than conceptual.[15]

---

from his evening out and in the passage in "Le ricordanze" ("The Recollections") that mentions the chiming of the bell tower carried by the wind: Giacomo Leopardi, *Canti*, translated and annotated by Jonathan Galassi (New York: Farrar Straus and Giroux, 2010), 111 and 183. See Franco Brioschi, *La poesia senza nome* (Milan: Il Saggiatore, 1980), 42, and Blasucci, "Paragrafi sull' 'Infinito,'" 114.

12. The accents all fall on the eighth and tenth syllables: *érmo cólle* ("solitary hill"), *tànta pàrte* ("such a large part"), *guàrdo esclùde* ("my view excludes"). See Mario Fubini, *Metrica e poesia* (Milan: Feltrinelli, 1962), 67.

13. The *siepe* ("hedge") of line 2 has no precedents in Petrarch's *Canzoniere*, but it is a typical feature of the bucolic landscape. On the other hand, the *ultimo orizzonte* ("farthest horizon") in line 3 appeared earlier in Petrarch (*Canzoniere*, 28, line 35). The *ermo colle* ("solitary hill") appears in line 1 of two sonnets by Galeazzo di Tarsia. See Blasucci, "Paragrafi sull' 'Infinito,'" 99–100, and the comment by Francesco Flora (1937) to Leopardi, in *Canti*, ed. Francesco Flora (Milan: Mondadori, 1945, 172).

14. Franco Ferrucci, "Lo specchio dell'infinito," *Strumenti critici* 4 (1970): 192.

15. Blasucci, "Paragrafi sull' 'Infinito,'" 99.

Line 4 begins a dynamic portion of the text, in which the conflict between meter and syntax becomes systemic, with emphatic enjambments separating the syntagms that express the experience of the infinite: *interminati | Spazi* ("interminable | Spaces"), *sovrumani | Silenzi* ("superhuman | Silences"), *quello | Infinito silenzio* ("that | Infinite silence"). The syntax is complicated by two anastrophes (lines 4–6 and 9–11) and by a fugue of subjects connected by the anaphora that repeats the conjunction "And" ("the eternal | And the seasons dead, and the present | And alive one, and the sound of it"). This *dispositio* is read by commentators as a form of mimesis of his thought: an attempt to imitate the experience of the infinite exactly as it presents itself to the mind of the experiencer in the moment, rather than being put into some order after the fact. The significance of the anastrophes in lines 4–6 and 9–11 is less obvious but perhaps identical: both put the object of perception before the act of perceiving and, in one case, before the subject of perception itself ("interminable | Spaces . . . I, in my thought, imagine"). If we were to follow the natural order, by writing "I imagine in my thought the interminable spaces beyond that and superhuman silences and the most profound quiet," we would destroy the effect of the poem, because Leopardi disturbs the natural sequence of speech in order to evoke the bewilderment of the speaker, who is overwhelmed by the object of his thought and thrown back to the end of the sentence, by using a stylistic element that seeks to be a formal equivalent of the experience described.[16] The vocabulary changes radically too: *interminati* ("interminable"), *sovraumana* ("superhuman"), *profondissma* ("most profound"), *infinito* ("infinite"), *immensità* ("immensity"), *naufragar* ("to be shipwrecked") have no connection with the Petrarchan tradition or the bucolic lexicon.[17] Like the enjambments that recall the perception of the infinite by dividing noun and adjective, the lexicon seems to aim for a similar effect. The words in the first three lines are all short, with the exception of "horizon," whereas almost all the words in the second segment are emphatically multisyllabic, as if to mimic the vastness of the mental object to which they refer, reinforcing the effect of the superlatives and the indefinite plurals.[18]

---

16. See Fubini, *Metrica e poesia*, 67.

17. Blasucci, "Paragrafi sull' 'Infinito,'" 100–101.

18. See the comment by Enrico M. Fusco in Giacomo Leopardi, *Canti* (Bologna: Cappelli, 1939), and Blasucci "I segnali dell'infinito," in *Leopardi e i segnali dell'infinito*, 124.

While the tone of the second part is emotional, the beginning of the last part ("Thus amidst this") proceeds logically, like an argument, and the sentence that follows sums up, at a distance, the perception that lines 4–13 describe with immediacy. The conflict with the meter settles down bit by bit and the powerful enjambment of lines 13–14 ("Thus amidst this | Immensity") is followed by a pause that does not break up the sentence. Indeed, the last line of the poem is also the only one that can stand on its own, apart from the opening line.[19] The fear aroused by the first sight of the infinite yields to the sweetness of being shipwrecked, and the chronological and sentimental distance between the experience and the writing about the experience, which in the central part of the poem appeared to be minimal, now returns with greater magnitude. The beginning is thus echoed in the end, but from a greater height.

Interpretations

No nineteenth-century Italian poem has attracted so many commentators[20] and so many translations into English.[21] A great deal of the comments emphasize one aspect specifically: the form of "The Infinite" seems inseparable from the experience it describes. "In my opinion," wrote Adriano Tilgher, "'The Infinite' is not the *analysis* but the *narrating* (something quite different) of a spiritual process."[22] Mario Fubini came to a similar conclusion after comparing the style of the poem to the equivalent passage in the *Zibaldone*: in the prose text, the work of the imagination follows a rational logic; in the poem, it is represented "with immediacy and accents of singular novelty, like someone discovering an unexplored region of his soul."[23] Blasucci builds on Fubini's observations and sees the *Zibaldone* passage as the critical, reflective

---

19. Blasucci, "Paragrafi sull' 'Infinito,'" 118; "I segnali dell'infinito," 129.

20. An anthology of critical responses to the poem can be found in *Interminati spazi sovrumani silenzi. "Un infinito commento." Critici, filosofi e scrittori alla ricerca dell' "Infinito" di Leopardi*, edited and with a critical essay by Vincenzo Guarracino (Grottammare: Stamperia dell'Arancio, 2001).

21. See *I canti di Giacomo Leopardi nelle traduzioni inglesi. Saggio bibliografico e antologia delle versioni nel mondo anglosassone*, ed. Ghan Singh (Recanati: Centro Nazionale di Studi Leopardiani, 1990).

22. Adriano Tilgher, *La filosofia di Leopardi* (Rome: Edizioni di religio, 1940), 149.

23. Giacomo Leopardi, *Canti*, with introduction and commentary by Mario Fubini, new edition in collaboration with Emilio Bigi (Turin: Loescher, 1964), 115.

summary of the mental process that the poem reenacts, mimicking the way thought unfolds, as if the text were not a description of the experience made after the fact but an authentic *itinerarium mentis in infinitum,* a journey of the mind to infinity, brought to the page.[24]

It is not difficult to pick up on a familiar Romantic paradigm in the critical responses of these readers. Fubini states it plainly in the "Introduction" to his commentary:

> The topics and forms of Leopardi's poems may be different, but the reader has the impression of recognizing a single subject in all of them: the poet's heart. . . . A lyric by Leopardi does not tell a story; it does not describe: it is the outpouring of a heart. . . . His language is not that of someone conveying to others an experience that has ended but that of someone who is addressing himself. Think of any of Petrarch's canzoni, such as "Di pensier in pensier" ("From thought to thought"): Petrarch who speaks to us about the perpetual undulations of his soul is not Petrarch who wanders from thought to thought, from mountain to mountain. The poet who composes the canzone has achieved complete understanding of himself and can therefore contemplate and describe each of his own contradictions, one by one. Not so Leopardi, who seeks to make the undulations of his soul perceptible in his verses, to convey feelings as they first take form in their original order. . . . In Leopardi's poetry, the *soul's time* takes sensible form: the reader is made to feel the action sung by the poet as something present.[25]

Here, we find all the Romantic *topoi:* Leopardi's poetry is "the outpouring of a heart" written in a language that ignores or is unaware of the presence of external interlocutors—it is the language of someone who "addresses himself," the poems in *Canti* are autobiographical, and the reflection of the self is reflected in the style. The syntax follows "the life of feelings," the meter rejects overly rigid rhyme schemes to allow the "heart's changing voice" to

---

24. Blasucci, "Paragrafi sull' 'Infinito,'" 104.
25. Leopardi, *Canti,* ed. Mario Fubini and Emilio Bigi, 8–13.

speak,[26] the "simple" lexicon" expresses an "ineffable inner turmoil," the poems tell "the story of a soul."[27] Incidentally, "Storia di un'anima" ("Story of a soul") was the title of the autobiographical novel that Leopardi was thinking about writing, and "the memoirs of a soul"(*les mémoires d'une âme*) was the expression Victor Hugo later used to describe his *Les Contemplations.*[28] The first edition of Fubini's critical commentary on the *Canti* came out in 1930. In the foreword to the second edition the author acknowledges the limits of such an ingenuously Romantic reading; in his collected essays, *Metrica e poesia* (1962), he uses more coldly technical tones but essentially repeats the same schemas: Petrarch's poetry orders experience in retrospect, whereas Leopardi shows "the undulations of thought."[29] In 1980, starting from very different assumptions, Franco Brioschi arrived at the same conclusions when he wrote that the metrical and syntactical structures of "The Infinite" do more than just describe the experience. They reproduce its most intimate form:

> The metrical and syntactical structures reproduce the journey [of thought] itself . . . The reader is not called upon to meet with the author on the 'public' level of the literary institution in order to witness this observatory of the experience portrayed. . . . This is how a profoundly new relationship of communication is born, intended to incite in the hearer a projective type of attitude: rather than *represent* an emotion, the poem is its *equivalent.*[30]

Critical writings that reflect on the novelty of "The Infinite" present the same design: they all say that the text has a close link with the author's experience and life history; they say that the style of the composition is opposite to the logical, rational style of other poems, in the same way that the desire for immediacy is opposite to mediation. Terms of comparison often crop up: Fubini compares "The Infinite" with the poetry of Petrarch, Della Casa, and

---

26. Ibid., 17.

27. Ibid., 20.

28. Victor Hugo, "Préface," in *Les Contemplations* (1830–1856), in *Œuvres poétiques*, vol. 2, ed. Pierre Albouy (Paris: Gallimard, 1967), 481.

29. Fubini, *Metrica e poesia*, 65–70.

30. Brioschi, *La poesia senza nome*, 104.

Foscolo; Blasucci compares the way Petrarch and the pastoral poetry tradition interpret the idyll genre with how Leopardi interprets it.[31] Behind such juxtapositions we glimpse the logic of the Romantic paradigm and the outline of its essential concepts autobiography and self-expression. But which parts of these critical readings are accurate?

Seriousness and Contingency

It is true that Leopardi's idylls, and to a lesser extent Alfieri's *Rime* and Foscolo's sonnets and *On Sepulchres*, are the first modern Italian lyric poems—the first Italian texts in which we glimpse the signs of the revolution that would transfigure European poetry in the century to come. From this point of view, "The Infinite" is special: judging it by the yardstick of novelty, in style and spirit, we might say that few other Italian poems in the first half of the nineteenth century came so close to what the lyric would later become. But it would be ingenuous to fetishize the novelty of a single case: the history of culture does not take leaps, even in its most revolutionary periods, and "The Infinite" is a revolutionary poem—not so much because of its novelties but, above all, because of the changes that it condenses within itself and those that it announces. Phenomena that run through the poetry of the eighteenth century and transformations that would become clear only in the periods after Leopardi's work, or even in the poetry of the early twentieth century, are crystallized in this poem in an initial form. What makes "The Infinite" a new type of poetry?

To begin with, its subject matter. One of the most longstanding constants of Western literature is the rule of the division of styles (*Stiltrennungsregel*), whose history Erich Auerbach reconstructed in *Mimesis* (1946). Auerbach traces out a philosophy of European literary history by following the changes in this written and nonwritten norm. In his view, the representation of reality in Greek and Latin literature is governed by a principle that acts as a habit or as a codified rule from one time to the next. We already find it in the *Iliad* and the *Odyssey*: the Homeric bards distinguished the narratable from the unnarratable in a hierarchical and classist way; significant deeds are performed for the most part by the ruling and warrior class, while the other parts of

---

31. Blasucci, "Paragrafi sull' 'Infinito,'" 99.

society have a secondary, servile function.[32] During the fourth century BCE, this tendency gave rise to a sort of law. The first illustrious text to proclaim the separation of styles as a simultaneously descriptive and normative principle is the second chapter of Aristotle's *Poetics:*

> The things that representative artists represent are the actions of people, and if people are represented they are necessarily either superior [*spoudaios*] or inferior [*phaulous*], better or worse, than we are. (Differences in character you see derive from these categories, since it is by virtue [*arete*] or vice [*kakia*] that people are ethically distinct from each other.)[33]

This three-part division gave rise to internal differences in every artistic discipline: among painters, Polygnotus portrayed people better than us; Pauson, people who are worse than us; and Dionysius, people just like us. Among the epic poets, Homer told tales of the actions of heroes, who are better than us; Hegemon of Thasos and Nicochares spoke of men who are inferior to us, while Cleophon talked about people "like us."[34] Classical rhetoric gave a systematic order to Aristotle's categories, formulating a schema that groups speeches and texts into three *genera elocutionis*—lowly or humble, medium or intermediate, and sublime—and linking them to the type of subject matter, according to a principle first expressed by Theophrastus. Based on this idea, ancient oratory tightly bound the qualities of the characters to the qualities of the story, the style, and the interest demanded of the reader. It did this by establishing a rule that mirrors their rigid social hierarchy, with only one possible exception, that of parody—a violation that overturns the rule without negating its value. The medieval *rota Vergilii* gives us a perfect illustration of these correspondences from a later period: Virgil's wheel condenses the genera of ancient rhetoric into a unified schema, linking together the social class of the hero, the type of action represented, and the type of *ornatus*.

---

32. Erich Auerbach, *Mimesis: Dargestellte Wirklichkeit in der abendländischen Literatur* (1946); English translation, *Mimesis: The Representation of Reality in Western Literature* (1946), trans. Willard R. Trask (Princeton, NJ: Princeton University Press, 2003), 21.

33. Aristotle, *Poetics*, 2.1448a.1–5, trans. Anthony Kenny (Oxford: Oxford University Press, 2013),

34. Aristotle, *Poetics*, 2.1448a.19–23.

This strict ordering principle allowed for styles to be alternated within the same speech, but not for them to be mixed up completely.[35]

In reality, this three-part schema is only theoretical. The text of the *Poetics* (at least in the version we know) already rests on a two-pronged antithesis, opposing tragedy and serious epic to comedy and comic epic, failing to mention any middle forms. In ancient Greek culture, the principles that enshrined the hierarchy between people were both social and moral: someone better than us possesses virtue (*arete*) and is *spoudaios*, meaning "worthwhile," "serious" but also "noble"; someone worse than us is marked by a vice (*kakia*) or a flaw (*hamartema*) and is *phaulos*, meaning "trivial," "lightweight," or even "ignoble." The intermediate case is not explicitly mentioned, but it is implied that people "like us" live in the realm of common life, that is, in the realm of activities that generate the well-being required to enter into the higher realms of public action and a theoretical life, but which grant no eminent virtue in themselves. While there may have been three genres of rhetoric, the ancient *Stiltrennung* proved to be asymmetric and binary, because the boundaries between the humble and the intermediate were never entirely certain. Indeed, the low style could include the comic, the satiric, the playfully erotic, the obscene, but also daily life, factual information, sketches, and trivia. The mime, the iambic, and the satire all belonged to the lowly genre as well, but so did the sections in a judicial oration that referred to private or economic matters.[36] There is no doubt that ancient Greek and Latin cultures reserved much less attention to people "like us" than what modern literature devotes to them. A large portion of reality that today we judge worthy of serious, tragic, or problematic mimesis, writes Auerbach, was confined to the domain of the comic or the intermediate style.

> [For the rule of division of styles] everything commonly realistic [*alles gemein Realistische*], everything pertaining to everyday life must not be treated on any level except the comic, which admits no problematic probing [*ohne problematische Vertiefung*]. . . . We are forced to conclude that there could be no serious literary treatment of everyday occupa-

---

35. See Erich Auerbach, *Literatursprache und Publikum in der lateinischen Spätantike und im Mittelalter* (1958); English translation, *Literary Language and Its Public in Late Latin Antiquity and in the Middle Ages*, trans. Ralph Manheim (Princeton, NJ: Princeton University Press, 1993), 37.

36. Ibid.

tions and social classes—merchants, artisans, peasants, slaves—of everyday scenes and places—home, shop, field, store—of everyday customs and institutions—marriage, children, work, earning a living.[37]

As the reflection of a hierarchical society, the ancient *Stiltrennung* dominated Greek and Latin literature and rhetoric, clashed with Christian creatural realism modeled on the Bible, and in the late Middle Ages combined with another form of stylistic separation that grew out of courtly literature. When Renaissance humanism rediscovered ancient poetics, the division of styles once again imposed its hegemony on the Western literary system: it spread during the period of European classicisms and finally dissolved forever when at the beginning of the nineteenth century the modern realistic novel propagated a new way of giving form to reality.[38] Only at that point did it become possible to do what ancient literature could never have done: represent the everyday life of common people, of people "like us," in a serious, tragic, and problematic way (Auerbach uses these three adjectives, *ernst, tragisch, problematisch*).

For centuries, the *Stiltrennung* was the most important *partage du sensible* in Western literature.[39] In reconstructing the history of this law, Auerbach produced the only philosophy of literary history that has stood up to the skepticism of our age, which is attentive to details and distrustful of the whole. However, although the overall plan of *Mimesis* remains valid, some of its general hypotheses do need to be corrected. Thomas Pavel is right when he observes that Auerbach associates two different precepts with the same name of *Stiltrennung*: the separation of styles in the strict sense and a corollary that should be treated apart. If we adopt the serious mimesis of everyday private life as our historical criterion, it could be said that bucolic-pastoral litera-

---

37. Ibid., 31.

38. Ibid., chap. 18.

39. The concept of *partage du sensible* comes from Jacques Rancière, *La Mésentente* (1995); English translation, *Disagreement*, trans. Julie Rose (Minneapolis: University of Minnesota Press, 1999), 24, but see especially *Le Partage du sensible* (2000); English translation, *The Politics of Aesthetics: The Distribution of the Sensible*, trans. Gabriel Rockhill (London: Continuum, 2004). Following his own path, Rancière comes to conclusions that are similar to Auerbach's. In his later work Rancière picks up on the reference to Auerbach. See Jacques Rancière, *Aisthesis: Scènes du régime esthétique de l'art* (2011); English translation, *Aisthesis: Scenes from the Aesthetic Regime of Art*, trans. Zakir Paul (London: Verso, 2013), xi.

ture and Hellenistic novels preceded the realism of Balzac and Stendhal by nearly two thousand years.[40] It could also be said that long before the arrival of novels, plays, and modern poems, New Comedy and Horatian-style lyric poetry spoke about the everyday affairs of private people—in the intermediate or noble styles but, in any case, in a serious tone. What distinguishes the ancient and classicist representation of everyday life from the representation that the realism of recent centuries has made familiar to us is the tendency to select the facts of reality through a filter that forces people and things to be stylized in order to adapt them to an *a priori*. Pavel calls this mode of representation "ideographic," because instead of trying to represent events as they happen, these works imitate reality based on the presuppositions of a preestablished Idea.[41] The division of styles, writes Pavel, is first of all an ideographic principle. One of its most important assumptions is the idea that contingencies, private details, minutiae, marginal data—what Roland Barthes called reality effects[42]—are suitable for genres in low or intermediate styles (Old Comedy, New Comedy, Menippean satire, satire, verse epistle, epigram, *nugae*, and so forth) but not for genres written in the high style. In Latin poetry, for example, the genres of comic style, such as satire in the strict sense of the word, the verse epistle, and the epigram, recount anecdotes about private people in a sarcastic or everyday-prose version. Conversely, biographical material that belongs to genres written in a noble style, especially the ode, is put through a filter that makes it more abstract. Similarly, in Italian literature of the late thirteenth century, it was normal for a genre with a comic style, such as the tenson in verse, to reveal details about someone's life, whereas the stories alluded to in lyrical love poems in the high style, even when written by the same author, remain generic, serial, and remote from any true individuation. This is a form of *Stiltrennung* that we find in Dante's *Rime*, for example.

Leopardi had a solid classicist background, and during the years he was composing "The Infinite" he reiterated the essential principles of the division

---

40. Thomas G. Pavel, *L'Art de l'éloignement: Essai sur l'imagination classique* (Paris: Gallimard, 1996), 273–274.

41. Thomas G. Pavel, *La Pensée du roman* (Paris: Gallimard, 2003), 111; English rev. ed., *The Lives of the Novel: A History* (Princeton, NJ: Princeton University Press, 2013), 72–73.

42. Roland Barthes, "L'Effet de réel" (1968); English translation, "The Reality Effect," reprinted in *The Rustle of Language*, trans. Richard Howard (Berkeley: University of California Press, 1989), 141–148.

of styles in the first pages of his *Zibaldone*.[43] When he decided to call the six pieces that make up his series an "idyll," he had a specific tradition in mind: the classic idylls of Moschus, the ancient bucolic, the modern pastoral, the sentimental idylls of Salomon Gessner.[44] These pieces share some common traits: typical situations, described in a medium or at most medium-high tone, the use of a pathetic-elegiac style, and a bucolic decor. This genealogy may perplex the modern reader, because the most important texts of the series named "Idylls" ("The Infinite," "The Evening of the Holiday," and "To the Moon") have little or nothing to do with the tradition that Leopardi draws on. Today, we see a fracture between these poems and the compositions of Moschus, the pastoral tradition, and Gessner.[45]

The first difference, as we were saying, lies in the subject matter. In "The Infinite" and "The Evening of the Holiday" a common individual speaker describes his experiences with a seriousness and existential density that would not be possible in Moschus, Gessner, or pastoral poetry.[46] The second difference involves the quality of the speaker and the nature of his experience: in Moschus, pastoral poetry, and Gessner the first person is an ideographic, stereotyped subject; the speaker in Leopardi has traits that are individual and cannot be interchanged. This union between biographical-testimonial realism and philosophical *pathos,* between minute details and existential *gravitas,* between contingency and seriousness, is a completely new factor. It breaks free of the limits that classicist poetics associated with a form such as the idyll, intended to accommodate typical situations described in a medium style with a pathetic-sentimental attitude. Leopardi's poems do not set limits on the import of the experiences they describe: his reflection on infinity, on the nature of memory, on death, on the twilight of all the things we find in "The Infinite," "The Evening of the Holiday,"

---

43. Karl Maurer, *Giacomo Leopardis "Canti" und die Auflösung der lyrischen Genera* (Frankfurt: V. Klostermann, 1957).

44. Marco Santagata, "Dagli idilli all'idillio," in *Quella celeste naturalezza* (Bologna: Il Mulino, 1994), 135–169.

45. See Blasucci, "Paragrafi sull' 'Infinito.'"

46. The union between contingency and seriousness is evident in "The Infinite," "The Evening of the Holiday," and "To the Moon" (even more after the variant that appears in the 1845 edition of the *Canti*). The other idylls, which are more tied to genre conventions, have been judged otherwise: "Il sogno" ("The Dream") recalls the medieval genre of the vision; "La vita solitaria" ("The Solitary Life"), and "Frammento XXXVII" ("Fragment XXXVII") recall various subgenres of bucolic poetry.

and "To the Moon" go beyond the limits of the models from which Leopardi claimed he took his inspiration.

In his "Literary Designs" of 1828, when he talks again about the idyll as a genre, the criterion he uses to define it is not classicist: idylls are poems "expressing situations, affections, historical adventures of my soul."[47] "Historical" is most probably a technical term: it refers to one of the cornerstones of ancient poetics, the antithesis between history and poetry set out in book nine of Aristotle's *Poetics*. Poetry relates the universal and the verisimilar, says Aristotle, what happens to a certain type of character *kata to eikos e to anankaion*, "in terms of verisimilitude and necessity"; history relates the particular and the true, what someone has done or has happened to him or her.[48] The Aristotelian and classicist concept of verisimilitude overlaps an empirical criterion of probability and a moral and social criterion of exemplarity: the first is similar to what reigns in the modern concept of realism; the second is completely different. In line with the latter, poetry's task is to show the world how it should be, not how it is. A noble character must behave nobly: although we know from experience that the opposite occurs at times, the task of the poet is to portray the ideal essence of aristocratic characters. Conversely, the historian has the option of recounting the imperfect behavior of a real aristocrat.

In ancient and classicist literary theory, compositions that follow the rules of poetry in Aristotle's terms are ideographic; those that are presented as history are not. Between roughly 1550 and 1800, in prefatory materials of texts that converge into the genre of the novel, the adjectives "poetic" and "historical" designate two classes of writings: the first represent characters and stories as they should be, according to the Aristotelian principles of verisimilitude; the second imitate the way of representing reality that is typical of historical works, which start from the real and its unpredictability.[49] When Leopardi writes "situations, affections, historical adventures of my soul," he means that his idylls talk about personally lived experiences. He is the first Italian writer to introduce an unprecedented amount of private contingency

---

47. Giacomo Leopardi, "Disegni letterari", in *Prose e poesie*, vol. 2, *Prose*, ed. Rolando Damiani (Milan: Mondadori, 1988), 1218.

48. Aristotle, *Poetics*, 9.1451b.9–10.

49. I write about this more extensively in Guido Mazzoni, *Theory of the Novel*, trans. Zakiya Hanafi (Cambridge, MA: Harvard University Press, 2017), 76–79.

into subjective poetry written in a high style, and "The Infinite" is the poem
where this novelty is revealed. Between 1824 and 1828, Leopardi stopped
writing poems;[50] after 1828, his new compositions would become increasingly autobiographical. Many private details (his years of study, the loves of
his youth, life in his village) would spill into his poems, and the novelty of
the content would become more evident. This is what De Sanctis is referring to in his still Romantic vocabulary when he writes that Leopardi, like
Foscolo, makes the man speak and not a mask, and this is what many modern
readers repeat when they argue that Leopardi's poems introduce a different
type of poetic autobiography, foreign to the previous literature and familiar
to the later.

Three Models of Lyric Poetry

Critics have used comparisons to illustrate this truth: De Sanctis opposed
Leopardi to Pietro Metastasio, while Fubini opposed Leopardi to Petrarch.
These antitheses are asymmetrical: Metastasio's speaker is almost always generic and interchangeable; Petrarch's speaker has a definite identity, and he
corresponds to the person whose name appears on the *Canzoniere*. In other
words, the comparisons that critics have used to explain Leopardi's novelty
refer to not two but three different models of poetic subject and lyric poetry:
the first two date from before the Romantic period, the third is absolutely
modern. In the first, the speaker is not a specific biographical person but a
generic collective persona, a replaceable *I* who has experiences that are individual (they are described in the first-person singular) but not individualized
(they are indistinct and emblematic). In archaic Greek poetry, in medieval love
poetry, or in improvised popular poetry, for example, the character who says
I is almost always a type, "the site of a role,"[51] and not an empirical individual. The experiences evoked by Alcaeus, or by most of the troubadours,
or by the improvised poetry accompanied by music that flourished in the
1700s, are serial in nature and could adapt effortlessly to a multiplicity of real

---

50. The only exception is an isolated, transitional composition—the verse epistle "Al Conte Carlo Pepoli"
("To Count Carlo Pepoli"), written in March 1826.

51. Jonathan Culler, *Theory of the Lyric* (Cambridge, MA: Harvard University Press, 2017), 54.

first persons. To give a name to writings conceived this way, we could use the word by which German Romance philologists define the poetry of the troubadours: *Gesellschaftslyrik,* social lyric.[52] From this point of view, archaic Greek lyric, the poetry of the troubadours, and eighteenth-century musical poetry intended for court and salon audiences are examples of *Gesellschaftslyrik.* Often, although not always, social verse is accompanied by music.

The second model arose in Latin literature of the first century BCE. When Paul Allen Miller writes that "the ego of Catullus, just as the 'Je' of 'Je est un autre' or the 'self' of 'Song of Myself,' must be rigorously distinguished in both its content and poetic function from the ego of the archaic poets of Greece," he traces out a boundary and underlines the birth of a new lyric subject. The first person we encounter in the work of Catullus, the elegiasts, Horace, and Ovid is a personal *I,* not a serial one.[53] The poetry of the Middle Ages experienced a similar transformation with Dante's *Vita nuova* and Petrarch's *Canzoniere,* which introduce into a love poetry marked until then by the traits of *Gesellschaftslyrik* individualized biographical experiences that escape the confines of seriality.[54] In terms of novel outcomes and the power of the model that dominated European poetry for centuries to come, the decisive example was Petrarch. The *Canzoniere* orders the poems in a book that does not tell the indefinite tale of two generic lovers but, rather, focuses on the ethical and psychological story of a first person endowed with a specific identity and a complex inner life. This is how the ritual space of erotic romance poetry, dominated by the relationship between love and the fixed characters of the beloved and the lover, was transformed into an introspective space.[55]

The opposition dividing *Gesellschaftslyrik* from personal lyric poetry is not rigid: the boundaries can be hazy and the two genres can coexist.[56] In Italy, social verse continued to be practiced widely before and after the *Canzoniere.*

---

52. On *Gesellschaftslyrik* in medieval poetry, see Claudio Giunta, *Versi a un destinatario: Saggio sulla poesia italiana del Medioevo* (Bologna: Il Mulino, 2002), chap. 4 ("Sulla lirica").

53. Paul Allen Miller, *Lyric Texts and Lyric Consciousness: The Birth of a Genre from Archaic Greece to Augustan Rome* (London: Routledge, 1994), 3–4.

54. See Giunta, *Versi a un destinatario,* 386–392.

55. See Roland Greene, *Post-Petrarchism: Origins and Innovations of the Western Lyric Sequence* (Princeton, NJ: Princeton University Press, 1991), chap. 1; Marco Santagata, *Dal sonetto al canzoniere* (Padua: Liviana, 1989), 131ff.; *I frammenti dell'anima* (Bologna: Il Mulino, 1992); and *Introduzione a Francesco Petrarca, "Canzoniere"* (Milan: Mondadori, 1996), liv.

56. See Wolfgang Rösler, "Persona reale o persona poetica? L'interpretazione dell'io' nella lirica greca arcaica," *Quaderni urbinati di cultura classica,* nuova serie 19, no. 1 (1985): 131–144.

Indeed, for centuries Petrarch—the first great introspective poet of European vernacular literature—became the model, imitated in letter but betrayed in spirit, that inspired the most extensive phenomenon of *Gesellschaftslyrik* ever known to European poetry: Petrarchism. In this regard, writes Joel Fineman,

> As the sonnet develops—as Petrarch, say, turns into Petrarchism— poetic subjectivity becomes increasingly artificial at the same time as, and in direct proportion to the way that, the sonneteering poet becomes increasingly thematically self-conscious about the rhetoricity of praise. This is why . . . it is necessary to introduce a distinction between the poetic person of Dante or Petrarch as opposed to the poetic persona of Sidney or Spenser. . . . As the sonnet form evolves—in the progress, if that is what it is, from Beatrice to Laura to Stella—it can be observed that poetic first person increasingly and, it seems deliberately presents itself in terms of what is understood to be a *merely literary* figure of a self.[57]

In the history of English literature, it was Shakespeare's *Sonnets* and John Donne's *Songs and Sonnets* that introduced a nongeneric model of subjectivity different from that of *Gesellschaftslyrik*. The fact that the former was rediscovered at the beginning of the nineteenth century and the latter a hundred years later is symptomatic.[58] What modern readers find in the poetry of Shakespeare and Donne, and what they cannot find in Sidney or Spenser, is a credibility, a biographic fullness that other Renaissance poets do not possess. And although twentieth-century criticism has shown that these sorts of works preserve many rituals of genre, a great deal of Shakespeare's and Donne's success as lyric poets hangs on the power with which these authors were able to inject new existential density into the web of conventions. It was precisely starting in the Romantic era that the subjective poetry of Sappho, Catullus, Horace, Dante, Petrarch, and Shakespeare began to be read in light of the new paradigm. And yet this very paradigm is what created the conditions

---

57. Joel Fineman, *Shakespeare's Perjured Eye: The Invention of Poetic Subjectivity in the Sonnets* (Berkeley: University of California Press, 1986), 10.

58. See Jane Kingsley-Smith, *The Afterlife of Shakespeare's Sonnets* (Cambridge: Cambridge University Press, 2019), chap. 4; and John R. Roberts, *John Donne: An Annotated Bibliography of Modern Criticism, 1912–1967* (Columbia: University of Missouri Press, 1973).

for a new way of saying *I* to develop, in a different way from the one we find in these authors. How are we to explain this transition?

Public and Private

I would begin by starting from the end and working backward, from the model of autobiographical lyric poetry that we have become accustomed to over the last two centuries. Let us look at two poems by Louise Glück. The first is from her debut book, *Firstborn* (1968), and the second from her 1999 book, *Vita Nova*:

Returning a Lost Child

Nothing moves. In its cage, the broken
Blossom of a fan sways
Limply, trickling its wire, as her thin
Arms, hung like flypaper, twist about the boy . . .
Later, blocking the doorway, tongue
Pinned to the fat wedge of his pop, he watches
As I find the other room, the father strung
On crutches, waiting to be roused . . .
Now squeezed from thanks the woman's lemonade lies
In my cup. As endlessly she picks
Her spent kleenex into dust, always
Staring at that man, hearing the click,
Click of his brain's whirling empty spindle . . . [59]

Formaggio

The world
was whole because
it shattered. When it shattered,
then we knew what it was.

It never healed itself.
But in the deep fissures, smaller worlds appeared:

---

59. Louise Glück, "Returning a Lost Child," in *Firstborn* (1968), reprinted in *Poems 1962–2012* (New York: Farrar, Straus and Giroux, 2013), 11.

it was a good thing that human beings made them;
human beings know what they need,
better than any god.

On Huron Avenue they became
a block of stores; they became
Fishmonger, Formaggio. Whatever
they were or sold, they were
alike in their function: they were
visions of safety. Like
a resting place. The salespeople
were like parents; they appeared
to live there. On the whole,
kinder than parents.

Tributaries
feeding into a large river: I had
many lives. In the provisional world,
I stood where the fruit was,
flats of cherries, clementines,
under Hallie's flowers.

I had many lives. Feeding
into a river, the river
feeding into a great ocean. If the self
becomes invisible has it disappeared?
I thrived. I lived
not completely alone, alone
but not completely, strangers
surging around me.

That's what the sea is:
we exist in secret.

I had lives before this, stems
of a spray of flowers: they became

one thing, held by a ribbon at the center, a ribbon
visible under the hand. Above the hand,
the branching future, stems
ending in flowers. And the gripped fist—
that would be the self in the present.[60]

Both poems seem like the visible shards of a biographical scene that remains cloaked to us in its entirety. They are made to be understood in slivers, and their meaning resides in the dialectic between what we understand, what we guess, and what we are unable to decipher completely. In "Returning a Lost Child," a reader without critical notes or commentary by the poet might understand that the speaker, perhaps while returning a lost child, has gone into the home of a family riddled with conflicts. In the first two stanzas of "Formaggio," the speaker reflects on the relationship between the world as a whole and small private worlds; in the third, we understand that the speaker is thinking about a specific place. Readers who know the places mentioned or the biography of the author can understand that Huron Avenue is in Cambridge, Massachusetts, and that Fishmonger, Formaggio, and Hallie's Flowers are stores on that street. Their names are probably mentioned because the lyric *I* is thinking about them. They are related to her life, but the reader cannot decipher every mental association and every detail.

These poems belong to the public sphere (that is, to literature, which is always a social and ritual affair), but they shift the axis of communication further inward, *in interiore homine*, into the inner person. It is as if biography had earned the right to appear on the page without too many mediations. This way of articulating private experience is absolutely modern, and the sign of this shift is the diffusion of a certain type of poetic obscurity that is accentuated in Glück's poem. To take another example,

La speranza di pure rivederti
m'abbandonava;

e mi chiesi se questo che mi chiude
ogni senso di te, schermo d'immagini,

---

60. Louise Glück, "Formaggio," in *Vita Nova* (1999), reprinted in *Poems 1962–2012*, 375–376.

ha i segni della morte o dal passato
è in esso, ma distorto e fatto labile,
un *tuo* barbaglio:

(a Modena, tra i portici,
un servo gallonato trascinava
due sciacalli al guinzaglio).

The hope of even seeing you again
was leaving me;

and I asked myself if this which keeps me from
all sense of you, this screen of images,
is marked by death, or if, out of the past,
but deformed and diminished, it entails
some flash *of yours:*

(under the arcades, at Modena,
a servant in gold braid led
two jackals on a leash).[61]

This is a motet from *Le occasioni* (1939, *The Occasions*), Eugenio Montale's second book. A reader unused to the language of modern poetry would probably find it incomprehensible. If they were familiar with the other poems in the collection, they would be able to understand that the "you" addressed by the first person is the same woman who appears in many other poems. They would also manage to decipher the meaning of the first two stanzas. Distant from his beloved, the speaker is afraid of losing even his hope of seeing her again, so he asks himself if the events that distract him from the woman's memory are a sign of death or a glimmer of her that resurfaces from the past but in a distorted and weakened form. But what does the servant in gold braid with the leashed jackals have to do with it? What is the

61. Eugenio Montale, "La speranza di pure rivederti," in *L'opera in versi*, ed. Rosanna Bettarini e Gianfranco Contini (Turin: Einaudi, 1980), 138; English translation "The hope of even seeing you again," in *Collected Poems 1920–1954*, 2nd rev. ed., trans. and ed. Jonathan Galassi (New York: Farrar, Straus and Giroux, 2000), p. 196.

relationship between the final words in parentheses and the lines that come before them?

"The hope of even seeing you again" was written in 1937. In February 1950 Montale published a newspaper article in *Corriere della Sera* with the title "Two Jackals on a Leash." In it he describes someone named Mirco, "a well-known poet who now has a different profession," and about his short lyric poems that remained for years in his vest pocket, addressed to a woman named Clizia who lived three thousand miles away. One summer day, Mirco was walking under the porticos of Modena, absorbed in his thoughts of her and annoyed by the distractions. At a certain point, two very strange dogs appeared in front of him, held on a leash by an old man in a gold-braided uniform. Mirco stopped and asked what breed of dog they were. The old man answered that they were jackals, not dogs. These very unexceptional words galvanized Mirco, because Clizia loved odd, amusing animals, and by calling them jackals, the old man had summoned her into his thoughts. From then on, Modena and jackals remained tied to his memory of the woman: "Could the two beasts have been sent by her, as if by emanation? Could they be an emblem, an occult citation, a *senhal*? Or maybe they were just a hallucination, the premonitory signs of her decline, of her end?" Sometime later, Mirco writes the first two stanzas of the motet; then he adds the third and puts it in parentheses, to isolate the episode and suggest a different tone of voice, "the astonishment of an intimate, distant memory."[62]

In the *Corriere della Sera* article, Montale ironically reenacts the bewilderment of his early readers in the face of such an obscure transition: "'who was the owner of the jackals?' someone asked, 'And what did Modena have to do with it? Why Modena and not Parma or Voghera? And the man with the jackals? Was he a servant? An adman?'"[63] What could average readers who knew nothing about the biographical background—like everyone who read the 1939 edition of *Le occasioni*—understand before Montale's work became an object of study and commentary? They could understand the situation, that the speaker in the poem is connected to a woman whom he

---

62. Eugenio Montale, "Due sciacalli al guinzaglio" (1950), in *Il secondo mestiere: Arte, musica, società*, ed. Giorgio Zampa (Milan: Mondadori, 1996), 1489–1493.

63. Ibid., 1493.

is desperate to see again; they can grasp the literal meaning of the second strophe; and they might guess that the jackals are not an allegory but a fact of reality related in some obscure way to the preceding lines. Nevertheless, the literal meaning of the poem remains indecipherable until a document external to it intervenes to explain the most intimate information in an individual's existence: a free mental association.

Montale's and Glück's poems are born from a metonymic framing that isolates a series of unrelated scenes from the totality, as if poems were lands that rose up out of invisible biographical waters, and as if the writing imitated the reticence typical of linguistic acts associated with the private sphere: diary pages and interior monologue. They are examples of modern autobiographical lyricism, which does not organize the data of experience with the aim of a public explanation, but seeks to put them on the page while preserving their only partially transitive nature. The explanation, when there is one, comes later, in notes appearing below the text, or in the practice of accompanying the poem with commentary written in retrospect by the poet. Montale sometimes did this in *Corriere della Sera*. To cite another example, in a book-length interview with Dennis O'Driscoll, Seamus Heaney clarifies, among other things, the biographical background of some of his poems and the data of reality that in certain texts remain obscure or in suspense because they are completely private and intended to be that way.[64]

In the last two centuries, this type of radically subjective poetry with a wealth of inward-looking mental associations has become the rule, changing readers' horizon of expectations. Today we perceive a gap between this model and most premodern autobiographical poetry. Subjective poems of the new type appear much more intimately private than the old types, because they are able to describe the inner life with an unprecedented wealth of details. Only in the modern era, though, did references become so intimate that they became indecipherable in some cases. Premodern allusions always have an implicit or explicit social context—perhaps social relations between two people, which often occurs in poems addressed to a second person, in occasional lyric

---

64. Dennis O'Driscoll, *Stepping Stones: Interviews with Seamus Heaney* (New York: Farrar, Straus and Giroux, 2008).

poetry, or in correspondence poems. In Horace's *Odes*, for example, we find
texts like this one (1, 33):

Albi, ne doleas plus nimio memor
inmitis Glycerae neu miserabilis
decantes elegos, cur tibi iunior
     laesa praeniteat fide.

Insignem tenui fronte Lycorida
Cyri torret amor, Cyrus in asperam
declinat Pholoen: sed prius Apulis
     iungentur capreae lupis,

quam turpi Pholoe peccet adultero.
Sic visum Veneri, cui placet imparis
formas atque animos sub iuga aenea
     saevo mittere cum ioco.

Ipsum me melior cum peteret Venus,
grata detinuit compede Myrtale
libertina, fretis acrior Hadriae
     curvantis Calabros sinus.

Tibúllus, do not grieve, obsessed with unkind
Glýcera, or drone sad elegies,
asking why she's broken faith and now
     prefers a younger man.

Her love for Cyrus burns Lycóris, fair
of brow, while Cyrus favors Phóloë
the harsh; but roe-deer will lie down
     with hungry wolves before

an ugly lover beckons Phóloë.
Thus Venus has decreed, whose pleasure is
to bend to her bronze yoke forms and hearts
     that do not match—cruel joke.

> Although a better love was seeking me,
> with pleasing bonds freedwoman Mýrtalë
> possessed me, fiercer than the Adriatic
>   curving Calabria's coast.[65]

The poem is most probably addressed to Albius Tibullus, who was one of Horace's friends. The identities of the other characters remain unknown, and this prevents us from understanding the literal meaning of some allusions that are presented almost as antonomasias (Lycoris, "fair of brow," and Pholoë, "the harsh"). And yet the reader knows with certainty that, at least in the literary fiction, Tibullus can decipher every clue. He knows why Glycera is unkind or why Pholoë is harsh, and he knows because the logic of the composition presupposes it: the text does not refer to a radically private knowledge but to a tight-knit form of sociability. There is a similar example in one of Dante's most famous sonnets:

> Guido, i' vorrei che tu e Lapo ed io
> fossimo presi per incantamento,
> e messi in un vasel ch'ad ogni vento
> per mare andasse al voler nostro e mio,
> sì che fortuna od altro tempo rio
> non ci potesse dare impedimento,
> anzi, vivendo sempre in un talento,
> di stare insieme crescesse 'l disio.
>
> E monna Vanna e monna Lagia poi
> con quella ch'è sul numer de le trenta
> con noi ponesse il buono incantatore:
> e quivi ragionar sempre d'amore,
> e ciascuna di lor fosse contenta,
> sì come i'credo che saremmo noi.

---

65. *The Odes of Horace*, trans. Jeffrey H. Kaimowitz (Baltimore, MD: Johns Hopkins University Press, 2008), 47.

Guido, I wish that Lapo, you, and I
were carried off by some enchanter's spell
And set upon a ship to sail the sea
where every wind would favor our command,
so neither thunderstorms nor cloudy skies
might ever have the power to hold us back,
but rather, cleaving to this single wish
that our desire to live as one would grow.

And Lady Vanna and Lady Lagia
borne to us with her who's number thirty
by our good enchanter's wizardry:
to talk of love would be our sole pursuit,
and each of them would find herself content,
just as I think that we should likewise be.[66]

"Guido, I wish that . . ." is not a soliloquy. Although critics have not un-
equivocally identified the woman "who's number thirty" mentioned by Dante
in line 10, the reader understands that the allusion was crystal clear to the
person to whom the sonnet is addressed, Guido Cavalcanti. Something similar occurs in the seventeenth of John Donne's "Holy Sonnets":

Since she whom I loved hath paid her last debt
    To nature, and to hers, and my good is dead,
    And her soul early into heaven ravished,
Wholly in heavenly things my mind is set.
Here the admiring her my mind did whet
    To seek thee God; so streams do show the head;
    But though I have found thee'and thou my thirst hast fed,
A holy thirsty dropsy melts me yet.
But why should I beg more love, when as thou
    Dost woo my soul, for hers off'ring all thine:

---

66. Dante Alighieri, *Rime*, ed. Gianfranco Contini (Turin, Italy: Einaudi, 1980): 35–36; English translation
Dante's Lyric Poetry: Poems of Youth and of the "Vita Nuova," ed. Teodolinda Barolini, trans. Richard Lansing
(Toronto: University of Toronto Press, 2012), 121.

> And dost not only fear lest I allow
>   My love to saints and angels, things divine,
> But in thy tender jealousy dost doubt
> Lest the world, flesh, yea, devil put thee out.[67]

"She whom I loved" is Anne More, the sixteen-year-old that Donne had married clandestinely in December 1601, ruining his career, already made difficult by his Catholic ancestry.[68] Their secret marriage created a scandal at court, where Donne had become quite well known, partly thanks to the early circulation in the late 1590s of some of the lyric poems later collected in *Songs and Sonnets*. At the time Donne was working as a secretary for Thomas Egerton, the Lord Keeper. Anne More was Egerton's niece and the daughter of another dignitary, George More, who, when the marriage was revealed, had Donne fired and thrown in jail. For many years Donne lived in poverty, with many children, aided by patrons such as Lady Magdalen Herbert, the mother of George Herbert, perhaps alluded to in "The Autumnal," and by the Countess of Bedford, perhaps alluded to in "Twicknam Garden." Anne More died in 1617, while giving birth to their twelfth child. This makes it possible to date the poem. Now, readers unfamiliar with Donne's personal history were able to read the poem by placing it in an illustrious literary tradition that has Petrarch as its archetype: the death of the beloved is transmuted into a greater closeness to God. Only readers familiar with Donne's background circumstances and personal history were able to decipher the private allusions and grasp all the implications. But in this case too, as for Horace and Dante, the text presupposes the existence of a group of people able to understand the literal meaning of the poem, in part because, having caused a scandal, the event referred to is a public one. When reading "Returning a Lost Child" by Glück, on the other hand, one cannot be sure that any reader would be able to fully grasp the biographical backdrop that the poem alludes to, whether real or imaginary, and which the speaker takes for granted; and

---

67. John Donne, "Since she whom I loved hath paid her last debt," in *John Donne's Poetry*, ed. Donald R. Dickson (New York: Norton, 2007). This sonnet circulated in manuscripts. It was discovered by Edmund Gosse in the Westmoreland Manuscript and included in Herbert J. C. Grierson's modern edition of Donne's works: *The Poems of John Donne, Edited from the Old Editions and Numerous Manuscripts, with Introduction and Commentary*, ed. Herbert J. C. Grierson (Oxford: Oxford University Press, 1912).

68. See Robert Cecil Bald, *John Donne: A Life* (Oxford: Oxford University Press, 1970), 93–142; and Dennis Flynn, *John Donne and the Ancient Catholic Nobility* (Bloomington: Indiana University Press, 1995).

the text is developed on the premise and introjection of this privateness into its structure. In the same way, one cannot be sure in "The hope of even seeing you again" whether the second person, *you,* will be able to understand the reasoning behind the last three lines. By addressing an absent second person, who is not expected to understand or respond, but simply to listen, the first person skips over all presuppositions and explanations to bring a completely private mental association into public, using a technique that has long belonged to the language of modern poetry. The same thing happens in Glück's poems: the situations can be described, but the literal meaning of the individual passages is known exclusively to the speaker: only the author's commentary would be able to clarify it completely. The poem plays on a dialectic between light and dark, between details that are illuminated and the whole that remains in shadow. Poems like "Returning a Lost Child," "Formaggio" or "The hope of even seeing you again" make much more space for the minute, the accidental, and the unmotivated details of personal life than that given to these aspects in the past. The differences between the premodern autobiographical lyric and that of the Romantic era are no less significant than the differences separating *Gesellschaftslyrik* from the subjective poems of Catullus, Horace, Dante, Petrarch, Shakespeare, or Donne.

Transcendental Autobiographism

Petrarch's most important interpreter, Gianfranco Contini, defined the way Petrarch talks about his life in the *Canzoniere* as "transcendental autobiographism."[69] Contini's critical writing almost never makes the premises of his discourse explicit, and in this case too the literary meaning of the Kantian adjective "transcendental" remains vague. Examining how Contini uses the term, one understands that it refers to the type of autobiographical experience recounted by the *Canzoniere:* Petrarch talks about himself, about an individuated *I,* but at the same time tells an openly allegorical story, which he assembles by adjusting the data of reality to construct an exemplary Stoic and Augustinian journey that leads the character from the errors of youth

---

69. Gianfranco Contini, "Preliminari alla lingua di Petrarca (1951)," in *Varianti e altra linguistica* (Turin: Einaudi, 1979), 178.

to the wisdom of maturity. Unlike medieval love *Gesellschaftslyrik*, Petrarch's speaker has a distinct identity and recounts specific autobiographical facts, such as when he praises the families of his patrons or inserts occasional pieces into the structure of the collection. Nevertheless, Petrarch always tries to preserve the universal value of his discourse by avoiding any references to overly particular circumstances.[70] The speaker is an individual but at the same time an *exemplum;* the experiences evoked are private but must also manage to be universally human.[71] To achieve this, Petrarch censors or blurs anything too detailed or contingent; for example, by reabsorbing occasional poems into the complex allegorical structure in such a way as to maximally conceal their ephemeral origins. For Petrarch, events that are too circumstantial always run the risk of proving transient—a reasoning consistent with what the *Stiltrennung* decrees for compositions written in the noble style: personal life can have a metaphorical sense only when it conceals or redeems its contingency and becomes ideographic, that is, transcendental.

The form of the poems appears to be governed by the same policy. The chief characteristic of Petrarch's style is his censorship of fortuitous details. The *Canzoniere* transmitted to European lyric poetry a hard-and-fast mechanism for selecting words and things. This mechanism is founded on a monolinguistic poetic vocabulary, which blots out the technical, prosaic, or spoken lexicon; and on an eternalizing representation of objects, transforming the data of reality into everlasting emblems and putting the indeterminate before the determinate and substances before accidents[72]—an approach aligned with the assumptions of the *Stiltrennung*. Censorship in the mimesis of the external world is matched by an identical attitude in the mimesis of the inner life. In the *Canzoniere,* the space of the conscience is composed of rigid forces, not fluid movements. The speaker is not torn apart by intangible psychological conflicts or by an abrupt overlapping of ideas and impressions but by weighty moral conflicts that the categories of medieval psychology and philosophy translated into concepts.[73] This form of mimesis is not new: it descends from an age-old tradition that started with Aristotle's *Nicomachean Ethics* and *Rhetoric* and

70. Santagata, *Introduzione,* lxx.

71. Ibid., lxxi.

72. Contini, "Preliminari alla lingua di Petrarca."

73. Santagata, *Introduzione,* lv.

continued up to the eighteenth century.[74] According to the schemas of this psychology, personal idiosyncrasy is transitory, like particular individuals: what counts is human beings caught in their essence and grouped under synthesizing categories that give form to the fluid flows of the mental life, attributing a single name to their dominant character trait ("astute," "courageous," "generous," "treacherous") and, even before that, to the forces that move it ("love," "hate," "pity," "envy"). The *Canzoniere* tells a tale that is at the same time individual and allegorical; the speaker smooths down the overly personal traits of its own story to turn itself into an emblem; the structure of the poems makes itself impermeable to the contingency of occasional events. In the world created by the text, what happens *in interiore homine* is transposed onto the page through a lexicon and a syntax that are public. The forms of allusion to private references that we find in Glück or Montale would be impossible in Petrarch.

The idea of transcendental autobiographism lends itself to a wider theoretical use that goes beyond Petrarch. Transcendental autobiographism exists every time the desire to introduce contingent biographical elements meets with the need to maintain an ideographic filter that allegorizes and generalizes particularities. From this perspective, poetic genres have long been the most solid transcendental structures of European lyric. As long as the classes into which lyric poetry were divided continued to have an implicit or explicit normative value, authors of an ode or an epigram, a satire or a love poem knew that they would have to inject their own real identity into the confines of a preestablished poetic identity, adapting the events and idiosyncrasies of their lives to a public, ritual mold:

> The composition of an epithalamium in archaic Greek poetry imposed certain limits on the author. He was conditioned by constraints on form and content that prevented him (to indicate extreme taboos) from using iambic trimeter for his meter as well as from arguing the idea, widespread in other contexts of archaic Greek poetry, that women represented the worst of all evils. This obstacle would

---

74. See Étienne Gilson, "La scolastique et l'esprit classique," in *Les Idées et les Lettres* (Paris: Vrin, 1955), 254–261; Louis Van Delft, *Le Moraliste classique: Essai de définition et de typologie* (Genève: Droz, 1982), 138ff.; and Lidiya Ginzburg, *O psikhologicheskoi proze* (1971, 1977); English translation, *On Psychological Prose*, trans. Judson Rosengrant (Princeton, NJ: Princeton University Press, 1991), 13–14 and 271.

present itself to the author even if, let us suppose, he found iambic trimeter to be the most congenial meter, or if he shared this misogynistic idea.[75]

This holds true for *Gesellschaftslyrik* and, more generally, for all poetic forms weighted down by conventions, that is, most of Western poetry up to the second half of the eighteenth century. Even though the great innovators of premodern autobiographical poetry, from Catullus to Petrarch and Horace to Shakespeare, were able to carve out spaces for introspection within the rules—by expanding the thematic range of Latin genres, for example, or by shifting the subject of the laud from the beloved to the poet's inner conflicts— their works did not entirely abandon the scaffoldings of genre and their transcendental function. For this reason especially, although Catullus's speaker differs from that of archaic Greek lyric, the subject of his *Liber* is not yet that of Rimbaud or Whitman. The same holds for Horace, Petrarch, Shakespeare, and Donne: the accidentality of their biographies is still filtered by genre structures that submit the contingency of life to public patterns.

The other decisive scaffolding, as we have seen, is the rule of the division of styles, which is internal to the system of poetic subgenres and runs throughout European literature. It reappears every time ancient models and poetics are assumed as a criterion of normative perfection. Another assumption belonging to the *Stiltrennung* stipulates that high-style genres are not suited to an overly detailed, documentary imitation of reality. The premodern attitude of transcendental autobiographism is always internal to the division of styles, whereas modern autobiographism tends to ignore it. Starting from a historical threshold that varies from one national literature to another but essentially coincides with the Romantic era, poets were able to recount ephemeral details of their contingent personal lives—real, self-fictionalized, or imaginary—with unprecedented confessional freedom, existential pathos, and seriousness.

This is what happens in Leopardi's work. When we compare the way *I* is said in "The Infinite" with the schemas of transcendental autobiographism, we realize that the reasoning behind the display of the self appears to have changed. For lyric poetry to have a universal value, for the *I* to mean *we,* it is

---

75. Rösler, "Persona reale o persona poetica?," 132.

no longer necessary for the first person to censor the details of its peculiarities and become a type, an *exemplum*, resting on an allegorical and ideographic framework. Between Petrarch's transcendental autobiographism and Leopardi's, one discerns the same difference that separates Augustine's *Confessions* from Jean-Jacques Rousseau's. How might we define this shift?

Differential Autobiographism

In the modern era, writes Georg Simmel, two different ideas of individuality took form. The first conceives of particular individuals as emanations of a general idea of the human being, who is the same in all times and places; the second values subjective differences, their peculiarities.[76] The first corresponds to Enlightenment rationalism and generated the idea of universal human rights; the second corresponds to Romantic and post-Romantic individualism, insists on particularities, and demands the right to bring each person's idiosyncratic traits into the public sphere.

The paradigm that we glimpse in "The Infinite," which then prevailed during the next two centuries, draws from such a model. This new type of autobiographism, which we might call *differential*, should not be understood in a naively Romantic sense. It is not the "spontaneous overflow of powerful feelings" or the "free and straightforward expression of any living and deeply held human feeling": it is not an unmediated confession, because there is no such thing as an unmediated confession—free, that is, of introjected mediations. The speaker in a lyric poem is always a pattern, a model of subjectivity constructed on the basis of inherited schemas and placed under the gaze of others.[77] It continues to be a persona and displays itself on the page in an implicit or explicit performance: self-exhibition and self-fashioning never

---

76. See Georg Simmel, "Die beiden Formen des Individualismus" (1901) in *Georg Simmel: Gesamtausgabe*, Band 7, ed. Rüdiger Kramme, Angela Rammstedt, and Otthein Rammstedt (Frankfurt: Suhrkamp, 1995), 49–56. This dichotomy and the Romantic idea of differential individualism were then picked up on and developed in many ways, especially by Richard Sennett and Charles Taylor. See Richard Sennett, *The Fall of Public Man* (New York: Knopf, 1977); and Charles Taylor, *Sources of the Self: The Making of the Modern Identity* (Cambridge, MA: Harvard University Press, 1989).

77. Werner Wolf, "The Lyric: Problems of Definition and a Proposal for Reconceptualisation," in *Theory into Poetry: New Approaches to the Lyric*, ed. Eva Müller-Zettelmann and Margarete Rubik (Amsterdam: Rodopi, 2005), 21–56; Culler, *Theory of the Lyric*.

disappear. But the awareness that lyric, like literature in general, always arises out of social patterns should not lead us to forget two fundamental differences: that not all patterns are the same, and that they have a different historical index, a different point of emergence, a different *kairos*. The personae of *Gesellschaftslyrik,* transcendental autobiographism, and differential autobiographism do not share the same nature. The paradigm of differential autobiographism is much closer to the biographical contingency of a private persona than the other two, because in the modern era the right of individuals to perceive, develop, and display their subjective difference is greater than what it was in the past. Differential autobiographism is the literary equivalent of this historical process.

The sign and symptom of this shift is the introduction into poetry of allusions, anecdotes, and private mental associations. In poems like "Returning a Lost Child" or "The hope of even seeing you again" the first person seems to talk to itself with a degree of solipsistic closure that is inconceivable for the schemas of transcendental autobiographism. In "Thoughts on Poetry and Its Varieties" (1833), one of the culminating theoretical texts of the Romantic lyric paradigm, John Stuart Mill argues that the sign of true poetry is its solipsistic and antitheatrical nature:

> Eloquence supposes an audience; the peculiarity of poetry appears to us to lie in the poet's utter unconsciousness of a listener. Poetry is feeling, confessing itself to itself in moments of solitude, and embodying itself in symbols, which are the nearest possible representations of the feeling in the exact shape in which it exists in the poet's mind. Eloquence is feeling pouring itself out to other minds, courting their sympathy, or endeavouring to influence their belief, or move them to passion or to action.
>
> All poetry is of the nature of soliloquy. It may be said that poetry which is printed on hot-pressed paper and sold at a bookseller's shop, is a soliloquy in full dress, and on the stage. It is so: but there is nothing absurd in the idea of such a mode of soliloquizing. What we have said to ourselves, we may tell to others afterwards; what we have said or done in solitude, we may voluntarily reproduce when we know that other eyes are upon us. But no trace of consciousness that any eyes are upon us must be visible in the work itself. . . . When the

expression of [the poet's] emotions, or of his thoughts tinged by
emotions, is tinged also by that purpose, by that desire of making an
impression upon another mind, then it ceases to be poetry, and becomes eloquence.[78]

For Mill, lyric poetry is the antithesis of oratory and theater, which are
designed to speak explicitly to an audience, to persuade or seduce it; poetry
seeks instead to reproduce the conditions of soliloquy, canceling out the presence of others. Taken literally, these ideas are easily contested. Mill himself
incorporates a decisive objection into his argument: poetry never completely
abolishes public mediations, for the good reason that no private soliloquy cir-
culates in a printed book. It may therefore be said that "poetry which is
printed on hot-pressed paper and sold at a bookseller's shop, is a soliloquy in
full dress and on the stage." Hence, his reference to soliloquy should not be
understood in a literal and factual sense; it should be understood in a stylistic sense. Although intended to be read, poetry acts as though its discourse
was removed from the gaze of others, in accordance with a rhetoric that is
diametrically opposed to that governing theater and oratory, which are designed as outward facing, to communicate something in the public sphere.
Now, if we historicized Mill's argument, we would notice that this is not the
case for all periods: the posture of the subject who speaks in *Gesellschaftslyrik*
and in transcendental autobiographism is always outward facing; every point
of its rhetoric is constructed to be understood by someone; the connections
of its discourse never become entirely private. The theory of poetry in
"Thoughts on Poetry and Its Varieties" is therefore not valid in all periods: it
describes the new way of saying *I* and the new attitude of differential autobiographism that Romanticism had made possible.

This brings us to the second point: the models of lyric subjectivity have a
different historical index; they represent different epochs. This is why the Romantic paradigm cannot be dismissed purely as a grand collective illusion.
The fact that during the same years authors who differ greatly from each
other, such as Hegel, Wordsworth, and Leopardi, came to think that subjective poetry is self-expression, and the fact that over the nineteenth century

---

78. John Stuart Mill, "Thoughts on Poetry and Its Varieties" (1833), in *Autobiography and Literary Essays*, ed.
John M. Robson and Jack Stillinger (Toronto / London: University of Toronto Press / Routledge, 1981),
348–349.

the idea solidified that Romantic poetry introduced a rupture between two epochs are not errors but symptoms: they indicate that a new model of subjectivity was being born during those decades. In *Gesellschaftslyrik,* the speaker does not have a true identity. In the poetry of Petrarch, as in that of Catullus, Horace, Dante, Petrarch, Shakespeare, and Donne, the speaker brings a personal biography into the text, or at least has a subjective density that the selves in the *Gesellschaftslyrik* do not possess; but its speech passes through transcendental structures that are still thick and filtering and that tend to transform contingency into an *exemplum.* Differential autobiography corresponds instead to the modern (that is, Romantic and post-Romantic) notion of subjectivity—a subjectivity that has conquered the right to publicly display associations of ideas, minimal anecdotes, and mental transitions that in other eras would be inexpressible. In doing so, it narrows the insurmountable distance between the persona who says *I* on the page and the real individual who puts his or her name on the book. The theoretical understanding that there is no such thing as unmediated self-expression should not cancel out the awareness that the quality of the mediation changes over time. *Gesellschaftslyrik* and transcendental autobiographism also survive in the modern age, but the paradigm that corresponds to the modern way of understanding subjectivity and its relationship with self-display, self-fashioning, and the presence of others is differential autobiographism.

Three Historical Thresholds

This shift is perceptible in "The Infinite" starting from the opening. "Always dear to me was this solitary hill | And this hedge, which such a large part | Of the farthest horizon excludes from my gaze." Petrarch's speaker tells his own story to an ideal community of listeners, according to a model that is implicitly theatrical—like a character giving a monologue in front of an audience. The first person in "The Infinite" adopts, in part, the rhetoric of private writings, making use of allusions that recall hints typical of diaries, which can only be deciphered entirely in reference to the lived experience. This aspect receives a great deal of emphasis from commentators on "The Infinite." And yet these signs of immediacy belong to a formal system still largely mediated by conventions. Leopardi's poetic vocabulary uses words that are far from the degree zero of communicative discourse—words that are loaded with the past and literature. His technique for composing poems is equally mediated: Leopardi usually wrote a first draft in prose and then coolly versified it—an approach that is antithetical to the idea of lyric poetry as an unmediated soliloquy and of style as spontaneous self-expression. If we were then to pose a truly radical question, we would have to ask why a poet who is simply expressing himself would do so in hendecasyllables? Why would he observe rules of meter, thereby preserving the traces of an ancient ritual? It might seem like a naive question, one that generally remains unanswered or is answered by citing the findings of literary history, and yet these apparently naive questions harbor essential issues.[79] Interestingly enough, they can be found in the *Zibaldone:*

> Usage has established that the poet write in verse. It is not of the essence that the poet write in verse. It is not of the essence of poetry or of its language and mode of expressing things. Of course, since this language and mode, and the things the poet says, are completely different from the ordinary, it is very appropriate, and extremely useful for his effects, that he employs a rhythm, etc., that is different from vernacular and common usage, in which things are expressed as they are, or as they are usually considered to be in life. I leave to one side the usefulness of harmony, etc. But in essence, in itself, poetry is not tied to verse.[80]

A common move in literary criticism, as we have seen, is to compare the poem with the passage from the *Zibaldone* in which Leopardi describes his perception of the infinite. Quite rightly, the commentators insist more on differences than similarities: "the work of the imagination that is rationally explained in prose is represented in poetry by Leopardi with immediacy and accents of extraordinary novelty, like someone discovering an unexplored region of the soul";[81] "in the first case, we have a point of view that is critical and reflective in character, in the second . . . evocative in character."[82] However,

79. See Culler, *Theory of the Lyric*, chap. 4.
80. Leopardi, *Zibaldone*, 1695–1696, September 14, 1821.
81. Leopardi, *Canti*, ed. Mario Fubini and Emilio Bigi, 115.
82. Blasucci, "Paragrafi sull' 'Infinito,'" 116.

the *Zibaldone* is not the only work that rewrites the ideas of "The Infinite" in prose; in fact, there is a passage in the notes for his autobiographical novel that closely resembles the text of the idyll. Here it is again:

> my observations on the plurality of worlds and the nothingness of us and this earth and on the greatness and force of nature that we measure by torrents, etc., which are nothing on this globe, which is nothing in the world, *and awakened by a voice calling me to dinner so that our lives seem like a nothingness to me and time and famous names and all of history, etc.,* on the biggest and most admirable buildings that do no more than roughen up this little globe the rough things that can't be seen from slightly above and slightly far away, but from slightly above our globe appears to be smooth. . . . [83]

When comparing these lines with the poem, one instantly notices the syntactic resemblance between the final part of the prose passage and lines 11–13 of "The Infinite" ("and what comes to me is the eternal, | And the seasons dead, and the present | And alive one, and the sound of it"): a sign that the syntax of the idyll sometimes closely follows the waves of thought, so much so that its paratactic shattering competes with the disorder of the notes, which are written in a form verging on interior monologue. Nevertheless, the logical and hypotactic development of lines 9–11 is incomparably more mediated and constructed than the corresponding prose passage. The form of the prose is a note that remains faithful to a stream of consciousness, to an interior monologue, whereas the syntax of "The Infinite," however evocative, ultimately organizes the discourse with a view to public understanding, because in 1819 it was impossible for an Italian lyric poem written in a serious tone to be constructed as a jumbled accumulation of thoughts.

A century later, of course, it would have been normal to read something of this sort in a poem. I randomly pick up *Ragazzo* (Boy) by Piero Jahier, published in 1919. Prose is mixed in with the verses. A high school student is attending a class. All of a sudden, a woman, his housemaid, comes to warn him that his father has left the house forebodingly. Knowing that his father means to die, the boy escapes from school and sets off running to find him.

---

83. Leopardi, "Ricordi d'infanzia e d'adolescenza," 1190 (emphasis added).

After a page of prose with no paragraph breaks, the boy's race through the streets is described in verse:

> Correre
> e perché invece tutte le cose inutili così lucide dal ponte
> campana che mesce mezzogiorno sporgendosi dal campanile
> scola l'acqua dalla pala il renaiolo
> penna di vapore sul fischio che si sentirà
>
> Correre
> tra i tanti visi frotteggianti forse uno che l'ha visto passare stamani:
> non mi riconosci se l'hai incontrato
> non vedi che sono il suo bambino
> perché ti dimentichi il viso che va a morire.[84]
>
> Running
> and why instead all the useless things so shiny from the bridge
> bell that pours out noon sticking out from the belltower
> the sandman drains the water from his shovel
> plume of steam on the whistle that will be heard
>
> Running
> among all the faces looking out maybe one that saw him pass this morning;
> don't you recognize me if you met him
> don't you see that I'm his child
> why do you forget the face that goes off to die?

While it is true that *Ragazzo* is not easy to assign to a specific genre, because it is a prose poem, these verses are very similar to poems Jahier published earlier, and to many other poems that appeared in Italy in the same years. In the most well known of the Italian collections to come out in 1919, Giuseppe Ungaretti's *Allegria di naufragi* (*Joy of Shipwrecks*),[85] we find the poem "Viaggio" ("Voyage") whose *dispositio* jumps from one sentence to the other without connections:

84. Piero Jahier, *Ragazzo* (Rome: La Voce, 1919), 8–9.

85. In the 1919 edition, the book was still called *Allegria di naufragi* (*Joy of Shipwrecks*). It would become *L'allegria* (*The Joy*) starting from the 1931 edition. See also Giuseppe Ungaretti, *Allegria*, trans. Geoffrey Brock (Brooklyn, NY: Archipelago Books, 2020).

Non mi posso accasare.
Ad ogni nuovo clima, mi ritrovo di averne già saputo.
In quali tempi andati?
Sempre me ne stacco forestiero.
Tornato nascendo da epoche troppo vissute.
Cerco un paese innocente.[86]

I can't find a home for myself.
At each new land, I find myself already knowing about it.
In what times gone by?
I always come away a stranger.
Returned being born from epochs too long lived.
I seek an innocent country.

Certain syntactical constructions and sudden juxtapositions that in 1819 might have been acceptable at most for jotting down some notes were now part of the Italian language of poetry in 1919. This occurred in all the Western literatures. Consider the ending of one of the most famous poems written in English in 1919, published the following year:

[. . .] De Bailhache, Fresca, Mrs. Cammel, whirled
Beyond the circuit of the shuddering Bear
In fractured atoms. Gull against the wind, in the windy straits
Of Belle Isle, or running on the Horn.
White feathers in the snow, the Gulf claims,
And an old man driven by the Trades
To a sleepy corner.
                              Tenants of the house,
Thoughts of a dry brain in a dry season.[87]

T. S. Eliot's "Gerontion" is a dramatic monologue and not a lyric poem in the narrow sense, but the way the speaker's thoughts are associated is cer-

---

86. Giuseppe Ungaretti, *L'allegria,* ed. Cristiana Maggi Romano (Milan: Fondazione Arnoldo e Alberto Mondadori, 1982), 233. "Viaggio" was not reprinted in the later editions of *L'allegria.*

87. Thomas Stearns Eliot, "Gerontion," in *The Poems of T. S. Eliot, Volume I: Collected and Uncollected Poems,* ed. Christopher Ricks and Jim McCue (London: Faber and Faber, 2015), 33. "Gerontion" was published in *Ara Vos Prec* (1920) and *Poems* (1920).

tainly much less structured than what was permitted by the conventions of the previous century. Assuming that the last verse is what ties the *explicit* to the *incipit* ("Here I am, an old man in a dry month, | Being read to by a boy, waiting for rain"), what is the link between the two preceding sentences? And the names mentioned—what do they refer to? In 1819, when Keats was writing his great odes and "La Belle Dame sans Merci," Shelley his "Ode to the West Wind," and Byron was publishing "Mazeppa" and "Ode on Venice," the finale of "Gerontion" would have been incomprehensible—both its literal meaning (and it still is for readers who are nonspecialists or lack critical commentary) and its significance as an artistic act. This means that the texts by Jahier, Ungaretti, and Eliot support the idea that poetry has more to do with unrelated subjectivity than "The Infinite" does. For poetry to lose its public mediations, the poet needs to escape from conventions and free himself or herself from the rituals of meter, lexicon, syntax, and rhetoric inherited from the past.

In other words, the birth of modern poetry was not an instantaneous change but a slow metamorphosis, a process that took place in three stages. The first changed the way of perceiving poetry. The modern concept of the lyric was born in the second half of the sixteenth century, later spreading throughout Europe between the second half of the eighteenth century and the beginning of the nineteenth. This shift included the nascent idea that writing in verse coincides with lyric poetry, and that the lyric is concerned with the writer's self-expression. The second transformed the way poetic personas were constructed in writing. A new type of autobiographism emerged, which did not cancel out the other models but gradually gained hegemony, overlapping with the development of genres that gave voice to the lived experiences of writers: modern autobiography, which, after the success of Rousseau's *Confessions* (1782–1789), spread quickly all over Europe; and the novel of the intellectual hero, with its archetype in the character of Saint-Preux in Rousseau's *Julie, or the New Heloise* (1761),[88] which came to full maturity with Goethe's *The Sorrows of Young Werther* (1774). Lyric poetry also moved closer to the writing of experience. The poetic subject was constructed in a different way, presenting itself increasingly as a differential individual, as the avatar of a biographical subject that talks about itself, reducing the mediations that in earlier poetry had transformed a private, individual story into a public,

---

88. See Victor Brombert, *The Intellectual Hero* (Philadelphia: Lippincott, 1961), 14.

exemplary story. But although the content of poetry changed in the first half of the nineteenth century, it would take at least a century for the form to transmute in consequence. The third change, involving style, was the slowest, since the metamorphosis of poetic form lasted throughout the nineteenth century and only came to an end with the first avant-garde movements of the twentieth century. This was when poets truly gained in principle the possibility of expressing themselves without the constraints that the Romantic poetics proclaimed but only partially achieved in the poems of their time. "The Infinite" is a new poem because of its subject matter, because of the way Leopardi says *I*, because of the poetic persona he constructs. The formal novelties are instead embryonic and can be grasped above all in retrospect, by a gaze informed by the literature of the twentieth century. These novelties are the harbinger of a transformation that would take place during the following decades and change the form of European poetry with a radicality that Romantic poetry experienced only in part.

CHAPTER THREE

A History of Forms

Theories of Style

We already have some familiarity with the theory of style that developed during the second half of the eighteenth century. One of the first memorable expressions of it in a text is Wordsworth's preface to the second edition of *Lyrical Ballads*. True poetry starts with the language "really spoken by men" and infuses it with passion, writes Wordsworth. What transforms style and makes the form of poetry different from the form of prose is a "spontaneous overflow of powerful feelings." Poetry is at the same time subjective and universal, unique and democratic, because poets do not differ from other people "in kind" but only "in degree"—the "degree" indicating greater expressive force. Fundamentally, the passions, thoughts, and feelings possessed by writers are the "passions and thoughts and feelings of men."[1] During periods of decadence, this natural creative process is supplanted by a cold-blooded replica that Wordsworth calls *poetic diction*.

With Wordsworth's preface, the great poetry of European Romanticism adopted an idea of style that had become widespread at the end of the eighteenth century, after gaining authoritative philosophical expression in theories on the nature of language by Giambattista Vico, Jean-Jacques Rousseau, and

---

1. William Wordsworth and Samuel Taylor Coleridge, *Lyrical Ballads*, 2nd ed., ed. R. L. Brett and A. R. Jones (London: Routledge, 1991), 261.

Johann Gottfried Herder.[2] When Wordsworth opposes spontaneous poetry to poetic diction, he defines a crucial shift in an admirably concise way. I will try to describe it using a passage equally admirable for its concision, written by Roland Barthes. In *Writing Degree Zero*, Barthes tells the story of how French poetry was transformed in the second half of the nineteenth century:

> In the classical period, prose and poetry are quantities, their difference can be measured; they are neither more nor less separated than two different numbers, contiguous like them, but dissimilar because of the very difference in their magnitude. If I use the word prose for a minimal form of speech, the most economical vehicle for thought, and if I use the letters a, b, c for certain attributes of languages, which are useless but decorative, such as metre, rhyme or the ritual of images, all the linguistic surface will be accounted for in M. Jourdain's double equation:
>
> $$\text{Poetry} = \text{Prose} + a + b + c$$
> $$\text{Prose} = \text{Poetry} - a - b - c$$
>
> whence it clearly follows that Poetry is always different from Prose. But this difference is not one of essence: it is one of quantity. . . . Classical poetry is felt to be merely an ornamental variation of prose, the fruit of an *art* (that is, a technique), never a different language, or the product of a particular sensibility.[3]

The vocabularies of Wordsworth and Barthes are very different, but the underlying paradigm is similar: the *poetic diction* of the former coincides with the *poésie classique* of the latter, that is, with the poetry of the French *âge classique* and, broadly speaking, all premodern classicist poetry. *Poetic diction* and *poésie classique* differ from ordinary language because they superimpose an *ornatus*, a series of decorative attributes, onto the minimal form of speech, the "most economical vehicle for thought." This type of verse writing is

---

2. Meyer H. Abrams, *The Mirror and the Lamp: Romantic Theory and the Critical Tradition* (1953) (New York: Oxford University Press, 1971), chap. 4; Paul de Man, "Lyric and Modernity," in *Blindness and Insight: Essays in the Rhetoric of Contemporary Criticism* (New York: Oxford University Press, 1971), 166–186.

3. Roland Barthes, *Le Degré zéro de l'écriture* (1953); English translation, *Writing Degree Zero*, trans. Annette Lavers and Colin Smith (New York: Hill and Wang, 1977), 41–42.

opposed to a completely different form: for Wordsworth, primitive lyric and *Lyrical Ballads*; for Barthes, fully modern poetry, which, according to his philosophy of literary history, was born with Rimbaud and the Symbolists. The style of *poésie classique* is "an ornamental variation" of prose, since the poet uses embellishments to ennoble degree-zero writing; the style of modern poetry is not mere veneer, but "the product of a particular sensibility." What does this difference imply?

Wordsworth and Barthes reflect on the same problem starting from the same premise. According to this schema, style arises either from subjective difference or ritual convention. In the case of subjective difference, the rhetorical departure from degree-zero writing reflects a lived experience that alters the ordinary way of saying things; in the case of ritual convention, figures are added deliberately without the impulse of genuine passion, using conventional devices. These ornaments have an origin and meaning that are collective: by rejecting poetic diction, Wordsworth knows that he has "cut [himself] off from a large portion of phrases and figures of speech which from father to son have long been regarded as the common inheritance of Poets";[4] Barthes knows that the *ornatus* of classical writing reflects a specific ritual of society.[5] The style of the primitive or modern poet is personal, whereas poetic diction is a group code. This antithesis opposes nature and culture, spontaneity and mediation, originality and habit, the self and society, individual talent and tradition, along the same lines as a two-part schema belonging today to what Theodor Adorno called "the specifically lyric spirit familiar to us."[6]

It must be noted that the essential texts of ancient poetics contain the ideas that the Romantic aesthetic would transform into commonplaces: that rhetorical figures express the passions, and that the poet is spoken by enthusiasm, divine folly, nature, and furor. In a well-known passage from Plato's *Ion*, the character of Socrates asserts that poets lose their wits when inspired by the divinity.[7] A controversial passage in Aristotle's *Poetics* states that since the imitator is more credible when he identifies with the passions he imitates,

---

4. Wordsworth and Coleridge, *Lyrical Ballads*, 251.

5. Barthes, *Writing Degree Zero*, 42.

6. Theodor W. Adorno, "Rede über Lyrik und Gesellschaft" (1957); English translation, "On Lyric Poetry and Society," in *Notes to Literature*, trans. Shierry Weber Nicholsen (New York: Columbia University Press, 1991), 40.

7. Plato, *Ion*, 533d–534e.

poetic art belongs to those who are gifted with (*euphues*) or given to madness (*manikos*), because the former are malleable (*euplastoi*) and the latter are able to go outside themselves, in an ecstatic trance (*ekstatikoi*).[8] The passage is not clear in every point but its overall meaning is as follows: for Aristotle, artistic creation includes a natural, irrational, and ecstatic element that not everyone possesses but which the imitator has received as a gift; as also stated in a passage from *Rhetoric* in which poetic speech is defined as *entheon*—inspired or, literally, inhabited by a god.[9] In Horace's *Odes* and *Ars Poetica*, we find references to the theory of enthusiasm, for example, when the lyric poet is described as an adept of Bacchus,[10] or when Democritus is reported to believe that poetic *ingenium* is superior to *ars*, and that those of sound mind should be excluded from Mount Helicon.[11] In the *Satires* we read that the ability to compose poetry is not enough to earn the title of poet, since the true poet needs not just *ars* but also *ingenium*, divine inspiration, and an eloquence capable of singing great deeds.[12]

As far as the relationship between style and pathos is concerned, Aristotle believed that the poet would do better by truly feeling the passions he attributed to his characters, taking for granted that natural feeling was superior to feelings re-created through artifice.[13] Horace applied a similar principle to dramatic poetry in a famous passage from *Ars Poetica*: if the actor wants the audience to cry when watching a tragedy, he must be the first to suffer, because language expresses the passions that nature forms inside us.[14] This theory would be taken up in Pseudo-Longinus's *On the Sublime*, a treatise almost completely unknown to ancient culture, which was rediscovered in

---

8. Aristotle, *Poetics*, 17.1455a.29–33.

9. Aristotle, *Rhetorics*, 1408b.18. When Aristotle speaks about the poet who goes "outside himself," he is not thinking about the changes that language undergoes when it becomes poetic, but about the plots that poets are able to invent when they transcend their own lives and lose themselves in those of their heroes. For Aristotle, the core of the poetic art is not the style (*lexis*) but the story (*mythos*), and the genre of reference is not dithyramb but tragedy. There is no reason, then, to find Romantic or Symbolist tones in the idea of the poet as a madman. Aristotle is not thinking of the Orphic seer who is spoken by language but is simply using the categories of his culture to describe the process of going outside oneself and identifying with characters, the process that makes *mythos* and *mimesis* possible. See Guido Morpurgo Tagliabue, *Linguistica e stilistica di Aristotele* (Rome: Edizioni dell'Ateneo, 1967), 208ff.

10. Horace, *Odes*, 3, 25.

11. Horace, *Epistles*, 2, 3, lines 295–302.

12. Horace, *Satires*, 1, 4, vv. 39–44.

13. Aristotle, *Poetics*, 17.1455a.31–33.

14. Horace, *Epistles*, 2, 3, lines 99–111.

the second half of the sixteenth century after the first printed edition by Francesco Robortello (1554) and transformed into a work of reference by pre-Romantic aesthetics.[15]

The ideas that passion influences the style of speech and that poetry contains an irrational element are thus well represented in ancient texts on poetics and rhetoric. The theorists of the eighteenth century, still suspended between classicism and pre-Romanticism, often refer to the expressivist passages in Plato, Aristotle, and Horace.[16] Nevertheless, this interpretation of poetry and form remains largely a minority view compared to the opposite interpretation. For Aristotle, the main element of poetic art, in logical and chronological order, is the mimesis of actions: the *lexis* is just one of the means by which the poet imitates. First come the things to be imitated and then only afterward comes the diction, which is chosen "according to appropriateness" (*kata to harmotton*), so that the quality of the content matches the quality of the form, following a specific system of implicit or explicit conventions that correspond to the *Stiltrennung*.[17] Since poets imitate people who are better than us, just like us, or worse than us, the style should conform to the nature of the characters. The form is an ornament to be superimposed on the degree-zero content in observance of a public codifiable ritual, and the difference between poetry and prose comes down to the kind of *ornatus* that one chooses. Aristotle addresses this subject in book three of *Rhetoric* while critiquing Gorgias's overly poetic style, in the name of the principle that "the language of prose is distinct from that of poetry."[18] Since the primary virtue of oratory is clarity, the rhetorician's prose must be neither inflated nor pedestrian but appropriate; conversely, the poet's language should not be too fitting (*prepousa*) to the speech or it loses its effect.[19] Although eloquence makes use of poetic ornaments in appropriate circumstances, it cannot afford to ignore norms; poetry, on the other hand, can stray further from common linguistic usage. Interestingly, when Aristotle distinguishes between poetry and prose, he assumes that they are contiguous:

---

15. Abrams, *The Mirror and the Lamp*, 72–78.

16. Ibid., 71.

17. Aristotle, *Poetics*, 4.1448b.32; 5.1449a.31–36; 6.1450b.13–15; 16.1455a.17–25; 22.1458b.15. See the commentary by Roselyne Dupont-Roc and Jean Lallot in Aristotle, *La Poétique* (Paris: Seuil, 1980), 363.

18. Aristotle, *Rhetoric* 1404a.28–29.

19. Ibid., 1404b.3–5.

while differing in the purpose they serve and in the kind of rhetorical figures appropriate to each, both conceive of style as a sort of clothing to dress the content and, to borrow from Barthes, they deviate in the quantity of ornaments but not in their essence.[20] We find this notion of style again in Horace: although there are plenty of passages in his works that mention lyrical rapture, his praises of *ingenium* are framed within a work that handed down to Western literature a hard-and-fast model of closely monitored classicism, attentive to the rules of the art, to customs, and to the weight of tradition. No wonder that in his *Ars poetica,* immediately after citing the opinion of Democritus, Horace feels the need to ironically dismiss poets who go so far as to allow their nails and beards to grow out in order to flaunt their ecstatic folly.[21]

The theory of style as ornament, which dominated classical and classicist poetics, respects the equation that Barthes attributes to Molière's Monsieur Jourdain—the bourgeois gentleman instructed by his master of philosophy that "everything that is not prose is verse, and everything that is not verse is prose."[22] "Antiquity did not conceive of poetry and prose as two forms of expression differing in essence and origin. On the contrary, both fall within the inclusive concept 'discourse.'"[23] They are distinguished by the quantity and quality of the *ornatus,* the choice of "a," "b," and "c" being governed by specific customs: the conventions of genre, the *aptum,* the norms of the *Stiltrennung.* Like a ritual garment that one adds to preexisting content, the form observes public measures and codified rules. The continuous exchange of concepts and words between the spheres of poetics and rhetoric, especially with regard to the theory and technique of *lexis,* or *elocutio,* is symptomatic. Even more symptomatic are certain ideas about poetry that modern culture would criticize. Verse writing is before anything else a *techne,* an *ars,* a technique that can be taught like oratory: consequently, if style in poetry is decoration added to degree-zero writing, the *colores* that compose it can be studied and reproduced. This is why paraphrasing poetry is viewed as an obvious practice: starting in the first century BCE, the schools of rhetoric

---

20. Ibid., 1404b.5–17.

21. Horace, *Epistles,* 2.3, lines 295–302.

22. Molière, *Le Bourgeois gentilhomme,* act 2, scene 4, in *Œuvres complètes,* vol. 2, ed. Georges Couton (Paris: Gallimard, 1976), 730.

23. Ernst Robert Curtius, *Europäische Literatur und lateinisches Mittelalter* (1948); English translation, *European Literature and the Latin Middle Ages,* trans. Willard R. Trask (Princeton, NJ: Princeton University Press, 2013), 147.

made it an exercise, combining it with translation into verse;[24] Quintilian recommends it in his *Institutio oratoria*.[25] This means that Greek and Roman literature tended to view poetry and prose as commensurate languages separated by a different quality of *ornatus*, different in quantity but not in essence. One of the ideas that accompanied the rise of the modern lyric is that poetry is supposedly impossible to translate or paraphrase. Not that classical poetics ignores the distance separating the text to be translated from the translated text, or between a poem and its paraphrase, but the emphasis given to the difficulties of this transformation by twentieth-century critics is completely foreign to ancient culture.

The success of this model surpassed the confines of Greek and Latin literature, for Monsieur Jourdain's equation actually describes the way Western poetry understood the difference between poetry and prose until at least the second half of the eighteenth century. Although the system of ancient rhetoric outlived the collapse of the culture that spawned it, poetics as an autonomous discipline disappeared for over a thousand years in the West, and its field of expertise was split between the disciplines of grammar and rhetoric. The oratorical interpretation of poetry was consolidated in the theoretical texts of the Early Middle Ages, which present poetry and prose as two variants of the same discourse, often indistinguishable even in their word choices. Later, the theory of their complementarity was strengthened even further, starting from the second half of the eleventh century, with the development of the *ars dictaminis* and a rhetoric that applied the idea of ornament to every form of diction, equally to prose and rhythmic prose, to rhythmic poetry and accentuated poetry.[26] In Brunetto Latini's *Tresor*, poetry is submitted to the teachings of rhetoric in the same way as prose;[27] in Dante's *De vulgari eloquentia*, the rhetorical model from which prose writers are expected to draw their inspiration comes from poets.[28]

---

24. Ibid., 148.

25. Quintilian, *Institutio oratoria*, 10, 5, 4.

26. Curtius, *European Literature and the Latin Middle Ages*, 147–148.

27. "The great division in all discourses (*parliers*) is in two manners: one in prose and another in rhyme. But the teachings of rhetoric are common to both. . . ." Brunetto Latini, *Li Livres dou Tresor*, ed. F. J. Carmody (Berkeley: University of California Press, 1948), 3.10, 327.

28. Dante, *De vulgari eloquentia*, ed. Pier Vincenzo Mengaldo, in *Opere minori*, vol. 2, (Ricciardi: Milan-Naples, 1979), 141–143.

Between the sixteenth and eighteenth centuries, the poetics of European classicism reintroduced the schema of ancient poetics in a pure form:

> According to the most fundamental neo-classic frame of reference, language is the 'dress' of thought, and figures are the 'ornaments' of language, for the sake of the pleasurable emotion which distinguishes a poetic from a merely didactic discourse. These elements must be joined to form a consistent whole according to the basic neo-classic unifying principle of the decorum or proportionableness of parts—a complex requirement, involving adjustment to the poetic kind, and the matter signified, as well as the character and emotional state of the speaker depicted.[29]

This theory lost prestige over the course of the eighteenth century. Little by little, after a transformation lasting a century, the idea prevailed that the rhetorical figures distinguishing a literary text from degree-zero writing were no longer embellishments chosen deliberately to respect certain customs but rather symptoms of a passion, a way of experiencing, a thought. The only classical author to openly support this position, Pseudo-Longinus, remained almost unknown to ancient culture and, in fact, only came under new consideration in the eighteenth century.[30]

Poetry and Prose

This change is entwined with another transformation that concerns the entire order of the literary space. During the seventeenth and eighteenth centuries, in many of the texts that would converge in the genre that gradually assumed the name of novel, *roman, novela, Roman,* or *romanzo,* the idea took hold that the work should be written in a simple style without ornaments. The model suggested was the way of telling things to be found in conversations between educated people.[31] This idea seems to fall back on the two

---

29. Abrams, *The Mirror and the Lamp,* 290.
30. Ibid., 72.
31. I have discussed this more extensively in Guido Mazzoni, *Theory of the Novel,* trans. Zakiya Hanafi (Cambridge, MA: Harvard University Press, 2017), 181–185.

cornerstones of ancient rhetoric (the assurance that it is possible to define an *ordo naturalis* and *verba propria,* that is, a degree-zero syntax and vocabulary;[32] and a belief in style as an ornament)—which, however, places degree-zero language outside the tradition of oratory. It is true that classical rhetoric had a place for *sermo humilis,* used in genres such as epistles and *commentarii,* but the appeals to naturalness and simplicity we find in the prefaces of many seventeenth- and eighteenth-century novels were completely unaware of this. Although the *ars litteraria* was indistinguishable from the art of eloquence during the early modern period,[33] as it had been in ancient poetics and during the long Latin Middle Ages,[34] the rise of the novel contributed decisively to the decline of rhetoric in European prose.[35] The novel was not the only discursive formation to emancipate itself from the model: early modern scientific prose between Galileo and the Royal Society and a substantial part of French philosophy between Pascal and the Enlightenment sought a new style, unmoored from the culture of eloquence and its rules, habits, and categories.[36]

Similar changes redefined poetry's place in the genre system as well, for two reasons. In the first place, with the development of the modern novel there came the idea that a certain kind of prose is the natural medium of speech and narrative. The rise of the novel was accompanied by a decline in the narrative poem and the didactic verse poem. Poe's verdict, still a prophecy in the 1840s, would come true: very few long poems would ever be popular again. Implicit in this first transformation was a more subtle shift. In the system of ancient poetics and rhetoric, *oratio prosa* is "speech that proceeds in a straight line," whereas poetry is *versus*—a "line" or "row" but also "that which is turned backwards": prose is degree-zero language; poetry is language dressed up in an ornament. According to ancient poetics

---

32. See Heinrich Lausberg, *Elemente der literarischen Rhetorik* (1949); English translation, *Handbook of Literary Rhetoric: A Foundation for Literary Study,* trans. Matthew T. Bliss, Annemiek Jansen, and David E. Orton (Boston: Brill, 1998), 213–214.

33. See Marc Fumaroli, *L'Âge de l'éloquence* (Paris: Droz, 1980).

34. See Curtius, *European Literature and the Latin Middle Ages,* chaps. 3, 4, 8; and Adrian Marino, *The Biography of "The Idea of Literature,"* trans. Virgil Stanciu and Charles M. Carlton (Albany: State University of New York Press, 1996), 1–5.

35. See Giorgio Manganelli, "Il romanzo" (1963), reprinted in *Il rumore sottile della prosa* (Milan: Adelphi, 1994), 58.

36. See Fumaroli, *L'Âge de l'éloquence,* "Introduction"; Michael McKeon, *The Origins of the English Novel 1600–1740* (1987) (Baltimore, MD: Johns Hopkins University Press, 1991), 108.

and rhetoric, though, when prose speech enters the public sphere, it too is clothed in an *ornatus* suited to the genre, subject, and occasion. Now, when the idea took root that there existed a natural style unfettered by the rules of rhetoric, this apparatus began to falter. The novel, *drame bourgeois,* and modern poetry all developed after the ritual conception of *ars litteraria* came to an end. This conception originated with ancient culture and was embraced by the classicist literature that arose with humanism between the fourteenth and fifteenth centuries, spreading throughout Europe during the early modern period. With one difference, though: while prose genres had no difficulty appealing to the idea of a natural style, it could not be argued that moderns should use verse in their ordinary writing. The notion of poetry that arose in the second half of the sixteenth century and prevailed in the Romantic era resolved this contradiction by means of a paradigm shift: poetry became identified with lyric poetry, and its style was no longer interpreted as the extension of an ancient ritual but as the expression of an individual—as a personal way of saying things that translates the writer's inner world into form. According to this model, which remains etched in conventional wisdom, the natural, objective, "realistic" way of saying things is the simple prose style, whereas poetry, by the very fact of breaking to a new line, represents a deviation from degree-zero writing, a form of estrangement no longer originating in a social ritual but in the writer's subjectivity.

Expressivism

The idea of style as self-expression became established very quickly in Romantic culture and was summed up perfectly in a famous maxim (much quoted although misinterpreted) by Buffon: *le style est l'homme même,* the style is the man himself.[37] At the end of the nineteenth century, Eduard Norden used this *topos* to underscore the distance between the ancient notion of form and the modern, Romantic, and post-Romantic conception:

---

37. Georges-Louis Leclerc de Buffon, *Discours sur le style* (1753, 1777), ed. Felix Hemon (Paris: Delagrave, 1894), 43.

what influence did the personality of the ancient writer have on style, or, in other words, what value did Buffon's saying, *le style est l'homme même,* have for those times? . . . Style was once an art that had to be learned, and its rules could not be transgressed in the name of one's own personality; after all, antiquity, much more than the modern era, has always demanded that the individual submit his or her own originality to the authority of tradition sanctioned by eminent critics—the mortification of genius.[38]

I would call the theory of style that emerged at the beginning of the nine-teenth century *expressivist.* I borrow the adjective from Charles Taylor, who used it to define the Romantic and modern attitude of those who place the meaning of life in the manifestation of their own subjective difference, in the "obligation on each of us to live up to our originality,"[39] according to the behaviors that Simmel identified when reflecting on the two forms of modern individualism. Expressivism, according to Taylor, is a framework that estab-lishes an ideal of the good life. At the beginning of the nineteenth century, the new moral standard began to gain ground among the cultural elites of the West, overlapping and clashing with other frames of reference that had lasted hundreds or thousands of years: the ancient ethics of honor, focused on the search for glory in the public sphere; the ethics of rational control over the passions, which exalts self-mastery achieved through discipline; the ethics of the ordinary life, for which the production and reproduction of existence, work, and family are absolute values that alone can justify a life. Like all frameworks, expressivism spread equally in the culture of the elites and in common knowledge. We need to distinguish between two versions of this ethos, one passive, the other active, summarized emblematically by two formulas that recur obsessively in contemporary mass communication, al-most as if they were moral rules: *be yourself* and *express yourself.* The first is limited to proposing the narcissistic ideal of being true to oneself, while the second is an invitation to express one's individuality in the public sphere; the first is an ethos of individuality and authenticity, while the second requires

---

38. Eduard Norden, *Die antike Kunstprosa. Vom vi. Jahrhundert v. Chr. bis in die Zeit der Renaissance* (1898, 1915) (Stuttgart und Leipzig: Teubner, 1995), 11.

39. Charles Taylor, *Sources of the Self: The Making of the Modern Identity* (Cambridge, MA: Harvard Univer-sity Press, 1989), 375. Abrams, as we have seen, called this same theory "expressive."

that this individuality be expressed among other people. Both owe much to the Romantic idea of the work of art as an emanation and mirror of the author, as a sensible trace of a personality. Accordingly, the new theory of style also had individualistic and, literally, egocentric consequences. *In fact, we need to distinguish between an expressivism in content—differential autobiographism—and an expressivism in form—the Romantic theory of style as the sensible expression of a self:* two symmetrical ways of manifesting personal difference and conveying it into the public space while dispensing with any mediations.

But the poetics of the early nineteenth century often gave a reductive interpretation of formal expressivism, as if showing oneself in style was simply a matter of externalizing one's passions. In reality, this theory soon took on a much more abstract and less psychological meaning. Rather than looking to a Romantic poet for an exemplary definition of it, we do better to turn to one of the greatest novelists of the twentieth century:

> For style for the writer, no less than colour for the painter, is a question not of technique but of vision: it is the revelation, which by direct and conscious methods would be impossible, of the qualitative difference, the uniqueness of the fashion in which the world appears to each one of us, a difference which, if there were no art, would remain for ever the secret of every individual. Through art alone are we able to emerge ourselves, to know what another person sees of a universe which is not the same as our own and of which, without art, the landscapes would remain as unknown to us as those that may exist on the moon. Thanks to art, instead of seeing one world only, our own, we see that world multiply itself and we have at our disposal as many worlds as there are original artists, worlds more different one from the other than those which revolve in infinite space, worlds which, centuries after the extinction of the first from which their light first emanated, whether it is called Rembrandt or Vermeer, send us still each one its special radiance.[40]

---

40. Marcel Proust, *Le Temps retrouvé* (1927); English translation, *Time Regained*, in *In Search of Lost Time*, vol. 6, trans. Andreas Mayor and Terence Kilmartin, rev. D. J. Enright (New York: Modern Library, 2003), 299.

Style is the product of a particular sensibility not so much because it expresses the passions of the writer but primarily because it embodies a personal way of seeing things: sedimented in form is a difference in outlook that separates individuals, a difference that would remain each person's eternal secret, writes Proust, were it not for art. As well as corresponding to the person, then, style "is a question not of technique but of vision." This is a metaphorical statement, since literature is not a visual art, but its meaning is clear: style translates a way of being and of conceiving reality into form; it is the textual equivalent of a worldview. We can situate this statement historically: for ancient culture, form was a question of *ars* more than anything, an ornament constructed according to codified rules; for post-Romantic culture, it was the trace of a particular sensibility, according to a principle that applied to all the arts and all literary forms but which finds special application in the most expressivist of genres—lyric poetry.

To truly understand the deep meaning of this theory, we need to rid Romantic poetics and Proust's definition of a few hidden implications that limit its universal scope. The idea of form that prevailed between the eighteenth and nineteenth centuries remained too closely tied to the psychic life and to the aesthetics of mimesis to develop the possibilities implicit in the triumph of expressivism. It continued to understand style as a reflection of the inner world, taking for granted that art is the representation of something: a subjective and untranslatable representation that is linked nevertheless to a preexisting content made of things, actions, thoughts, and passions. We have come across countless variations of this idea when commenting on some authoritative readings of "The Infinite": the syntactic order of the central part is said to express the speaker's astonishment at the sudden appearance of immensity; the enjambments or the polysyllabic words are said to evoke a perception of the infinite, and so on. By choosing the work of a few painters, Proust strips his reference of psychological content. However, he does not depart from Romantic assumptions, since Vermeer certainly does not paint the forces that move the psyche; nor, however, do his paintings depict things as they are, but rather a personal way of seeing them, "the qualitative difference, the uniqueness of the fashion in which the world appears to each one of us."

In reality, the autonomy to choose one's style that the Romantic revolution made available allowed both the limits of psychology and the limits of imitation to be transcended. When artists are granted the right to freely choose their own style and to use form to express a vision of the world, they are permitted not only to break written and unwritten customs but also to surpass the aesthetics of mimesis. At one level, expressing oneself without constraints may mean expressing one's inner life by trespassing on the conventional limits placed on creative anarchy; on another, it may imply a deeper and more general rupture. When taken to heart, the obligation to live and write at the height of one's originality actually implies the right to ignore the two constraints that opposed creative anomie for thousands of years. The first is what T. S. Eliot or Curtius would have called Tradition: that complex of forms, habits, canons, and *topoi* that coursed through Western literature until the Romantic era, when "individual talent" (Eliot), the idea of *tabula rasa* and "creative imagination" (Curtius) began to overwhelm respect for inherited rules and imitation of the ancient model authors.[41] The second is the web of shared meanings that Ortega y Gasset defines as "lived reality" (or "human reality") and opposes to the dehumanization of art.[42] It is the set of prereflexive certainties on which we base our linguistic and social understanding with others, the implicit belief that we are perceiving time, space, things, people, and logical processes in a reasonably similar manner—what Husserl would call the "lifeworld" and Freud the "reality principle." One can debate whether and to what extent the lifeworld and the reality principle have a universal foundation; the fact remains that modern Western culture developed this basis of understanding. By the authority of this conventional wisdom, we distinguish rational thought from magical thought, conscious logic from the logic of the unconscious, the literal from the metaphoric, and reality from imagination. Leopardi's moderate interpretation of the right to autonomy allowed him to bend the relationship between meter and syntax to mimic the form of experience. A century later, Filippo Tommaso Marinetti's and André Breton's literal and extremist interpretation of the same principle allowed them to proclaim the end of psychology and the triumph

---

41. Thomas Stearns Eliot, "Tradition and the Individual Talent," (1919) in *The Sacred Wood: Essays on Poetry and Criticism* (1920) (Mineola, NY: Dover Publications, 1998), 67–88; Curtius, *European Literature and the Latin Middle Ages*, 396, 398. On the concept of tradition in Eliot and Curtius, see Claus Uhlig, "Tradition in Eliot and Curtius," *Comparative Literature* 42, no. 3 (January 1990): 193–207.

42. José Ortega y Gasset, *La deshumanización del arte* (1925); English translation, "The Dehumanization of Art," in *The Dehumanization of Art and Other Essays on Art, Culture, and Literature* (Princeton, NJ: Princeton University Press, 2019), 17 and 11.

of the unfettered imagination,[43] the death of logic and the rejection of common sense.[44] Although what Proust saw in the perfectly mimetic paintings of Vermeer and Rembrandt was a revelation of "the qualitative difference, the uniqueness of the fashion in which the world appears to each one of us," and therefore the appearance of new, original worlds, many of the painters of his age decided to express their difference by filling their canvases with figures, lines, or blots that lacked any relationship with the sensible appearance of the external world. Generally, the culture of the early nineteenth century interpreted expressivism as a rejection of classicist rules and as an expansion of mimesis to include representation of the conscious life of the mind. Nevertheless, when the Romantic idea of style as the product of a particular sensibility was faithfully interpreted, it went beyond the limits of Romanticism and found its own entelechy between the aesthetics of Symbolism and the age of the avant-gardes—in the process that Ortega y Gasset calls the dehumanization of art. This process applied the poetics of expressivism to the full, thereby complicating the relationship with ordinary ways of saying or seeing things that the art of the early nineteenth century psychologized but never relinquished.[45] Expressing oneself freely can also mean hanging any object whatsoever on the wall of a museum or composing a text by cutting up linguistic materials chosen at random and rearranging them. Although all literary genres went through such a process and experienced the extreme version of modern creative anomie, poetry writing engaged with it the most. The symptoms of this engagement were, first, the emergence of the idea that modern poetry is obscure; and, second, the loss of interest in poetic texts on the part of the average educated audience—in other words, the loss of poetry's social mandate.[46]

The extreme consequences of creative freedom implicit in the Romantic principle of originality began to show between the second half of

---

43. Filippo Tommaso Marinetti, "Manifesto tecnico della letteratura futurista" (1912); English translation, "Technical Manifesto of Futurist Literature," in *Let's Murder the Moonshine: Selected Writings*, ed. Robert Willard Flint (Los Angeles: Sun and Moon Classics, 1991), 119–125.

44. André Breton, "Manifeste du Surréalisme" (1924); English translation, "Manifesto of Surrealism," in *Manifestoes of Surrealism*, trans. Richard Seaver and Helen R. Lane (Ann Arbor: University of Michigan Press, 1972), 1–48.

45. Ortega y Gasset, *The Dehumanization of Art*.

46. See Walter Benjamin, "Über einige Motive bei Baudelaire" (1939); English translation, "On Some Motifs in Baudelaire," in *Illuminations*, trans. Harry Zohn (New York: Schocken Books, 2007), 103–148.

the nineteenth century and the beginning of the twentieth; this is when the lengthy crisis in formal rules that started in the late eighteenth century and continued throughout the following century finally came to an end. In order to describe its effects in literature, I will turn once again to the equation that Barthes attributes to Monsieur Jourdain. If practice strictly followed theory, and if style really were the product of a particular sensibility, the conventions that for millennia dictated the choice of "a," "b," and "c" would no longer make sense. The letters of Barthes's equation stand for the backbones of poetic form: *meter, lexicon, syntax,* and *tropes.* For a long time, these components conformed to a specific collective ritual: poetry was degree-zero writing to which were added a metrical cage, words, turns of phrase, and ornaments established by a public *nomos* and codified rituals. Then, beginning in the second half of the eighteenth century, these rituals began to crumble and the genre entered a phase in which anarchy became the norm.[47] It is as if modern poetry went through two parallel changes, both tending toward unrestrained individuation: on the side of content, *subjective difference entered fully into poetry as the consequence and allegory of a new form of individualism;* on the side of form, *individual talent was liberated by the right to compose poems without adhering to preestablished rules, and to understand style as an anarchic expression of the self.* The first was accomplished early on with the Romantic lyric: purely in terms of its content, "The Infinite" is already a modern poem. The same cannot be said for its style, because Leopardi remains in many ways a classicist, and because the advent of stylistic freedom occurred much later than when it was announced in poetics texts. The spread of subjectivism in the world of form was not a sudden change but a process that unfolded through the nineteenth century in stages, coming to an end only when poets truly had, in the abstract, the opportunity to express their originality, as the Romantic poetics had wanted to but only partly achieved. Between the end of the eighteenth century and the age of the historical avant-gardes, writers of poetry acquired unprecedented possibilities: they could use any word, break to a new line whenever they wanted,

---

47. On the "institutionalization of anomie" and on the "regime of singularity" of modern and contemporary art, see, respectively, Pierre Bourdieu, *Les Règles de l'art* (1992, 1998); English translation, *The Rules of Art: Genesis and Structure of the Literary Field,* trans. Susan Emanuel (Stanford, CA: Stanford University Press, 1996), 132 and 214–283; and "L'institutionnalisation de l'anomie" (1987); English translation, "Manet and the Institutionalization of Anomie," in *The Field of Cultural Production,* ed. Randal Johnson (New York: Columbia University Press, 1993), 238–253; and Nathalie Heinich, *Le triple jeu de l'art contemporain* (Paris: Minuit, 1998), 19ff.

violate grammar rules in their sentence construction, and use rhetorical figures that were so original as to be obscure. Each of these movements on its own may seem tortuous, but the change went in only one direction: the triumph of individual talent in the choice of "a," "b," "c," and "d"—lexicon, syntax, meter, and tropes.

Lexicon

Wordsworth's preface to *Lyrical Ballads* announces a change that affected all European literature and subverted an age-old custom: for the first time, poetry dispensed with a language different from common vocabulary; for the first time, poetry was no longer written in a separate and anomalous language. Writers and schools that reinstated this distance certainly abounded, but the idea that the vocabulary of poetry must necessarily be distinct from that of prose, in the name of a convention that had become second nature, was no longer valid. Alongside the poetics that restored separateness, there also arose others that praised the mixing of registers.

The process was the same in all European literatures, but each national literature has its own linguistic history. In Italy the lexical revolution transpired slowly and violently. The rule of the division of styles had been applied rigidly for centuries in the Italian poetic system, and the gap between high-style genres, serious but distant from the prose of everyday life, and low-style genres, open to contingency but condemned to remain in the comic register, remained unbridgeable. Lyric poetry written in a high register was influenced for a long time by the Petrarchan lexicon, which was restricted, sublimating, and censorious: at least until the seventeenth century, there were few exceptions to the implicit rule that the register of serious poetry must be detached from the contingent and the ordinary. The first writers to introduce everyday objects copiously into the vocabulary of high lyric poetry were Giovan Battista Marino and the Baroque poets: it is not unusual to find words like *pollami* ("poultry"), *grandine* ("hail"), *vermi* ("worms"), and *carbone* ("coal") in their works.[48] Until then, this sort of vocabulary could never have appeared in the register of serious lyric poetry. The context in which these terms appear,

---

48. These citations come from leafing through the Giovanni Getto anthology, *Lirici marinisti* (1962) (Milan: TEA, 1990), 198, 208, 225, 225, and 412.

though, is almost never descriptive and flat, as it is for lyric poetry that breaks away from poetic diction, but rather emblematic and estranged. When Montale writes that "acetylene torches throb | from the scattered dories" (*dai gozzi sparsi palpita | l'acetilene*),[49] he does nothing more than present a fact of reality with its *verba propria*. Instead, when Bernardo Morando mentions "silk moths" (*bombici*), he does so to compare the beauty of a silk spinner to the ugliness of the worms from which she draws out gossamer threads for her weaving. Montale's scene is realistic; Morando's is allegorical. In the 1920s one can call objects by their names simply because certain objects exist, whereas Baroque poetry has no notion of contingency as such—the idea of a detail that points only to itself, acting as a reality effect. This impression is reinforced by the way the texts represent prosaic objects, which are sometimes named openly but more often remain concealed behind a veil of periphrasis; or they are ennobled by heightening the literary tone through anastrophes and hyperbatons, epithets, and truncations. To take examples once again from Morando, if the title of a sonnet mentions the poet-lover's "eyeglasses" (*gli occhiali*), in the body of the text they become the "spherical crystals" (*sferici cristalli*) with which the lover arms "the lights [of his eyes]" (*i lumi*).[50] The crisis in poetry as a separate language does not correspond to the broadened register. What happens is quite the opposite: the introduction of prosaic elements is compensated for by reinforcing the ritual signs, as if to balance the weight of the unpoetic lexicon by shoring up the literary register.

Eighteenth-century literature imitates these procedures, expands the scope of things that can be written about in a poem, and compensates for the inclusion of prosaic words by increasing the *ornatus*.[51] The lexicon of Parini's lyric poems, for example, is remarkably wide-ranging and includes words such as "lung" (*polmone*), "bitumen" (*bitume*), and "gain" (*guadagno*), but only because these prosaic terms are almost always embellished with ornaments that transform the lung into a "capable lung" (*polmon capace*) (*Odes*, 2, line 7), the bitumen into a "horrible bitumen" (*orribil bitume*) (2, line 33), and gain

---

49. Eugenio Montale, "Arsenio," from *Ossi di seppia* (1925, 1928), in *L'opera in versi*, ed. Rosanna Bettarini e Gianfranco Contini (Turin, Italy: Einaudi, 1980), 82; English translation, "Arsenio," in *Collected Poems 1920–1954*, 2nd rev. ed., trans. and ed. Jonathan Galassi (New York: Farrar Straus and Giroux, 2000), 113.

50. Getto, *Lirici marinisti*, 223, 410, 412.

51. See Vittorio Coletti, *Storia dell'italiano letterario* (1993) (Turin: Einaudi, 2000), 196–201.

into a "public gain" (*pubblico guadagno*) (10, line 66).[52] When not relying on epithets or truncations, difficult metrics and twisted syntax suffice to restore decorum to the form, using a technique to compensate for the prosaic elements that would last for another century, as long as Italian poetic diction continued to exert its influence. We find the same stylistic features in Leopardi, in "Aspasia," for example, but especially in his "Palinodia al Marchese Gino Capponi" ("Recantation for Marchese Gino Capponi"), in adherence to the classicist conventions from which he had not completely freed himself. Although Foscolo and Leopardi were new poets in terms of their subject matters and syntactic choices, they still believed firmly in poetic diction: not a single passage of their work in verse deviates from the language of tradition. However, it is significant that the author of "The Infinite," while remaining a classicist, understood classicism as a choice and not a given.[53] For Leopardi, the modern world, prosaic and disenchanted, is capable of truth and incapable of beauty: poetry can continue to exist only if it remains a separate language, faithful to the words of the past.[54] This classicist choice is hardly compatible with the theory of lyricism that Leopardi developed from 1826 on. It is as if his work were caught between two opposing tendencies: one Romantic and subversive, which led him to introduce biographical details into the rituals of poetry, thereby altering them; and another that is classicist and conservative, which prompted him to remain faithful to his inherited norms.

Giosuè Carducci still uses Italian poetic diction in a regular fashion, as do authors such as Emilio Praga and Vittorio Betteloni, who, starting in the

---

52. Giuseppe Parini, *Il Giorno e le Odi*, ed. Gianna Maria Zuradelli (Turin: UTET, 1965).

53. Developing an idea mentioned in Cesare Beccaria's treatise *Intorno alla natura dello stile* (*Research on the Nature of Style*), Leopardi distinguishes between the "words" (*parole*) of poetry and the "terms" (*termini*) of science: words present the bare idea of the object they signify but also communicate accessory images; terms aridly define their objects without leaving any semantic auras. Since beauty is the enemy of precision, poetry will use words, not terms; its language will therefore be ancient, conventional, indeterminate, and distant from the language of everyday use. In Italy, this separate vocabulary had existed for only a few centuries, because the early writers had not yet refined literary language by distancing it from the everyday use of speech. Although this philosophy of literary history came to different conclusions, it is very similar to what we find in Wordsworth: Leopardi ends up justifying poetic diction despite knowing, like Wordsworth, that it is a conventional language. See Giacomo Leopardi, *Zibaldone di pensieri* (1817–1832); English translation *Zibaldone*, trans. Michael Caesar and Franco D'Intino (New York: Farrar, Straus and Giroux, 2013), 1806–1815, September 30, 1821; 1226, June 26, 1821; 1807, September 30, 1821; 3016–3017, July 23, 1823.

54. Leopardi, *Zibaldone*, 2945–2946, July 11, 1823.

1860s, began to introduce significant amounts of *verba propria* into the lexicon of the lyric, by referring to trades, foods, and everyday objects by their common names. And yet they do not give up on poetic synonyms, linguistic archaisms, or figures of inversion; nor do they seem to realize that the solemn and everyday registers end up clashing with each other, with unintentionally comic results.[55]

In Italy, the real lexical revolution took place with Giovanni Pascoli's *Myricae* (1891–1900). Introducing a huge amount of jargon, pregrammatical, and everyday language into the vocabulary of lyric poetry, Pascoli names contingency with a precision that was unprecedented for Italian poetry written in a high or middle register: "for the first time, there was a shift from the special language of poetry to the poetic use of the language of *all*, or to the poetic use of *all* languages";[56] for the first time the vocabulary of poetry became indistinguishable from prose. An essential aspect of this critical change remained incomplete, though: Pascoli violates the laws of poetic diction, but he does not discard the poetic vocabulary of tradition altogether. He continues to use prosaic and everyday words alongside the old archaic forms, as if they were still a poetic register of common use and not a linguistic fossil. Examples of such overlapping can be found throughout *Myricae*. In "O vano sogno" ("O Vain Dream"), for example, *mortella* ("myrtle"), *radicchio, pimpinella* ("salad burnet"), and *ruminanti* ("ruminants"), softened by the epithet *dolci* (sweet), stand next to the adjective *aulente* ("fragrant"), referring to *fieno* ("hay"):

> Al camino, dove scoppia la mortella
> tra la stipa, o ch'io sogno, o veglio teco:
> mangio teco radicchio e pimpinella.
>
> Al soffiar delle raffiche sonanti,
> l'aulente fieno sul forcon m'arreco
> e visito i miei dolci ruminanti.

---

55. See Antonio Girardi, "La lingua poetica tra Scapigliatura e Verismo," in *Giornale storico della letteratura italiana*, 98 (1981): 581ff.

56. Antonio Girardi, "Nei dintorni di *Myricae:* Come muore una lingua poetica?," in *Paragone—Letteratura* 40, no. 14 (470) (1989): 70.

In the fireplace, where the myrtle bursts into flame
amid the kindling, I either dream or stay awake with you:
I eat salad burnet and radicchio with you.

When resounding gusts of wind blow,
I fetch fragrant hay on my pitchfork
and visit my sweet ruminants.[57]

In reality, Italian poetic diction only truly dies when the bookish vocabulary of the past becomes archaic sounding, when poets feel that the traditional vocabulary and morphology are a dated code, to be avoided or used only as a deliberate poetic choice. It took until the 1910s for this process to conclude.[58] Only then would Italian poetry be able to call itself free from premodern poetic diction.

Syntax

In the syntax of sentences and in the syntax of the composition as a whole, premodern poetry adopts a public and regular diction: the text is not constructed as a real soliloquy but as a discourse that respects the grammatical norms of collective communication—as if it were being spoken in front of an invisible audience and was theatrical or oratorical in nature. The literature of the last two centuries has instead taught its readers that the original structure of thought is pregrammatical: it follows a private and irregular syntax, whose extreme forms are the inner monologue and the montage principle. Take Shakespeare's Sonnet 27:

Weary with toil, I haste me to my bed,
The dear repose for limbs with travel tired,
But then begins a journey in my head
To work my mind, when body's work's expired.
For then my thoughts, from far where I abide,

---

57. Giovanni Pascoli, *Myricae,* ed. Giuseppe Nava, 2nd rev. and enl. ed. (Rome: Salerno, 1991), 116.
58. Girardi, *Nei dintorni di* Myricae, 76.

> Intend a zealous pilgrimage to thee,
> And keep my drooping eyelids open wide,
> Looking on darkness which the blind do see.
> Save that my soul's imaginary sight
> Presents thy shadow to my sightless view,
> Which like a jewel hung in ghastly night,
> Makes black night beauteous, and her old face new.
> > Lo thus by day my limbs, by night my mind,
> > For thee, and for myself, no quiet find.[59]

When I read this, the text before me brings an inner process to the page, according to the literary *topos* of the meditation or nocturnal reverie. Worn out by love, the speaker falls asleep, hoping to be refreshed, but his thoughts return continually to his beloved, preventing him from sleep and keeping his eyes wide open. His soul's imaginary sight presents him with the shadow of his beloved who, like a jewel, illuminates the black, ghastly night and rejuvenates its appearance. A complex thought process is broken down into parts and adapted into a rational, hypotactic syntax, marked by oppositions ("To work my mind, when body's work's expired," "And keep my drooping eyelids open wide," "by day my limbs, by night my mind"). Every passage has a grammatical foundation; every junction follows logically in a public and comprehensible way. Contemporary poetry, on the other hand, has accustomed us to reading texts that are estranged from the ordinary rules of collective communication. The spread of private syntax affects both the sentence structure and the structure of the composition as a whole: the first results in an interior monologue; the second in a construction that holds together thanks to the montage principle. In "The hope of even seeing you again" or "Returning a Lost Child" (to cite the texts in Chapter 2), the sentence syntax is shattered but grammatical, while the syntax of the composition follows chains that are partially private and allusive, held together by juxtaposing fragments, through transitions that are not always decipherable.

At the beginning of the twentieth century, private syntax became a permanent feature of the spectrum of possibilities that authors had at their dis-

---

59. William Shakespeare, *Sonnets*, ed. with analytic commentary by Stephen Booth (New Haven, CT: Yale University Press, 1977), 27.

posal when writing. It was then that interior monologue and the montage principle became grammaticalized, to use a category of linguistics: authors could use them or continue to rely on more traditional forms of syntax when constructing sentences and texts; and yet they perceived these forms as open possibilities, as practicable solutions. The most conspicuous change occurred more in prose than in poetry, since private syntax spread in literature primarily from narrative fiction. One of the first great examples of montage in literature is the scene of the agricultural rallies in *Madame Bovary* (1857), and one of the first extensive examples of the application of interior monologue is the short novel *Les lauriers sont coupés* (1887, *We'll to the Woods No More*) by Édouard Dujardin. Forgotten for decades, Dujardin's work reappeared in 1924, after Joyce publicly acknowledged its influence on him. A few years later, Dujardin wrote an essay in which he laid claim to the invention of the interior monologue.[60] It is true that the expression *monologue intérieur* preceded *Les lauries sont coupés*,[61] that the first limited examples of this technique can be found in Dostoevsky (*Notes from Underground* and his short story "A Gentle Creature") and in Tolstoy (the monologue of Anna Karenina before her suicide), and that Bettina von Arnim, in *Dies Buch gehört dem König* (1843, *This Book Belongs to the King*), had earlier loosened logical and syntactic links.[62] Nevertheless, there is no precedent in earlier literature of the degree of syntactic deconstruction to be found in *Les lauriers sont coupés*. Although Dujardin developed the device and claimed it as his own, it is possible that a first embryonic example of interior monologue comes from poetry, namely, from the last texts of a friend of Dujardin, Jules Laforgue,[63] to whom Dujardin also attributed the invention of free verse:[64]

Et quoi encore? Oh du génie,
Improvisations aux insomnies!

---

60. Édouard Dujardin, *Le Monologue intérieur: Son apparition, ses origines, sa place dans l'œuvre de James Joyce et dans le roman contemporain* (Paris: Messein, 1931).

61. They actually appear in *La Parole intérieure* (1881) by Victor Egger. See Laura Santone, *Voci dall'abisso: Nuovi elementi sulla genesi del monologo interiore* (Bari: Edipuglia, 1999), 7, 81.

62. See Peter Bürger, *Prosa der Moderne* (1988), with the collaboration of Christa Bürger (Frankfurt: Suhrkamp, 1992), 312.

63. Anne Holmes, "Laforgue's *Derniers Vers, X:* Interior Monologue and 'Vers libre,'" *Modern Language Review* 108, no. 3 (July 2013): 802–811.

64. Édouard Dujardin, *Les Premiers Poètes du vers libre* (Paris: Mercure de France, 1922), 56–59.

Et puis? L'observer dans le monde,
Et songer dans les coins:

"Oh, qu'elle est loin! Oh, qu'elle est belle!
"Oh! qui est-elle? A qui est-elle?
"Oh, quelle inconnue! Oh, lui parler! Oh, l'emmener!"

And what else? Oh, some genius,
Improvisations on insomnia!

And then? To observe her in the world
And contemplate in corners:

"Oh, she's so distant! Oh, she's so beautiful!
"Oh! who is she? Who is she with?
"Oh, what a mystery woman! Oh, to speak to her! Oh, to take her away!"[65]

Three decades later, the "Technical Manifesto of Futurist Literature" (1912) would list the deconstruction of syntax as one of Futurism's technical principles,[66] while the loosening of *dispositio* through montage would become a common practice in the founding texts of European poetic modernism. Apollinaire's "Zone" (1913), for example, is composed in part of unrelated segments with no connections:

Voilà la jeune rue et tu n'es encore qu'un petit enfant [. . .]
Maintenant tu marches dans Paris tout seul parmi la foule [. . .]
Aujourd'hui tu marches dans Paris les femmes sont ensanglantées [. . .]
Maintenant tu es au bord de la Méditerranée [. . .].

Te voici à Marseille au milieu des pastèques

Te voici à Coblence à l'hôtel du Géant

Te voici à Rome assis sous un néflier du Japon

---

65. Jules Laforgue, *Derniers Vers*, 10, in *Œuvres complètes*, vol. 2, ed. Maryke de Courten, Jean-Louis Debauve, Pierre-Olivier Walzer, and David Arkell (Lausanne: L'Âge d'homme, 1995), 330.

66. Marinetti, "Technical Manifesto of Futurist Literature," 119.

Te voici à Amsterdam avec une jeune fille que tu trouves belle et qui
   est laide.

Here is the young street and you are still a baby [. . .]
Now you stride alone through the Paris crowds [. . .]
Today in Paris the women are bloodstained [. . .]
By the Mediterranean [. . .].

You in Marseilles among piles of watermelons

You in Coblenz at the Giant's hotel

In Rome sitting under a Japanese medlar tree

In Amsterdam with a girl you find pretty who is ugly . . . [67]

In some cases, punctuation is omitted and the associations between ideas
and images are unrelated: "Bergère ô tour Eiffel le troupeau des ponts bêle
ce matin" ("Shepherdess O Eiffel Tower whose flock of bridges bleats at the
morning"), "Soleil cou coupé" ("Sun slit throat"). A few years later we find
the same phenomena in *The Waste Land,* featured even more prominently in
the *Cantos.* Once this metamorphosis is complete, it becomes clear that poets
can use a syntax that is "wholly different from syntax as understood by logi-
cians and grammarians."[68]
But although the full display of this new model may have taken place
during the time of the avant-gardes, the process began in the Romantic age.
It followed different timelines depending on the national literature and was
based on ancient precedents, starting with Pindar, whose sudden juxtapositions were a model for the ancient and classicist ode. Although Hölderlin
translated and commented on Pindar and was influenced by him in many
ways, the logical steps in his texts reach a far greater degree of dislocation
than in the ancient author. One of the modern and revolutionary aspects of

67. Apollinaire, "Zone," from *Alcools* (1913), in *Œuvres poétiques,* ed. Marcel Adéma et Michel Décaudin
(Paris: Gallimard, 1990); English translation, "Zone," in *Alcools,* trans. Anne Hyde Greet (Berkeley: University
of California Press, 1965), 2–13.

68. Donald Davie, *Articulate Energy: An Inquiry into the Syntax of English Poetry* (London: Routledge and
Paul, 1955), 148.

Hölderlin's poetry is his tendency to deconstruct argumentative connections by means of sudden paratactic juxtapositions, which follow a very different mode of reasoning than that of ordinary speech. This may affect the syntax of the sentence or that of the composition. Take one of his most famous poems, "Hälfte des Lebens" ("The Middle of Life"):

Hälfte des Lebens

Mit gelben Birnen hänget
Und voll mit wilden Rosen
Das Land in den See,
Ihr holden Schwäne,
Und trunken von Küssen
Tunkt ihr das Haupt
Ins heilignüchterne Wasser.

Weh mir, wo nehm' ich, wenn
Es Winter ist, die Blumen, und wo
Den Sonnenschein,
Und Schatten der Erde?
Die Mauern stehn
Sprachlos und kalt, im Winde
Klirren die Fahnen.

The Middle of Life

With yellow pears the land,
And full of wild roses,
Hangs down into the lake,
O graceful swans,
And drunk with kisses,
You dip your heads,
Into the hallowed-sober water.

Alas, where shall I find when
Winter comes, flowers, and where
Sunshine,

And the shadows of earth?
The walls stand
Speechless and cold, in the wind
Weathercocks clatter.[69]

Here, the intermediate passage that should connect the two stanzas of the poem is omitted. By doing this, as Adorno writes in his essay on Hölderlin's parataxis, "the mediation is set within what is mediated instead of bridging it" and "each of the two stanzas . . . has an inherent need for its opposite."[70] Adorno sees in this a sign of the union between form and content in the structure of the text itself, "the antithesis of sensuous love and being cast out, an antithesis of content, breaks the stanzas apart, just as conversely it is only the paratactical form itself that produces the caesura between the halves of life."[71] The abrupt, enlightening transition that links the two parts of the text is an immediate subjective association, a primary form of montage. It anticipates a way of constructing texts that was still unusual in 1804 when the poem was published by Friedrich Wilmans in the *Taschenbuch für das Jahr 1805,* but which was destined to create a permanent place for itself on the horizon of possibilities. The history of its reception is interesting and symptomatic: when the *Taschenbuch* came out, some reviewers panned the nine poems by Hölderlin that composed it, calling them obscure and rambling.[72] Two centuries later, when the journal *Text+Kritik* asked a group of German and Austrian poets to compile an anthology of the most important poems of the twentieth century, they opened their anthology with "The Middle of Life," an early nineteenth-century text that, in their view, already belonged to the lyric poetry of the future.[73]

---

69. Friedrich Hölderlin, "Hälfte des Lebens," in *Sämtliche Werke. Zweiter Band, Gedichte nach 1800,* ed. Friedrich Beißner, vol. 1, (Stuttgard: Kohlhammer, 1951), 117; English translation, "The Middle of Life," in *Hölderlin: His Poems Translated by Michael Hamburger* (London: Harvill Press, 1952), 159.

70. Theodor W. Adorno, "Parataxis: Zur späten Lyrik Hölderlins" (1963–1964); English translation, "Parataxis: On Hölderlin's Late Poetry," in *Notes to Literature,* vol. 2, ed. Rolf Tiedemann, trans. Shierry Weber Nicholson (New York: Columbia University Press, 1992), 133.

71. Ibid.

72. Henning Bothe, *Ein Zeichen sind wir, deutungslos: Die Rezeption Hölderlins von ihren Anfängen bis zu Stefan George* (Stuttgart: Metzler, 1992), 19ff.

73. "50 Gedichte des 20. Jahrhunderts," selected by Durs Grünbein, Barbara Köhler, Friederike Mayröcker, Peter Waterhouse, in *Lyrik des 20. Jahrhunderts,* special issue of *Text+Kritik* (1999), 5–6.

Two landmark poets in the history of modern American poetry were also great syntactic innovators. Reflecting on the novelty of Whitman's enumerative syntax, Leo Spitzer picks up on an idea by Detlev Schumann and develops it in a classic text from the *Stilkritik*. The chaotic enumeration in *Leaves of Grass* is a syntactic figure of modern plurality and, at the same time, of the pantheistic unity of the multiple:[74]

Sex contains all, bodies, souls,
Meanings, proofs, purities, delicacies, results, promulgations,
Songs, commands, health, pride, the maternal mystery, the seminal milk,
All hopes, benefactions, bestowals, all the passions, loves, beauties,
    delights of the earth,
All the governments, judges, gods, follow'd persons of the earth,
These are contain'd in sex as parts of itself and justifications of itself.[75]

This model would set an example: Schumann reconstructed the biblical and Christian genealogy of this syntactic figure and found traces of it in Rainer Maria Rilke and Franz Werfel; Spitzer in Paul Claudel, Rubén Darío, Pedro Salinas, and Pablo Neruda:

Los jóvenes homosexuales y las muchachas amorosas,
y las largas viudas que sufren el delirante insomnio,
y las jóvenes señoras preñadas hace treinta horas,
y los roncos gatos que cruzan mi jardin en tinieblas,
como un collar de palpitantes ostras sexuales
rodean mi residencia solitaria,
como enemigos establecidos contra mi alma,
como conspiradores en traje de dormitorio
que cambiaran largos besos espesos por consigna.

The young homosexuals and languishing girls,
the tall widows frantic with sleeplessness,
the matrons still tender in years, now thirty hours pregnant,

---

74. Leo Spitzer, *La enumeración caótica en la poesía moderna* (Buenos Aires: Imprenta y casa editora Coni, 1945).

75. Walt Whitman, "A Woman Waits for Me" (1856–1867), in *Leaves of Grass and Other Writings,* ed. Michael Moon (New York: Norton, 2002), 87–88.

the gravel-voiced tomcats that cross in the night of my garden
like a necklace of sexual oysters, atremble,
encircle my lonely environs—
antagonists stalking my soul,
schemers in nightgowns,
exchanging long kisses, packed in like a countersign.[76]

Unlike stream of consciousness or modernist montage, chaotic enumeration does not skip logical steps or break with the rules of grammar, but its overall effect is similar: it leads to a loosening of control and hierarchy. While Whitman plays with lists and the trope of congeries to dissolve syntax, Dickinson works on elision and inversion:

Further in Summer than the Birds
Pathetic from the Grass
A minor Nation Celebrates
Its unobtrusive Mass

No Ordinance be seen
So gradual the Grace
A pensive Custom it becomes
Enlarging Loneliness.

Antiquest felt at Noon
When August burning low
Arise this spectral Canticle
Repose to typify.

Remit as yet no Grace
No Furrow on the Glow,
Yet a Druidic—Difference
Enhances Nature now.[77]

---

76. Pablo Neruda, "Caballero solo," in *Residencia en la tierra (1925–1931),* ed. Hernán Loyola (Madrid: Cátedra, 1997); English translation "Gentleman Alone," in *Five Decades: A Selection (Poems: 1925–1970),* ed. and trans. Ben Belitt (New York: Grove Press, 1974), 13.

77. Emily Dickinson, "Further in Summer than the Birds" (1866) in *Emily Dickinson Poems as She Preserved Them,* ed. Cristanne Miller (Cambridge, MA: Belknap Press, 2016), 534.

Conjunctions, cuts, anastrophes, and unmarked verbs break the rules of public syntax and create effects of obscurity that, as Cristanne Miller writes, are consubstantial to the architecture of the text:

> The unusual use of the opening conjunction, omitted words and phrases, and syntactic inversions help to create a sense of the delicate momentary Grace the speaker finds it so difficult to describe. . . . In the last two stanzas inverted phrase order, the omission of several words, form / class substitution, and uninflected verbs make the poem even more difficult to decipher. . . . We might suppose that the poet means something like: "This custom or grace is felt to be oldest at Noon, when the August sun is burning low and this spectral canticle arise(s), typifying repose; up until this moment, no grace has been remitted and the glow remains unfurrowed (unblemished); yet a druidic difference enhances nature now." There are other ways to reconstruct the syntax here, however, and one must take into account the puzzling "Yet," Dickinson's unmarked verbs (arise and remit) and the general lack of connections regardless of how one finally reconstructs it. There is no causal or temporal relation, for example, between the August noon and the verb "Arise," and there is no clear subject or agent for "Remit."[78]

To my knowledge, no examples of private syntax exist in Italy before the time of Foscolo and Leopardi. Strongly paratactic texts or texts with rough and approximate connections can be found, but there are no poems built on an associative logic that strays from the rules of public speech, whether this involves the form of the sentences or the form of the composition. The only writings that approach the aesthetic of words in freedom—some of Burchiello's sonnets, for example—fall under the separate domains of comic or nonsense poems and do not constitute true exceptions. An early change took place during the period when the poetics of Romanticism gained full hegemony.[79] Foscolo and Leopardi remain faithful to poetic diction, but

---

78. Cristanne Miller, *Emily Dickinson: A Poet's Grammar* (Cambridge, MA: Harvard University Press, 1987), 88–89. See also John Schmit, "'I Only Said-the Syntax-': Elision, Recoverability, and Insertion in Emily Dickinson's Poetry," *Style* 27, no. 1 (1993): 106–124.

79. Wolf-Dieter Stempel, *Syntax in dunkler Lyrik (Zu Mallarmés "À la nue accablante")*, in *Immanente Ästhetik, ästhetische Reflexion: Lyrik als Paradigma der Moderne*, ed. Wolfgang Iser (Munich: Fink, 1966), 33–46.

they modernize the *dispositio* and sentence structure of lyric poetry. Some readers of *On Sepulchres* were struck by the freedom of its transitions: the connections could appear unfounded to the eyes of its contemporaries. Foscolo himself felt the need to justify the boldness of certain logical transitions by recalling the freedom to frame arguments that classicist literature recognized in lyric poetry, following Pindar's example.[80] Leopardi was perhaps the first Italian poet to exhibit a syntax that, in his most innovative texts, partly follows associative waves of thought.

These changes were destined to evolve much further. Once again, Pascoli proved to be a revolutionary poet. Consider "Mezzanotte" ("Midnight"), in *Myricae:*

> Otto . . . Nove . . . anche un tocco: e lenta scorre
> l'ora; ed un altro . . . un altro. Uggiola un cane.
> Un chiù singhiozza da non so qual torre.
>
> È mezzanotte. Un doppic suon di pesta
> s'ode, che passa. C'è per vie lontane
> un rotolìo di carri che s'arresta
>
> di colpo. Tutto è chiuso, senza forme,
> senza colori, senza vita. Brilla,
> sola nel mezzo alla città che dorme,
> una finestra, come una pupilla.[81]

> Eight . . Nine . . . one more stroke: and slowly passes
> the hour; and another . . . another. A dog yelps.
> An owl cries out from who knows which tower.
>
> It's midnight. A double sound of footsteps
> can be heard, which passes by. From distant roads there's
> a rolling of wagons that stops

---

80. Ugo Foscolo, "Lettera a Monsieur Guillon" (1807), in *Scritti letterari e politici dal 1796 al 1808,* ed. Giovanni Gambarin (Firenze: Le Monnier, 1972), 508.

81. Pascoli, "Mezzanotte," in *Myricae,* 1:6.

suddenly. Everything is shut down, formless,
colorless, lifeless. Shining out,
alone amid the city that sleeps
a window, like an iris.

The impressionistic structure of the poem breaks the scene down into multiple fragments, placed side by side: the striking of the clock, the dog, the crying owl, the chiming of the hour, the sound of footsteps, the rolling of the wagons, the perception that everything is shut down, the window that lights up. How are we to classify such a text? The first verses can perhaps come to our aid. Clearly, the sequence "Eight . . . Nine . . . one more stroke: and slowly passes | time; and another . . . another" is a mental soliloquy on the part of the speaker, who is counting the strokes of the belltower. In Leopardi's poems, the shift from public to private syntax always stops short before the speech becomes a true interior monologue. In "Le ricordanze" ("The Recollections"), lines 50–52, when Leopardi describes a scene similar to Pascoli's, the sentence structure never becomes impressionistic:

Viene il vento recando il suon dell'ora
Dalla torre del borgo. Era conforto
Questo suon, mi rimembra, alle mie notti [. . .].

The wind comes, with the hour that tolls
from the town tower. This sound, I can recall,
was a comfort to my nights [. . .].[82]

The broken sentence structure in "A se stesso" ("To Himself") also recalls the form of soliloquies in Alfieri's tragedies—a model of theatrical syntax in which the hero must make himself understood by the audience in order to clarify hidden meanings and comment in detail on what he thinks, even though he pretends to speak to himself. In Pascoli's poems, instead, the speech is privatized: the first two lines of "Midnight" are constructed as a monologue

---

82. Giacomo Leopardi, "Le ricordanze," in *Canti*, ed. Emilio Peruzzi (Milan: Rizzoli, 1981); English translation, "The Recollections," in Giacomo Leopardi, *Canti*, ed. and trans. Jonathan Galassi (New York: Farrar, Straus and Giroux, 2010), 183.

without an audience that notes perceptions while they take place. This practice has no precedent in Italian literature.

This progressive movement toward a mental syntax stops only when poets come to associate words in total autonomy. By that I mean when they can write sentences in the form of stream of consciousness and freely arrange the parts of the text without following an argumentative or narrative order, relying instead on unconscious analogies or on a conscious but entirely subjective montage. Singing the praises of words in freedom and mocking "the ridiculous inanity of the old syntax inherited from Homer,"[83] the "Technical Manifesto of Futurist Literature" has an emblematic value. In Italy, the crisis of public syntax, like the crisis of the traditional poetic lexicon, came to a peak during the first avant-garde movements.

Meter

In the long run, the most sensational effect of Romantic poetics was the invention of free verse. An essential principle of premodern Western literature is that writing in verse is distinguished from ordinary speech by virtue of metrical rules: even genres most similar to prose in terms of vocabulary and the use of figures were still separated on the basis of this criterion. Nevertheless, the principle that meter did not suffice to make a composition true poetry was well known to ancient culture. As Aristotle argues in the first pages of his *Poetics,* although Empedocles wrote in verse, his work has nothing in common with Homer's: if the latter deserves the name of poet, Empedocles should be called, rather, a *physiologos,* a scholar of nature;[84] because, as stated in book nine, "the poet must be a maker of stories rather than verses, in so far as it is representation that makes him a poet, and representation is of actions."[85] And yet, while admitting that it is possible to use verses for nonpoetic purposes or to write artistic prose, ancient aesthetics did not conceive of a poetry that is "poetic" but not amenable to the laws of meter, to a fixed, public, agreed-upon measure. Whatever the meter, everyone was

83. Marinetti, "Technical Manifesto of Futurist Literature," 119.
84. Aristotle, *Poetics,* 1.1447b.17–20.
85. Ibid., 9.1451b.27–29.

expected to know how a verse was composed and when to break to the next line. According to this reasoning, the two greatest revolutions of modern prosody—free verse and the prose poem—would be simply inconceivable.

This time-honored principle began to falter as early as the eighteenth century, when the rhythmic prose of *The Works of Ossian* (1765) changed readers' and writers' habits, when a few British poets began to imitate the irregular metrics of the English Bible, and when a few German poets began to adopt fluid prosodic patterns called *Freie Rhythmen*. In July 1796, *Monthly Magazine* published an article entitled "Is Verse Essential to Poetry?" It was signed anonymously by someone who called himself "The Enquirer," probably the Unitarian minister William Enfield—essayist, writer, and author of a treatise on taste. It is a very interesting article, because it shows how much readers' horizon of expectation had been changed by the aesthetics of the eighteenth century and how new Romantic ideas were altering their perception of metrics. Enfield questions whether verse is necessary for poetry. He first repeats the typical schema of ancient literature, writing that the essence of poetry is imitation, not versification, and then follows with his new ideas. He adds that the work of the poet is above all enthusiasm, inspiration, and "the immediate offspring of a vigorous imagination and a quick sensibility":[86] small wonder, he notes, that long before versification was known, primitive people expressed their strong passions in a vehement language that produced "a kind of wild and unfettered melody."[87] But because the only criteria of literary value are truth and nature, the rules of art do not state that sophisticated authors are better than primitives, or that poets must write and speak in verse. Enfield stops short of explicitly theorizing free verse, but his essay already contains arguments that will be used in the second half of the nineteenth century to legitimize the dissolution of regular metrics: namely, if poetry is unmediated self-expression, then it is not clear why traditional measures should communicate spontaneous passions any better than the rhythmic prose adopted by Macpherson; or any better than a versification that follows the poet's internal rhythm by ignoring the external rule of meter.

A significant difference separates modern and classical theories. For Greek and Latin culture, and for the classicist cultures that continued to rewrite

---

86. "Is Verse Essential to Poetry?," *Monthly Magazine* 2, no. 6 (July 1796): 454.
87. Ibid.

ancient concepts until the second half of the eighteenth century, the crucial opposition separates *mimesis* from *metron:* the emphatic name of poet is reserved for those who are able to represent people's actions, speech, and characters while conforming to an apparatus of traditional customs; those who merely set a nonimitative subject matter to regular verse must be called something else. Thus, there may be prose writers who fit the name of poet, but there is no possibility for poets to break up their lines as they please, because the regular norms governing verse composition do not allow for the irregular practice of free verse. In the burgeoning conventional wisdom of the second half of the eighteenth century, on the contrary, anyone capable of original and meaningful self-expression could be called a poet. The thinking behind this new outlook was that meter represents an inherited convention, which artists have the full autonomy to accept or reject according to their personal tastes.[88]

Wordsworth's preface to *Lyrical Ballads* shows that challenging the legitimacy of meter was integral to Romantic poetics. Like Enfield, Wordsworth believed that the essential opposition is not between prose and verse, but between poetry—whether poetic or prosaic—and ordinary language and scientific prose. Following the implications of his argument, Wordsworth cannot avoid asking "an obvious question": "why, professing these opinions, have I written in verse?"[89] His answer is rather confused: at first, he argues that once poetic diction has been abolished there is no reason to deprive oneself of the pleasure, universally acknowledged, that meter brings to the reader. Then he adds that the principle of order conveyed by regular verse harmoniously tempers the disorder to which the mind tends when it is excited by passion. Finally, he asserts that feeling is what gives rise to rhetorical figures and produces spontaneous rhythms. One is left with the impression that Wordsworth skirts around a problem without really addressing it. Rhythm may well be judged a natural element, but it is undeniable that meter is a convention: just as poetic phraseology transforms the spontaneous figurativeness of passionate language into a congeries of increasingly cold formulas, so meter rigidifies the natural rhythms of inspired speech, compressing

---

88. On the history between the opposition between poet and versifier, see Timothy Steele, *Missing Measures: Modern Poetry and the Revolt against Meter* (Fayetteville: University of Arkansas Press, 1990), chap. 3.

89. Wordsworth and Coleridge, *Lyrical Ballads,* 262.

them into a conventional measure. If Wordsworth had been consistent with the principles he professed, he would have reached a conclusion shared by many eighty years later, namely, *that meter is the poetic diction of rhythm.* Even Leopardi, despite his classicism, was far from believing that meter was a necessity: although lyric poetry is "inspired writing," metrical schemes arise out of habits that have become second nature: "Usage has established that the poet write in verse. . . . But in essence, in itself, poetry is not tied to verse."[90] Taken literally, Romantic expressivism heralded a metrical revolution, the same revolution that spread into literary practice during the late 1800s, when the two genres accompanying the decline of traditional prosody—the prose poem and poetry in free verse—became established definitively.

It would be wrong to interpret the former as a mere continuation of ancient artistic prose. The prose poem has nothing to do with the tradition of ancient rhetoric: it is a direct consequence of Romantic aesthetics. Starting from the time when lyric poetry gained hegemony over verse writing and being a lyric poet no longer depended on obeying an external metrical norm but on allowing oneself to be carried away by the "spontaneous overflow of powerful feelings," it became difficult to explain why feelings must necessarily overflow into verse. Between the second half of the eighteenth century and the beginning of the nineteenth, the popularity of poetic prose—Gessner's *Idylls* (1756, 1772) and *The Works of Ossian* (1765)—shows that the horizon of expectations for writers and readers was ready to accept a revolutionary novelty: the possibility of expressing poetic pathos without having to break up lines, and of creating poetry while writing in prose—as in one of the most influential texts of German Romanticism, Novalis's "Hymns to the Night," in the version that appeared in *Athenaeum* in 1800. It was French literature that developed the idea of poetry in prose most extensively, to the point of exporting the term *poème en prose* to other languages.[91] In France, the notion

---

90. Leopardi, *Zibaldone*, 1695–1697, September 14, 1821.

91. The first extended critical reflections on prose poetry are also about French literature: see Franz Rauhut, *Das französische Prosagedicht* (Hamburg: Friederichsen, de Gruyter und C., 1929); Vista Clayton, *The Prose Poem in French Literature of the Eighteenth Century* (New York: Columbia University Press, 1936); Albert Cherel, *La Prose poétique française* (Paris: L'Artisan du livre, 1940); and Suzanne Bernard, *Le Poème en prose de Baudelaire jusqu'à nos jours* (Paris: Nizet, 1959). For a history of criticism of the *poème en prose,* see Steven Monte, *Invisible Fences: Prose Poetry as a Genre in French and American Literature* (Lincoln: University of Nebraska Press, 2000), 5–6.

of poetic prose was recognized in the *Encyclopédie*, in the entry "poème en prose" written by Louis de Jaucourt in 1765,[92] and, before that, in *Les Aventures de Télémaque* (1699) and *Dialogues sur l'éloquence* (1718) by Fénelon.[93] The genre entered the modern phase of its history in the mid-nineteenth century with Baudelaire, to whom we also owe the rediscovery of *Gaspard de la nuit* (1842) by Aloysius Bertrand. For the first time, the poet was not defined by mimesis or meter but by subjective feeling, the "lyric motions of the soul" expressed in the choice of content and style, as Baudelaire put it in his dedicatory letter to Arsène Houssaye, which he used as a preface to his *Petits Poèmes en prose*:

> Which of us has not, in his ambitious days, dreamt the miracle of a poetic prose, musical without rhythm or rhyme, supple enough and striking enough to suit lyrical movements of the soul, undulations of reverie, the flip-flops of consciousness.[94]

The other effect of the modern revolution in metrics was the spread of free verse into literatures that, during the Romantic age, had not experienced a loosening of prosodic patterns comparable to the free rhythms of the Germans. This is what took place in English-language poetry between the second half of the nineteenth century and the beginning of the twentieth, after Whitman's first edition of *Leaves of Grass* (1855) had conspicuously renounced any form of metrical regularity, drawing inspiration from the free prosody of biblical translations. In French-language poetry it happened after the magazine *La Vogue* launched the fashion of *vers libre* in the second half of the 1880s (earlier, Rimbaud had not followed any predictable line-break patterns in the versified parts of his *Illuminations*, also published for that matter in *La Vogue*, in 1886).[95] In Spanish-speaking literature, the modern

---

92. "Poème en prose," in *Encyclopédie, ou Dictionnaire raisonné des sciences, des arts et des métiers* (1751–1780), vol. 12 (Neuchâtel: Samuel Faulche, 1765), 396. The example of a *poème en prose* that Jaucourt has in mind is Fénelon's *Télémaque*.

93. Nathalie Vincent-Munnia, *Les Premiers Poèmes en prose: Généalogie d'un genre dans la première moitié du dix-neuvième siècle français* (Paris: Champion, 1996), 21ff.

94. Charles Baudelaire, *Petits Poèmes en prose* or *Le Spleen de Paris* (1869); English translation, *Paris Spleen: Little Poems in Prose*, trans. Keith Waldrop (Middletown, CT: Wesleyan University Press, 2009), 5.

95. See Clive Scott, *Vers libre: The Emergence of Free Verse in France 1886–1914* (Oxford: Clarendon, 1990), 54ff.; Michel Murat, *Le Vers libre* (Paris: Champion, 2008), chaps. 1 and 3.

metrical revolution is often traced back to "Nocturno" (1894) by José Asunción Silva. One of the first examples of Russian free verse is *Aleksandrijskie pesni* (*Songs of Alexandria*) by Mikhail Kuzmin (1908).[96] The origin of Italian free verse is usually attributed to Gian Pietro Lucini, who made a regular practice of violating metrical rules.[97] As the practice spread, so did reflection on the momentous value of this new literary fashion. Whitman had a good grasp of the historical and political significance of the phenomenon:

> In my opinion, the time has come to essentially break down the barriers of form between prose and poetry. I say the latter is henceforth to win and maintain its character regardless of rhyme, and the measurement-rules of iambic, spondee, dactyl, etc., and that even if rhyme and those measurements continue to furnish the medium for inferior writers and themes . . . the truest and greatest *Poetry*, (while subtly and necessarily always rhythmic, and distinguishable easily enough,) can never again, in the English language, be express'd in arbitrary and rhyming metre. . . . While admitting that the venerable and heavenly forms of chiming versification have in their time play'd great and fitting parts—that the pensive complaint, the ballads, wars, amours, legends of Europe, etc., have, many of them, been inimitably render'd in rhyming verse . . . , it is, notwithstanding, certain to me, that the day of such conventional rhyme is ended.[98]

Today's Muse, and the American Muse above all, must jettison "the literary, as well as social etiquette of overseas feudalism and caste"[99] and express itself in prose or in a new poetic form more agile and more open to reality: behind the invention of free verse, we glimpse a philosophy of history. In 1897, Mallarmé published one of his most important writings in poetics, "Crise de vers" ("Crisis in Poetry"), gathering together thoughts that he wrote at

---

96. See M. L. Gasparov, *Ocherk istorii evropeiskogo stikha;* English translation, *A History of European Versification,* trans. G. S. Smith and Marina Tarlinskaja (Oxford: Clarendon, 1996), 284.

97. See Alberto Bertoni, *Dai simbolisti al Novecento: Le origini del verso libero italiano* (Bologna: Il Mulino, 1995), 100.

98. Walt Whitman, "Notes Left Over," in *Complete Prose Works* (1892), in *Complete Poetry and Collected Prose,* ed. Justin Kaplan (New York: Library of America, 1982), 1056.

99. Ibid.

different times from 1886 onward. The author of *Un coup de dés* was one of the first to grasp the significance of what was happening:

> But the truly remarkable fact is this: for the first time in the literary history of any nation, along with the general and traditional great organ of orthodox verse which finds its ecstasy on an every-ready keyboard, any poet with an individual technique and ear can build his own instrument. . . . Each poet has his flute or viol, with which to do so.[100]

His response to Jules Huret's *Enquête sur l'évolution littéraire* (Survey on Literary Evolution), published in *Écho de Paris* in 1891, is more explicit:

> We are witnessing a spectacle, . . . which is truly extraordinary, unique in the history of poetry: every poet is going off by himself with his own flute, and playing the songs he pleases. For the first time since the beginning of poetry, poets have stopped singing bass. Hitherto, as you know, if they wished to be accompanied, they had to be content with the great organ of official meter. Well, it was simply overplayed and they got tired of it! . . . [I]n a society without stability, without unity, there can be no stable or definitive art. From that incompletely organized society—which also explains the restlessness of certain minds—the unexplained need for individuality was born. The literary manifestations of today are a direct reflection of that need.[101]

Until then, the writing of poetry had bowed to the orthodoxy of prosodic rules, which unified the scattering of personal styles into the norm of a collective music. The revolution in metrics to which Mallarmé bore witness liberated the melody in each person. It allowed poets to follow their ear and transform an art governed by ritual into one that was individualistic, designed

---

100. Stéphane Mallarmé, "Crise de vers" (1886–1896); English translation, "Crisis in Poetry," in *Selected Prose Poems, Essays & Letters*, trans. Bradford Cook (Baltimore, MD: Johns Hopkins University Press, 1956), 37.
101. Stéphane Mallarmé, "Sur l'Évolution littéraire" (1891); English translation, "The Evolution of Literature," in *Selected Prose Poems, Essays & Letters*, 18–19.

to give voice to each poet's "flute or viol" and to display, as Proust would have said, a personal way of seeing things.

As profound as it is spectacular, this innovation changed readers' horizon of expectation: for poets to write poetry without a fixed structure and to begin and end their lines as they pleased was truly an unprecedented novelty. With the fall of the last and most important technical residue of the ancient art of versification, writers could really, at least in theory, express themselves autonomously, as if their style was a matter of pure vision. Conversely, when a poet chose to adhere to the inherited metrical forms, the choice took on a different meaning from what it had before free verse became the norm. It is easy to understand that this metrical triumph of individual talent over tradition points to a profound historical transformation and reflects that "unexplained need for individuality" that distinguishes the modern world. Almost two decades after Mallarmé's writings, the magazine *Poesia,* founded and directed by Marinetti during the years leading up to the birth of the Futurist movement, published an *Enquête internationale sur le Vers libre* (International Investigation into Free Verse). It brings together a number of interesting remarks, including a succinct and incisive contribution by Marie Dauguet.

> In literary aesthetics, free verse is the last effort of the individualist evolution started by Romanticism. It is the ultimate fruit of what is most independent in humanity, not just thought . . . but the way of perceiving [*la façon de sentir*]. This is precisely why it has provoked such protests. It is the very form of the emancipated inner self.[102]

Dauguet grasps the significance of the phenomenon when she writes that free verse is the last stage of Romantic individualism, the literary equivalent of the most intimate personal life. In the opening comments to the *Enquête internationale sur le Vers libre,* Gustave Kahn, who at the time was considered to be the main exponent of the new poetics of free verse, makes explicit claim to the historical continuity mentioned by Dauguet: "the Romantics . . . partly emancipated poetry. We have resumed their laborious effort, picking up at

---

102. *Enquête internationale sur le Vers libre et Manifeste du Futurisme par F. T. Marinetti* (Milan: Éditions de *Poesia,* 1909), 39.

the point where they stopped making technical progress and innovating."[103]
In this case too, the movement toward unrestrained individuation started by
Romanticism ran throughout the nineteenth century and came to maturity
in the age of the avant-gardes.

Tropes

The gap between modern poems and a minimal form of speech, the most
economical vehicle of thought, is often so great as to make texts indecipherable. This indecipherability is partly new, though, and different from the kind
readers were used to. Classical poetics and rhetoric were well aware of the
notion of *obscuritas,* and many verse writers in ancient literature earned the
name of *ainigmatodes* or *obscurus.* Oracular and mantic poetry is enigmatic,
as is that of Orpheus and Epimenides; Xenophanes, Parmenides, and Empedocles are judged indecipherable, along with Pindar and Lycophron; Callimachus and Propertius are deliberately difficult poets, while the incomprehensibility of Helvius Cinna and Persius actually becomes the object of irony.[104]
The obscurity of ancient poetry usually stems from a specific source: it is a
sign that the text communicates elitist or initiatory knowledge, whether in
content or form. The oracle speaks in riddles because it safeguards a divine
knowledge that humans understand only partially; the philosopher speaks
to savants who can understand him fully; Pindar is inspired by a god and addresses an inner circle; the Alexandrian poet writes for a refined audience that
shares his tastes. "If we wanted to generalize, [the forms of obscurity in classical
poetry] are manifestations of a style that asserts the gap between those who
know more and those who know less."[105] And if we were to continue general-
izing, we might say that this also explains the most important manifestation of
obscuritas in medieval poetry: the Provençal *trobar clus.* In these cases, anyone
able to decipher or appreciate the text gains access to an elitist knowledge or
taste, while anyone incapable of deciphering or appreciating it is excluded

103. Ibid., 29.

104. See Manfred Fuhrmann, "Obscuritas: Das Problem der Dunkelheit in der rhetorischen und literaräs-
thetischen Theorie der Antike," in *Immanente Ästhetik, ästhetische Reflexion,* 47–72; Franco Montanari, "Appunti
per lo studio dell'oscurità nella poesia classica," *L'Asino d'oro* 2, no. 3 (1991): 31–52.

105. Montanari, "Appunti per lo studio dell'oscurità nella poesia classica," 46.

from a knowledge that, despite being the privilege of the few, has a universally human value.

In addition to picking up the already-existing forms of obscurity, modern poetry developed new ones. Let us take two very different examples. We have already talked about the first one: if Montale had not explained the events alluded to in "The hope of even seeing you again," the last stanza would have been incomprehensible in its literal reading. The second is a poem by Rimbaud, "L'étoile a pleuré rose au cœur de tes oreilles" ("The Star Wept Rose into the Heart of Your Ears"), which was written on the same sheet of paper as the vowel sonnet:

> L'étoile a pleuré rose au cœur de tes oreilles,
> L'infini roulé blanc de ta nuque à tes reins;
> La mer a perlé rousse à tes mammes vermeilles
> Et l'Homme saigné noir à ton flanc souverain.

> The star wept rose into the heart of your ears,
> An infinity of white rolled between your nape and hips;
> The sea spumed red onto your vermilion breasts,
> And Man bled black onto your sovereign side.[106]

The overall meaning and choice of genre are easily deciphered: this is a laud of the female body, similar to those found in Renaissance or Baroque poetry, in more or less direct imitation of the Song of Songs. The middle verses can be understood (the second one means that the woman's white back is like an infinity, the third that her nipples are like drops of a red sea), but the beginning and the end are obscure. What do they allude to? The first line is thought to be a metaphorical description of an earring or part of an ear; the last could mean "the man at your side is like a stain of black blood." If we were to venture an interpretation, we might imagine that the blood stands for the wound of love suffered by the man, and that the black indicates, by metonymy, the color of his clothes. In this case the verse would mean "the man dressed in black who stands beside you is like a stain of

---

106. Arthur Rimbaud, "L'étoile a pleuré rose au coeur de tes oreilles," in *Œuvres complètes*, ed. Jean-Luc Steinmetz, 2nd rev. ed., (Paris: Flammarion, 2016); English translation "The Star Wept . . . ," trans. Wyatt Mason, in *Rimbaud Complete* (New York: Modern Library, 2002), 101.

blood, because his heart is metaphorically wounded." But it is by no means certain that this is right: in fact, there is nothing to prevent the closing from being read in a completely different way, for example, as a sexual metaphor. We easily understand that as long as the author's commentary is lacking, any literal interpretation would be risky, and that the figures making up this text cannot be reduced univocally to a degree-zero sentence. The reader of Montale's poem can decipher each segment but remains in the dark about the relationship between the parts; the reader of Rimbaud's poem easily grasps the sense of the whole but cannot decipher the individual images. And yet the mechanism that makes the two poems partially obscure is in many ways similar. While the pre-Romantic lyric usually refers to a knowledge or style that is public but only comprehensible to a few, the post-Romantic lyric is unintelligible because it exhibits a personal way of seeing, connecting, and deforming things—as does the speaker in Montale's motet when it associates jackals with the woman it addresses, or the speaker of Rimbaud's quatrain when he superimposes a play of impenetrable metaphors onto a hypothetical visible reality. We could say that the distinction between ancient and modern indecipherability is *a resistance to paraphrase:* for ancient poetry it is almost always possible to dissolve the figurative language into a prosaic degree-zero sentence, but for the poetry of the last two centuries this can sometimes prove impossible. As long as the reference code is public, the gap of knowledge separating the text from the reader can always be bridged; when the code is private, however, the reader can only hope for commentary from the poet.

The growing popularity of author notes, especially in the last century, is symptomatic of this need. Some of the most famous author notes are those at the end of the Boni and Liveright edition of *The Waste Land*. Many years later, Eliot tended to downplay their importance, claiming that he had added them only because the book was too short. Reading his correspondence with Gilbert Seldes and James Sibley Watson, the editors of *The Dial,* which published *The Waste Land* in the November 1922 issue, we learn that the notes existed before the Boni and Liveright edition. Clive Bell claims that it was Roger Fry who suggested to Eliot that he add them.[107] In any case, the notes became a permanent part of later editions of the text. The simpler ones provide sources

---

107. See Michael North's commentary to T. S. Eliot, *The Waste Land*, ed. Michael North (New York: Norton, 2001), 21.

for some of the quotations embedded in the text (Ezekiel, Ecclesiastes, *Tristan and Isolde,* Baudelaire, Dante, Shakespeare, and so on); the more complex ones add information that readers would be unlikely to understand on their own, beginning with references to Jessie L. Weston's *From Ritual to Romance* and James Frazer's *The Golden Bough.* They serve above all to clarify and specify associations between characters and parts of the poem that Eliot himself views as arbitrary:

> I am not familiar with the exact constitution of the Tarot pack of cards, from which I have obviously departed to suit my own convenience. The Hanged Man, a member of the traditional pack, fits my purpose in two ways: because he is associated in my mind with the Hanged God of Frazer, and because I associate him with the hooded figure in the passage of the disciples to Emmaus in Part V. The Phoenician Sailor and the Merchant appear later; also the "crowds of people," and Death by Water is executed in Part IV. The Man with Three Staves (an authentic member of the Tarot pack) I associate, quite arbitrarily, with the Fisher King himself.[108]

In other words, the notes to *The Waste Land* primarily have the purpose of unraveling a web of associations that, without notes, would remain indecipherable because they are subjective. Marianne Moore's "Note on the Notes" that she published in the first edition of *The Complete Poems* (1967) includes a broader reflection:

> A willingness to satisfy contradictory objections to one's manner of writing might turn one's work into the donkey that finally found itself being carried by its masters, since some readers suggest that quotation-marks are disruptive of pleasant progress; others, that notes to what should be complete are a pedantry or evidence of an insufficiently realized task. But since in *Observations,* and in anything I have written, there have been lines in which the chief interest is borrowed, and I have not yet been able to outgrow this hybrid method of composition, acknowledgments seem only honest. Perhaps those

---

108. Ibid., 22.

who are annoyed by provisos, detainments, and postscripts, could be persuaded to take probity on faith, the will for the deed, the poem as a self-sufficiency, and disregard the notes.[109]

Moore justifies the inclusion of her notes by the need to make clear what "is borrowed" in her poems: points of departure and quotations taken from others that inspire the text and with which it dialogues. Allusive poetry has a very long history, but the problem that Eliot, Moore, and many other modern authors face is new. In the twentieth century it became clear that tradition had grown frayed and multiple: no one could take it for granted that other people would understand references that were crucial and obvious to the writer. This also means that ever since the cultural repertory exploded, less canonical references should be considered to all intents and purposes personal associations and private allusions—hence the need for notes to explain them.

The spread of author commentary is a symptom of a new sort of indecipherability. To understand a poem, it is no longer enough to possess a collective, cohesive knowledge of a historical, mythological, political, or broadly cultural nature; one must also know the private anecdotes scattered throughout the text, understand the quotations that only the author and a few others can grasp, or decipher associations that the poet establishes "quite arbitrarily" between parts of the text. Unlike the unintelligibility that occurs in occasional and epistolary rhymes, what we have here goes beyond any shared social life (even the minimal social bond that connects the poet of occasion to his interlocutor, or two poets who correspond with each other). It leaves the reader all alone with purely subjective associations—the impenetrability of another person's consciousness that only notes can render less impenetrable.

But modern poems are not all indecipherable in the same way. Franco Fortini, who dedicated one of his last essays to this topic, distinguishes two types of resistance to interpretation: *obscurity* and *difficulty:*

> "Obscurity" is therefore the condition of a text or part of it that does
> not allow for a quick paraphrase capable of satisfying the needs of

---

109. Marianne Moore, *New Collected Poems,* ed. Heather Cass White (New York: Farrar, Straus and Giroux, 2017), 295.

the paraphrase; namely, to reduce as many self-referential elements as possible in favor of referential ones. The metaphor "Achilles is a lion" can be translated (understood, clarified) more easily than "Achilles is a fly," at least for a cultural context that has made the lion into a traditional stereotype. . . . If we then look at the stylistic–expressive and cognitive function of the (always relative) incomprehensibility or impenetrability of a text or part of it, we can say that the "obscurity" must never (nor can it) be defeated or overcome, because its reason for being, ultimately, is a particular category of figure, such as reticence or euphemism. Unless we want an essential part of the message to disappear, this obscurity must remain; moreover, and as we know, it is a mimesis of the obscurity of relations between human beings.

"Difficulty," on the other hand, is a characteristic of obscurity that is momentary rather than constitutive, which can be resolved by a certain degree of reader expertise. "Difficulty" is also a stylistic trait; indeed, it is organized and intentional in many literary traditions. But it differs from "obscurity" in that it accepts and even demands interpretation and paraphrasing. Poetic "obscurity" presents itself as insurmountable, . . . at its height, it escapes expressive language and culminates in the chaos or silence of all hermetic knowledge, which, in our century, has been popularized by avant-garde and surrealist procedures. "Difficulty," on the other hand, arises as a *provisional* riddle that can be solved using specific tools and therefore by means of critical exegesis or *hermeneusis,* manifesting the (typically allegorist) divide between an infinitely translatable linguistic object and its provisional rational–communicative translation.[110]

Obscurity arises from a purely subjective deformation of the degree-zero discourse based on daytime logic and common sense, as happens when we invent metaphors that bear no correspondence to what the senses perceive or what we are used to associating with a certain thing, person, or situation. If I say "Achilles is a fly" or "this table is an apple," I replace the commonly accepted semantic fields with a completely intransitive semantic field—a

---

110. Franco Fortini, "Oscurità e difficoltà," *L'asino d'oro* 2, no. 3 (1991): 87.

symbolic projection of my subjective difference and the obscurity of relations between human beings. Difficulty is instead a provisional riddle,
grounded in a knowledge gap that can be bridged by paraphrase, putting
readers in a position to access the information referred to by the poet. When
Donne writes "she whom I loved hath paid her last debt" or when Montale
closes "The hope of even seeing you again" with an apparently incongruous
image, readers can solve the mystery by reading the notes for the missing
information. There are two types of difficulties and two types of paraphrases
in this regard, because one cannot confuse a text that alludes to public information to which everyone has access with a text that alludes to private anecdotes. Nonetheless, it is true that when explaining the identity of "she whom
I loved" and what the jackals on the leash mean, we are solving a provisional
riddle, a knowledge gap: the text remains paraphrasable in both forms of
difficulty. Obscurity and difficulty are not mutually exclusive conditions but
rather relative magnitudes, tied to the reader's degree of competence; they
also communicate with each other, like the extremes of a graduated scale.
Both have always existed (difficulty is actually inherent in the language of
poetry, given that poetic diction is nothing more than an apparatus of "difficult" synonyms that serve to distance writing in verse from ordinary language), but their nature and incidence have been changed by modern poetry,
increasing the number of difficult allusions because they are private, and fu-
eling a search for striking imagery. When reading the line "And Man bled
black onto your sovereign side" in Rimbaud's poem, one might think that the
line was produced by altering the minimal form of speech or by defamiliar-
izing a represented action, event, or object. But one might also believe that
Rimbaud transcribed onto paper an obscure mental process that cannot be
reduced to our shared language and to the common perception of things.
Obscurity became even more profound and irreducible during the age of the
historical avant-gardes. Here is the beginning of a poem by André Breton,
"Le Soleil en laisse" ("The Sun on a Leash"), taken from *Clair de terre* (1923,
Earthlight):

> Le grand frigorifique blanc dans la nuit des temps
> Qui distribue les frissons à la ville
> Chante pour lui seul
> Et le fond de sa chanson ressemble à la nuit

Qui fait bien ce qu'elle fait et pleure de le savoir
Une nuit où j'étais de quart sur un volcan
J'ouvris sans bruit la porte d'une cabine et me jetai aux pieds de la lenteur
Tant je la trouvai belle et prête à m'obéir
Ce n'était qu'un rayon de la roue voilée
Au passage des morts elle s'appuyait sur moi

The big white cold storage room in the mists of time
That sends out shivers to the city
Sings to itself
And the musical background of its song resembles the night
Which does what it does well and weeps because it knows it
One night when I was keeping watch over a volcano
Without a sound I opened the door of a cabin and threw myself at the
feet of slowness
I found it that beautiful and that ready to obey me
It was only a spoke of a bent wheel
When the dead passed by it leaned against me.[111]

The style deviates from degree-zero writing so strongly that the text is impenetrable. What is "the big white cold storage room in the mists of time | That sends out shivers to the city"? Is it an image that adorns a *verbum proprium* or a metaphorical creation that has lost all connection to the natural way of saying things? Regardless of the meaning of the individual passages, it seems clear to me that Breton's poem does not merely add metaphorical disguises or metonymic cuts to a perceptible datum: it functions according to a different form of reasoning than that of rational discourse. It does not seem as if Breton has a degree-zero sentence, scene, or story in mind, except in a very vague way, that the poem then coats with figures or ornaments. Rather, he seems to let himself be guided by a chain of impenetrable psycho-linguistic associations, the "imitation of a consciousness that is inarticulate and therefore obscure, first to itself

---

111. André Breton, "Le Soleil en laisse," in *Clair de terre* (1923), in *Oeuvres complètes*, ed. Marguerite Bonnet (Paris: Gallimard, 1988), 188; English translation, "The Sun on a Leash," in *Earthlight*, trans. Bill Zavatsky and Zack Rogow (Copenhagen: Green Integer, 2004), 93.

and then to its intended audience,"[112] creating a subjective chain that is intransitive and therefore obscure, and which eludes paraphrase. It "escapes from articulate language" and expresses "the chaos or silence of all hermetic wisdom," or more simply "the obscurity of relations between human beings."[113] Ever since it became grammatical to use tropes freely, modern poetry has accustomed us to a mixed regimen of reading, to alternating the decipherable and the undecipherable: parts, lines, details that the reader interprets according to a referential logic, and portions of text that are impossible to paraphrase. When I read "La aurora" ("Dawn"), a poem by García Lorca from *Poeta en Nueva York* (1929–1930), from the context and the collection as a whole, I can tell that we are in a specific place:

La aurora de Nueva York tiene
cuatro columnas de cieno
y un huracán de negras palomas
que chapotean las aguas podridas.
La aurora de Nueva York gime
por las inmensas escaleras
buscando entre las aristas
nardos de angustia dibujada.
La aurora llega y nadie la recibe en su boca
porque allí no hay mañana ni esperanza posible.
A veces las monedas en enjambres furiosos
taladran y devoran abandonados niños.
Los primeros que salen comprenden con sus huesos
que no habrá paraíso ni amores deshojados;
saben que van al cieno de números y leyes,
a los juegos sin arte, a sudores sin fruto.
La luz es sepultada por cadenas y ruidos
en impúdico reto de ciencia sin raíces.
Por los barrios hay gentes que vacilan insomnes
como recién salidas de un naufragio de sangre.

112. Fortini, "Oscurità e difficoltà," 87.
113. Ibid.

Dawn in New York
has four columns of filth
and a hurricane of black doves
splashing in putrid waters.

Dawn in New York whimpers
down the huge stairs
seeking in the chaff
flowers of sketched anguish.

Dawn comes and no one receives it in his mouth
because there is no tomorrow or possibility of hope.
Sometimes furious swarms of coins
drill and devour the abandoned children.
The first to leave understand in their bones
there'll be no paradise or leafless loves;
they know they go to the filth of numbers and laws,
to artless games, to fruitless sweat.

The light is buried by noises and chains
in the obscene challenge of rootless science.
In the neighborhoods are people who wander unsleeping
like survivors of a shipwreck of blood.[114]

The dawn he describes probably existed in reality, and the last two lines refer to scenes of poverty and urban conflict that recur in other poems of the book. Everything else obeys a different logic. According to Barthes, modern lyric poetry is no longer an ornamental variation on prose, like *poésie classique,* but "a different language or the product of a particular sensibility." Before Symbolism and the avant-gardes gave greater freedom to the use of tropes, style was seen primarily as the product of a particular sensibility; after this turning

---

114. Federico García Lorca, "La aurora," in *Poeta en Nueva York* (1929–30), 1st ed. with introd. and notes by Andrew A. Anderson (Barcelona: Galaxia Gutenberg, 2013), 209; English translation "Dawn," in *Poet in New York,* trans. Pablo Medina and Mark Statman (New York: Grove Press, 2008), 73.

point, we can understand why and how poetry became, in some cases, a different language.

Although obscurity and difficulty are not mutually exclusive, every text has its dominant: some poems are mainly obscure, some are mainly difficult, and some manage to escape this opposition. One of the hallmarks of obscure texts is the arbitrariness with which metaphors are used. Since metaphor juxtaposes two different semantic fields and eliminates the mediation of the "like," it is the most risky figure for logic: it unites what rational discourse keeps distinct or approaches with caution.[115] Extending metaphorical freedom therefore means reducing the space of daytime communication and distancing art from the shared world, as Ortega y Gasset understood when he defined metaphor as "the most radical instrument of dehumanization."[116] In contrast, difficulty does not completely destroy the logical connections of shared discourse; it leaves the job of restoring them to the paraphrase. If it is true that these two forms of incommunicability have always existed, it is also true that modern lyricism has transfigured them. In little more than a century, the territory that literature conceded to autobiographical content and to the subjectivity of style has expanded out of all proportion. Today, thanks to our reigning idea of lyric poetry, poets can in theory say whatever they want, inventing continually new forms of private incommunicability. Before Romanticism, Symbolism, and the historical avant-gardes, what Fortini calls obscurity was a rare anomaly; today it is part of the horizon of expectation with which we approach books of poetry. Similarly, the difficulty that stems from private sources, something unusual in premodern poetry, is now the norm in post-Romantic lyric poetry. Taken together, these two phenomena mean one thing: the triumph of subjective estrangement over mimesis, of personal diction over public speech, and of individual talent over tradition.

---

115. See Francesco Orlando, *Illuminismo e retorica freudiana* (Turin: Einaudi, 1982).
116. Ortega y Gasset, *The Dehumanization of Art*, 35.

CHAPTER FOUR

The Literary Space of Modern Poetry

Poetry as Estrangement

As we have seen, between the second half of the eighteenth century and the beginning of the twentieth, the form of European poetry underwent an extraordinary metamorphosis. In theory, poets gained complete lexical, metrical, syntactic, and rhetorical freedom; expressivism in content was accompanied by expressivism in form; and style could be interpreted as the product of a particular sensibility, or even as a different language. Although many writers tried to limit the ensuing anarchy, choosing to return to order was now a personal choice, no less fragile and arbitrary than choosing not to. We have also seen that modern poetry is a literary space with a center and two main peripheries: the center is occupied by lyric poetry, the outlying areas by two diametrically opposed attempts to surpass its primacy—long narrative or essay poems on nonautobiographical subjects, and poetry that aspires to resolve itself into pure form or pure sound. The main border lies in the relationship with the author's differential autobiography, but what holds the territory together is the nature of the form.

Poetry is unsuited for mimesis because "imitation has much of the servile about it," writes Leopardi in the *Zibaldone*.[1] Contrary to the writer who effaces

---

1. Giacomo Leopardi, *Zibaldone di pensieri* (1817–1832); English translation, *Zibaldone*, trans. Michael Caesar and Franco D'Intino (New York: Farrar, Straus and Giroux, 2013), 4357–4358.

himself to let facts speak for themselves, the "man of genius . . . will have his own feelings to express"; "he will be averse to clothing another character, to speaking in the voice of another person, to imitating." He will want, rather, to be at the text's center, talking about himself in a style that differs from the degree-zero of prose, which is best suited for representing the external world.[2] Leopardi is rewriting a commonplace of the Romantic aesthetic—the antithesis between imitation and expression. According to this paradigm, literature has two tasks: to recount the actions of human beings in the external world, and to express—to press out—the writer's internal world. The first requires the author to focus on the reality that is considered objective by common sense, which requires the medium of prose, as in modern novels; the second allows the writer to express himself or herself and involves versification, as in poetry. On the page preceding the passage just cited, Leopardi wrote that, due to their length, epic poems require a plan set out coldly in advance, distorting the momentary impetus that constitutes the essence and secret of true poetry. This chain of automatic associations, as we have seen, came into being at a specific time: at the same time, in fact, as the development of modern genres, when poetry became specialized toward the lyrical. When poetry was still "prose + a + b + c," narrating in verse according to the rules of prosody meant following a custom that had become second nature, governed by specific collective norms. However, once prose written in a simple style became perceived as the degree-zero medium, once the modern novel and the bourgeois drama supplanted narrative in verse and theater in verse, and once the expressive theory of style gained hegemony over the Western literary system, the act of breaking to a new line before the typographical end of the page became a form of estrangement, which distanced poetry from the natural way of telling stories or constructing arguments. Once verse writing became divorced from its ritual origin, the very act of starting a new line before its natural end represented a way of detaching from degree-zero communicative writing by shifting the reader's attention from content to form. More generally, for the conventional wisdom that prevailed when the Romantic paradigm became hegemonic, a text's form became the creation, expression, and trace of a person: the author. For this reason, *all texts that draw attention to a stylistic deviation from the ordinary, that is, the "natural" and prosaic way of saying things, are implicitly*

---

2. Ibid.

egocentric. Although many forms of estranged prose have existed and still exist—beginning with novels that are read for how they are written and not for the story they tell—when it became unnatural to tell stories in poetry, a purely mimetic verse could no longer survive.[3] *This means that no poems today, even antilyric ones, can escape the subjectivism of style.* All types of writing in verse have become opaque: even poems that strive to break out of the confines of the lyric by telling stories and presenting arguments do so in a form that, to our reading habits, appears overtly estranged. This is why the form of modern poetry subsists in a kind of paradox, a double bind: its devices, starting with the idea that it can break to a new line before reaching the natural end of the row, arise from ancient collective conventions whose original meaning has been lost, and which have subsequently been reinterpreted as personal ways of seeing things, as traces of an authorial subjectivity. Something that originated in ritual was reinterpreted (and rewritten) as a sign of self-expression. The appeal of modern poetry derives in part from this ambiguity.

There exists an egocentrism of content and an egocentrism of form: expressly autobiographical poems combine both, whereas texts devised from expressly impersonal poetics, such as *Un coup de dés* or *The Waste Land,* reject the former but flaunt the latter. While the mimetic novelist strives to be the mediator of a story that, in theory, speaks for itself, stylistic estrangement is inherent in modern verse writing—a genre in which the author retains absolute dominion over the writing, even while proclaiming the elocutionary disappearance of the poet or pure impersonality. Over the last two centuries, mimetic prose genres have in many ways placed the writer in the forefront of the work once again (with humorous novels, the *roman personnel,* essay novels, and novels based on style) but all of them leave aside verse. Today, when you walk into a bookstore you know you will find fiction shelves (all written in prose, with very rare exceptions) and the poetry shelf, mostly filled with lyric poetry. The *epos,* the romance, and novels in verse have disappeared. It may happen in English-speaking countries that Vikram Seth's *The Golden Gate* (1986) becomes a bestseller, that Derek Walcott writes a postcolonial epic in verse (*Omeros,* 1990), that John Ashbery publishes the 216-page *Flow Chart* (1991), and that Anne Carson (*Autobiography of Red,* 1998), Les Murray (*Fredy*

---

3. On this shift in functions, see also Dominique Combe, *Poésie et Récit: Une rhétorique des genres* (Paris: Corti, 1989), especially 151–154. Prose poems incorporate forms of estrangement that perform the same function as the ritual of meter.

Neptune, 1998) or Brad Leithauser (*Darlington's Fall,* 2002) successfully devote themselves to the novel in verse,[4] but these are texts that intentionally defy reader expectations. Usually, versified stories are rare and end up stacked in any case with the poetry books, which is to say, mainly lyrical texts, not novels. At least, this is what happened to all the texts in Italian bookstores described as verse novels on their back cover or on the publisher's sleeve during the period when I was preparing the Italian version of this book.[5] Besides, novel readers know very well that they will not find what they are looking for in these texts. Amazon's editorial review advertising Vikram Seth's *The Golden Gate* in February 2002 is a good example: "Can 690 sonnets, rhyming a-b-a-b-c-d-e-f-e-g-g, be a novel? Definitely!" The question sounds like a blatant denial, betraying a fear that what is so confidently asserted may not be true. Bob Brandeis, the Amazon.com reviewer of *Fredy Neptune,* puts it candidly: "Despite laudable efforts by Vikram Seth and Anne Carson, the novel in verse isn't exactly a fashionable genre."[6] Although willing to leave some space to the author's speaking voice, novel readers expect the book to tell a story, and when diction overpowers content, the work might even prove annoying. Poe's prophecy has come true: epic and didactic poetry are relics from which future readers will extract short lyric poems by cutting out the connecting passages.[7] When toned down and with some exceptions allowed, this idea continues to be true on the whole, and it signals a momentous change.

Lyrical Romanticism

Although opacity of form ties the currents of modern poetry together, the genre remains a vast forcefield frayed at the edges. So far I have mentioned the difference between the center and the peripheries; now I would like to

---

4. On the verse novel tradition and its recent developments, see Catherine Addison, *A Genealogy of the Verse Novel* (Cambridge: Cambridge Scholars Publishing, 2017).

5. *La camera da letto* (1984 and 1988) by Attilio Bertolucci, *Giovanna d'Arco* (1990) by Maria Luisa Spaziani, *L'infermiera di Pisa* (1991) and *Il palazzo e il pazzo* (1993) by Ottiero Ottieri, *La sorella dell'ave* (1992) and *Rosabianca e la contessa* (1994) by Ludovica Ripa di Meana, *La comunione dei beni* (1995) by Edoardo Albinati, *Suora Carmelitana* (1997) by Franco Buffoni.

6. This review is at https://www.amazon.com/Fredy-Neptune-Novel-Verse-Murray-ebook/dp/B013P2ESWA.

7. Edgar Allan Poe, "The Poetic Principle" (1850), in *Essays and Reviews,* ed. Gary Richard Thompson (New York: Library of America, 1984), 72.

try to draw a rough map of it. It will be a very approximate attempt, for two reasons. The first stems from the difficulty of writing a literary history of the *longue durée*. A project of this sort has become problematic over recent decades. The culture of our times is increasingly skeptical of canons and unifying syntheses, whose unilateral, simplifying, and violent character has been deconstructed repeatedly. The rise of new collective subjects that were once silent or treated as a minority, the expansion of geographical spaces, the spread of relativism, the increase in the number of researchers, and the amount of research and empirical data have called into question any confidence one might have in writing a philosophy of literary history that for Bakhtin, Auerbach, Adorno, or Szondi still had a clear path forward. The second reason concerns specifically the genre of modern poetry, which seems more resistant to the claims of a comparative literary history than the novel. There is a "stubbornly national" element in modern poetry:

> Poetry has primarily to do with the expression of feeling and emotion: and . . . feeling and emotion are particular; whereas thought is general. It is easier to think in a foreign language than it is to feel in it. Therefore, no art is more stubbornly national than poetry.[8]

> Due to the Curse of Babel, poetry is the most provincial of the arts, but today, when civilization is becoming monotonously the same all the world over, one feels inclined to regard this as a blessing rather than a curse: in poetry, at least, there cannot be an "International Style."[9]

In poetry, writes Auden, there cannot be an International Style. For this reason, what Hans Magnus Enzensberger called the "world language of modern poetry"[10] does not exist except in rough form. In addition to the bond with the poet's mother tongue, two other factors serve to keep national traditions locked up inside themselves, making poetry "the most provincial of the

---

8. Thomas Stearns Eliot, "The Social Function of Poetry" (1945), in *On Poetry and Poets* (New York: Farrar, Straus and Cudahy, 1957), 8.

9. Wystan Hugh Auden, "Writing," in *The Dyer's Hand and Other Essays* (1962) (New York: Random House, 1989), 23.

10. Hans Magnus Enzensberger, "Weltsprache der modernen Poesie" (1960–1962); English translation, "World Language of Modern Poetry," in *The Consciousness Industry: On Literature, Politics and the Media*, selected and with postscript by Michael Roloff (New York: Seabury Press, 1974), 42–61.

arts." The most obvious is the relationship with the publishing industry. In Western countries, the number of foreign-language poetry books translated, distributed, and read is substantially smaller than the number of foreign-language fiction works: this becomes obvious from a quick look through publisher catalogues. The most important factor lies in the history of poetry itself: each linguistic–literary area has developed versions of modern poetry that are markedly more vernacular than versions of the novel, a genre that more easily and more frequently absorbs international influences. For these reasons, any maps are necessarily approximative and not very detailed on a small scale.

The point of departure for the historical and morphological history I sketch out here is suggested by the internal logic of poetry itself. Since the genre is characteristically egocentric, one can reasonably order the axes of its development on the basis of the weight and role that the first person has in the world depicted by the poem. One could consider the evolution of expressivism separately in terms of content and form, but this would entail adopting a mechanical criterion that does not approximate the real connection of the phenomena. Rather, subject matter and style need to be united in a single examination, focusing on the place that the speaker occupies in the text.

At the center of our literary space we find the subjective genre par excellence: lyric poetry. In the system of literary forms that arose with the Romantic revolution, the modern lyric has a kinship with prose autobiography; however, while the medium used by prose autobiography is associated in our conventional wisdom with mimesis, the determining factor in modern poetry is the weight of style. This means that ever since form was interpreted as reflecting a particular sensibility, the family of modern lyric texts has appeared to be marked by subjectivism. To echo Leopardi's observation, we could say that if imitation in prose has much of the servile about it, then modern lyric poetry is typically a noble genre—a literary form that, by evoking thoughts or slivers of personal life in a style far removed from the ordinary way of telling things, conveys a doubly egocentric image of the world. The structure of theater and the novel easily transcends the sphere of an individual life: the hero of drama speaks and acts alongside other heroes in the common space of the stage; the narrator can make his or her own words conflict with those of the characters, or shift the action in time and space. Even the most lyrical of novelists has a hard time ignoring the constants of a genre constructed to show simultaneously the truth of the protagonist and the truth of what transcends the protagonist—the external world, the gaze of others, the psychological and social forcefields on which the identity and destiny of individuals depend. Conversely, modern poets find it difficult to step outside the sphere of the self. Whenever they attempt to do so, they seem to trespass beyond the measure that is intrinsic to the logic of the genre, venturing into a territory that our horizon of expectations judges as experimental.

But if lyric poetry represents the center around which the genre conglomerates, this core is in its turn so frayed and extended over time that it merits further segmentations. The model of subjective poetry that emerged in recent centuries, as we noted, arose between the second half of the eighteenth century and the beginning of the nineteenth. Applying a category of political philosophy to literature, we might call this archetype *lyric Romanticism*. What I am thinking of is not a specific set of texts but an ideal type that I will try to describe starting with a concrete individual example. In a famous essay, Meyer H. Abrams observed that the literature of Romanticism revamped the genres of poetry by inventing a lyrical form that would become wildly popular in the second half of the nineteenth century and into the twentieth, but which did not exist before Romanticism except in embryonic form. For lack of a better definition, Abrams called it the *greater Romantic lyric,* wanting to emphasize a theoretical continuity between this form and the Pindaric ode, which neoclassical critics called the *greater ode* to distinguish it from the Horatian *lesser ode.* The text of a greater Romantic lyric contains the monologue of an individuated poetic speaker who moves through an individuated landscape and holds a conversation with itself, with a silent interlocutor, or with things. Usually the first person begins by describing what it sees, and then delves into a broadly philosophical reflection that prompts it to make a moral decision, resolve an emotional problem, deal with a tragic loss, or reflect on the human condition.[11] Some of the most canonical poems of English Romanticism follow this structure: Coleridge's "The Eolian Harp," "Frost at Midnight," "Fears in Solitude," and "Dejection: An Ode"; Wordsworth's "Tintern Abbey"

---

11. See Meyer H. Abrams, "Structure and Style in the Greater Romantic Lyric," in *From Sensibility to Romanticism: Essays Presented to Fredrick A. Pottle,* ed. F. W. Hilles and Harold Bloom (New York: Oxford University Press, 1965), 527–528.

and "Ode: Intimations of Immortality"; Shelley's "Stanzas Written in Dejection" and "Ode to the West Wind." But it is not hard to come up with dozens
of other canonical examples in other literatures, from Leopardi's "The Infinite" to Hölderlin's "The Middle of Life" and Lamartine's "L'Isolement."

What distinguishes these Romantic poems from the premodern lyric
written in a tragic style is their connection with contingency and individuation: the poetic discourse refers to a specific place and time, the speaker has
a proper name, its identity coincides largely with that of the real person whose
name appears on the book of poetry. This way of writing presupposes an
ethos that is difficult to define in terms of form or content but which contemporary readers grasp easily, especially when they compare these poems
to the subjective poems they have become accustomed to by twentieth-
century literature. We could say that the greater Romantic lyric arose out of a
form of *confidence:* the confidence with which the *I* speaks about itself, in the
conviction that its personal life has an immediate universal value or, to use
Hegel's expression, a world-historical value—in the dual sense of "recognized
by all" but also "essential for our understanding of reality." This lyrical subject
could be described the same way Wordsworth's preface to *Lyrical Ballads* describes the poet: namely, an individual who is not extraordinary in position,
prestige, or deeds; a normal person, perhaps a bit more gifted in expressing
thoughts and passions but for the most part equal to everyone else.[12] Since
every detail of the lyric subject's life can be known to us, from his or her name
to a slew of incidental little anecdotes, readers who identify with the subject
do not identify with a transcendental model. Rather, they superimpose their
own subjective world onto the subjective world of the lyric speaker, as if the
latter's private idiosyncrasies were collective singularities.

At the level of content, then, this is a pure model of expressivism: differential autobiographism, immediate reader identification with another person,
and triumph of the individual over the type. We would expect topics such as
these to be accompanied by a corresponding form, one that is entirely subjective; instead, this kind of poetry comes nowhere near the excesses that

---

12. William Wordsworth and Samuel Taylor Coleridge, *Lyrical Ballads,* 2nd ed., ed. R. L. Brett and A. R.
Jones (London: Routledge, 1991), 261. Wordsworth always has a strong awareness of the universal and social
value of the lyric: Jacques Rancière, *La Chair des mots: Politiques de l'écriture* (1998); English translation, *The
Flesh of Words: The Politics of Writing,* trans. Charlotte Mandell (Stanford, CA: Stanford University Press, 2004),
chap. 1; and Jonathan Culler, *Theory of the Lyric* (Cambridge, MA: Harvard University Press, 2015), 321–331.

Symbolism and the avant-garde movements would make familiar. Individual talent has to do battle with two forces: tradition, which would insist on respecting customs handed down from the past; and common sense, which would advise against subverting normal appearances. In theory, Romantic poetry breaks free from both; in actual fact, though, at least until the second half of the nineteenth century, the texts do not completely abandon them, as if this poetry with its strongly subjective content sought a reformist balance between tradition and the lifeworld. When we think of the ideal type of Romantic poetry, we think of this form of *self-confident and measured individualism:* self-confident in claiming the universal value of a personal experience, and measured in balancing expressivism and anti-expressivism—the rights of individual talent and respect for certain structures of public discourse that are rooted in common sense or tradition. Not surprisingly, although Romantic theory actually legitimized all experiments, only more than half a century later would true experimentalism explode. Apart from the early spread of free verse in pre-Romanticism and German Romanticism, the most important formal novelty in early nineteenth-century European lyricism remains the crisis in poetic diction. This self-confident and measured subject is also quite *whole* when compared to what would happen to it a century later.[13] Between the second half of the nineteenth century and the age of the avant-gardes, the speaker in modern lyric poetry became progressively disharmonious, dissonant, and divided, as compared with the first person of Romantic poetry, which generally still possessed the inner hierarchical structures that give order to the flow of consciousness.

But the greater Romantic lyric was not the only major form in the period during and after Romanticism. Differential autobiographism was the new and ultimately hegemonic paradigm, but other first-person models continued to be reinterpreted and blended with the new model. European poetic Romanticism reused and rewrote the apparatus of themes and genres handed down by ancient poetry, creating a form of Romantic classicism. Much of the work of Hölderlin and Novalis, and some of the work of Foscolo, Keats, and Shelley, consists of texts in which, at least in the first instance, the speaker seems to move within the structures of transcendental

---

13. See Pier Vincenzo Mengaldo, "Grande stile e lirica moderna" (1983), in *La tradizione del Novecento: Nuova serie* (Florence: Vallecchi, 1987), 8–9.

autobiographism, reinterpreting ancient or medieval genres within the framework of a Romantic aesthetic: the ode, hymn, elegy, *ekphrasis,* lament, prosopopoeia, sonnet. Reading the entirety of Hölderlin's poems does not yield many biographical details, and yet one has the sense of a voice that reuses ancient materials in a novel, modern, and wholly personal way to create an absolute lyrical voice. In 1819, while Leopardi was working on his idylls, Keats wrote his six great odes. In none of them do we find specific details from a contingent biography, any more than we do in Petrarch or Shakespeare. Five of the odes appeared in *Lamia, Isabella, The Eve of St. Agnes, and Other Poems* (1820), a volume containing short narrative poems and other sorts of texts, all still conceived (like the earlier *Poems* of 1817) according to the principle of separating genres, which Romanticism strove to leave behind. Keats's six odes seem closer to the greater odes of classicist descent than to the greater Romantic lyric; yet whoever reads them notices an overload of subjectivity that cannot fit into the inherited schemes, partly because one cannot help but overlay them across the *Poems* of 1817, which offer a wealth of autobiographical details, and partly because the quality of the voice has changed. Behind the matter expressed in schemes descended from the tradition of the ode stands a contingent, unique speaker. It is no accident that Keats—like Novalis, Hölderlin, or Shelley—immediately created a biographical legend, and the first person in his poems overlapped with the person whose name appears on the covers of his books. Their tragic lives facilitated this process, but it never would have happened without the peculiarity of their diction.

Alongside the greater Romantic lyric, the other major tradition of lyrical Romanticism is the modern reinterpretation of forms that, in theory, contain no differential autobiographism and yet are charged with a voice that is singular and individuated but at the same time absolute and vertical. In this case too, the speaker in the text claims a universal value for the particular experience that it seeks to voice. When Adorno imagines lyricism as a genre that "hopes to attain universality through unrestrained individuation," he is thinking of these first persons,[14] who are thoroughly modern subjects,

---

14. Theodor W. Adorno, "Rede über Lyrik und Gesellschaft" (1957); English translation, "On Lyric Poetry and Society," in *Notes to Literature,* trans. Shierry Weber Nicholsen (New York: Columbia University Press, 1991), 38.

meaning Romantic and post-Romantic: "the manifestations in earlier periods of the specifically lyric spirit familiar to us are only isolated flashes."[15]

Wholeness, security, and measure are qualities we recognize after the fact, from the vantage point of a later age when these characteristics cease to be obvious, when the individual who possessed them and the social conditions that legitimized them have faded away. From this point of view, Baudelaire's and Whitman's stances are quite interesting. Although Baudelaire's speaker maintains a relatively traditional declarative posture, he was the first author to decry the "lost halo," a crisis in the poet's traditional role. He was also the first to introduce forms of experience and discursive constructions into his poetry that would become typical features of modernism, such as the epiphany ("À une passante"), as well as texts composed using associative methods that evade classical forms of narrative or argumentation ("Le Cygne").[16] Baudelaire was the first European poet to transport lyric poetry of a serious style, traditionally placed in a rural setting, into the city and into a modern physical space. Whitman, on the other hand, never faced the problem of having to legitimize his poetry: no poet has ever shown such confidence in his role, not even Victor Hugo, perhaps, who owed his immense popularity especially to his novels and public figure. The assumption behind *Leaves of Grass,* repeated constantly in the book, is that there is no gap between *I* and *us:* the speaker is a "comrade" to everyone ("these tend inward to me, and I tend outward to them");[17] in singing himself he also writes the epic of a people. This gesture simultaneously embodies the modern lyrical dream ("to attain universality through unrestrained individuation") while overcoming some of its assumptions. The first is wholeness: Whitman's speaker seeks to be plural and multiple. In reality, the overall effect is quite different from that of divided modernist subjects: in *Leaves of Grass* there is a correspondence between self and world; in the end Whitman's multiplicity has an extraordinarily cohesive tone. The second is the relationship to inherited tradition. Whitman consciously abandons the forms he associates with the literary and political Ancien Régime, with European feudalism, and renews the meter, lexicon, and syntax of English-language poetry. In this regard, he

---

15. Ibid., 40.

16. "À une passante" and "Le Cygne" were published in the second edition (1861) of *Les Fleurs du Mal.*

17. Walt Whitman, "Song of Myself," in *Leaves of Grass and Other Writings,* ed. Michael Moon (New York: Norton, 2002), 39.

certainly exhibits confidence but not measure—if by measure we mean a balance with the forms of the past. He does not innovate in order to break with the public at large, as the European avant-gardes of the early twentieth century would do, in the name of pure, individual stylistic freedom, a subjectivism to which an indemonstrable political significance is perhaps attributed; instead, he tries to invent another tradition, another language, that is at the same time personal and collective. To this end, he relies on two great cornerstones of general culture: the oratorical tradition and, most of all, the Bible, whose heir he seeks to be, literally.[18] His goal is to give an account of a plural nation that heralds a new world, based on an intermingling. The stylistic correlates of this project are multilingualism, inclusive lists, and the long line.

From the vista of more than a century and a half later, such a project seems unattainable. Ben Lerner puts it most aptly: "the Whitmanic program has never been realized in history, and I don't think it can be."[19] The explosion of differences, a fundamental trait of the modern world that Whitman wants to sing about, makes it unthinkable for one voice to speak on behalf of everyone else, for a first person to be large enough to contain multitudes without trampling on other points of view.[20] But even if such an inclusive work of art could still exist, it is highly unlikely to be a book of poetry. Since the second half of the nineteenth century, "only in rare instances," writes Benjamin, speaking of Baudelaire, "is lyric poetry in rapport with the experience of its readers":[21] it is a niche genre that speaks to a specialized group.

For a long time, twentieth-century poetry and poetics made a certain meta-literary idea habitual: the embarrassment or shame of writing poetry—the development and consequences of that "loss of the halo" that Baudelaire described in one of his *Petits Poèmes en prose* and, with different emphases, in

---

18. Herbert J. Levine, "Song of Myself as Whitman's American Bible," *Modern Language Quarterly* 48 (1987): 145–161; Elisa New, *The Regenerate Lyric: Theology and Innovation in American Poetry* (Cambridge: Cambridge University Press, 1993), chap. 4 ("Crossing Leviticus: Whitman"); William C. Harris, "Whitman's *Leaves of Grass* and the Writing of a New American Bible," *Walt Whitman Quarterly Review* 16, no. 3 (1999): 172–190.

19. Ben Lerner, *The Hatred of Poetry* (New York: Farrar, Straus and Giroux, 2015), 49.

20. Ibid., 49–50.

21. Walter Benjamin, "Über einige Motive bei Baudelaire" (1939); English translation, "On Some Motifs in Baudelaire," in *Illuminations*, trans. Harry Zohn (New York: Schocken Books, 2007), 156.

Mon cœur mis à nu (*My Heart Laid Bare*).[22] More than a static commonplace, this is a family of recurring themes that appear in two versions, one dysphoric and the other euphoric. In Italy, poetry was fully launched into the twentieth-century period of its history by the generation of authors born in the 1880s. Some of them wrote poems expressing their shame at writing poetry, at the loss of its social mandate. One of Aldo Palazzeschi's most famous poems, "E lasciatemi divertire" (1910, "So Let Me Have My Fun!"), stages an ironic dialogue between a poet and the members of a respectable bourgeois audience. The poet provokes them by writing nonsense verses ("Tri tri tri, | fru fru fru, | ihu ihu ihu, | uhi uhi uhi"); the audience is outraged and questions whether this is poetry. The poem resembles a modern equivalent of a medieval tenson and can be read as a preview or transcription of what happened during "Futurist soirées," performances that the Futurists held in theaters to provoke their audiences. Palazzeschi, who was one of the first to join Marinetti's avant-garde, was also among the first to attend these events. "So Let Me Have My Fun!" is written in a comic register, but the intent, revealed in the final stanza, is serious:

> Infine io ò pienamente ragione,
> i tempi sono molto cambiati,
> gli uomini non dimandano
> più nulla dai poeti,
> e lasciatemi divertire!

> In the end I am plenty right,
> times have changed,
> men don't ask anything anymore
> from poets:
> so let me have my fun![23]

---

22. Charles Baudelaire, "Perte d'auréole"; English translation, "Lost Halo," in *Paris Spleen: Little Poems in Prose*, trans. Keith Waldrop (Middletown, CT: Wesleyan University Press, 2009), 88; and "Fusées XVII"; English translation, "Squibs XVII," in *Intimate Journals*, trans. Christopher Isherwood (Mineola, NY: Dover Publications, 2006), 45.

23. Aldo Palazzeschi, "E lasciatemi divertire! (Canzonetta)," in *L'Incendiario* (1910), reprinted in *Tutte le poesie*, ed. Adele Dei (Milan: Mondadori, 2002), 238. I am citing from the 1910 edition of *L'Incendiario*. Some years later, the poem would be slightly revised and titled "Lasciatemi divertire"; the final version is from 1925. English translation "So Let Me Have My Fun! (Pop Song)," in *A Selection of Modern Italian Poetry in Translation*, trans. and ed. Roberta L. Payne (Montreal: McGill-Queen's University Press, 2004), 69.

We find a similar declaration in a contemporary text, "La signorina Felicita" by Guido Gozzano: "io mi vergogno, | sì, mi vergogno di essere un poeta" ("I'm ashamed to be— | yes, I confess, I'm ashamed to be a poet!").[24]

From then on, the number of Italian poets who wrote poems expressing their shame at writing poetry only grew. Lyric poetry is the only literary genre to experience such a phenomenon, and it is easy to understand why. Since poets are able to speak in public about their personal experience, they give voice to the embarrassment that intellectuals feel in the face of people who do "real" work: Gozzano explicitly opposes his own "life of dreams, this life of sterility" to the "rude rough" life of the "merchant after cash."[25] There are two sides to this, though: on the one hand, the poets' shame matches that of all intellectuals; on the other, modern poets are also the most vulnerable to a sense of guilt. In addition to the hubris of creativity, they suffer from the hubris of self-expression: they claim to speak in the first person and to do so in a form charged with subjectivity; they also claim that readers will find a universal truth in the idiosyncrasy of another particular being. Modern poetry harbors an element of exhibitionism, which can be experienced as an aggression or, at any rate, as a gesture destined not to be understood, eliciting boredom, annoyance, or displeasure. In English-language poetry, the text that memorably encapsulates this crisis is Marianne Moore's "Poetry," first published in 1919 in the literary magazine *Others* and rewritten repeatedly. Here are the first lines:

> I, too, dislike it: there are things that are important beyond all this fiddle.
> > Reading it, however, with a perfect contempt for it, one discovers
> > > that there is in
> > it after all, a place for the genuine.[26]

---

24. Guido Gozzano, "La Signorina Felicita ovvero la Felicità," in *I colloqui* (1911), reprinted in *Tutte le poesie,* ed. Andrea Rocca (Milan: Mondadori, 1980), 178; English translation "Signorina Felicita," in *The Man I Pretend to Be: The Colloquies and Selected Poems of Guido Gozzano,* trans. and ed. Michael Palma (Princeton, NJ: Princeton University Press, 1981), 86–87.

25. "Oh! questa vita sterile, di sogno! | Meglio la vita ruvida concreta | del buon mercante inteso alla moneta, | meglio andare sferzati dal bisogno, | ma vivere di vita! Io mi vergogno, | sì, mi vergogno d'essere un poeta" ("This life of dreams, this life of sterility: | better to find a rude rough row and hoe it, | to be a merchant after cash and show it, | better to be lashed by necessity, | but living, but alive! I'm ashamed to be— | yes, I confess, I'm ashamed to be a poet!"). Gozzano, *La signorina Felicita ovvero La Felicità;* English translation "Signorina Felicita," in *The Man I Pretend to Be,* 86–87.

26. Marianne Moore, "Poetry," in *Others* 5, no. 6 (July 1919): 5.

What makes it proverbial is the "too," the naturalness with which it is taken for granted that no one likes poetry and that the important things lie "beyond all this fiddle." Immediately afterward comes a "however" and a response to the crisis of legitimacy, but the line that expresses the common perception of the literary genre, and that has remained in the memory of many, is the first.[27]

Legitimizing poetry is an issue for many twentieth-century writers. Grouping their responses around cardinal points, we might say that there are two opposing ways of reacting to the loss of balance that the Romantic archetype was able to preserve. In the first case, those who speak up feel that they do not have the right to give themselves too much importance and tend to deflate the pathos in an ironic, sarcastic, or cynical way; in the second case, expressing oneself means violating the rules of social life, as if the affirmation of oneself and one's style were an inherently provocative act that takes place *against* the world, against the norms of public discourse and conventions. Here, then, is where the confidence and measure of Romantic poetry, its harmonious egocentrism, neither excessive nor marginal, acquire a retrospective clarity and historical value—because our primary idea of lyric poetry, as we said, is based on that model, and because it somehow represents the entelechy of a genre that is structurally individualistic, the center of its literary space.

Expressionism and Irony

The forcefield of modern poetry can be described by using lyric Romanticism as the term of comparison, and by studying how the representation of the world and the speaker changed beginning in the second half of the nineteenth century, when it became more difficult for poets to defend the confidence and measure inherent in the idea of confession. The peripheral areas of the forcefield, born out of the crisis in lyric Romanticism, branch out from the center and are almost always defined by negation, as are some of their most famous watchwords ("the elocutionary disappearance of the poet,"[28] "the

---

27. See Lerner, *The Hatred of Poetry*, 3–5.

28. Stéphane Mallarmé, "Crise de vers" (1886–1896) in *Œuvres complètes*, ed. Henri Mondor and Georges Jean-Aubry (Paris: Gallimard, 1945); English translation "Crise de vers'," in Rosemary Lloyd, *Mallarmé: The Poet and His Circle* (Ithaca, NY: Cornell University Press, 1999), 232.

extinction of personality"[29]), which can easily be read as the reversal of Romantic watchwords.

While the peripheries were taking form, the center of the territory was also being renewed: the first result of the metamorphosis that transformed the style of European lyric poetry between the second half of the nineteenth century and the period of the avant-gardes was precisely the change in subjective poetry. The main direction of this development is easily grasped by rereading some of the texts we have looked at. The fifteen lines of "The Infinite" describe the experience of an empirical individual with absolute seriousness, but although its diction is full of personal elements, it does not disrupt conventional wisdom and tradition. The poems that Rimbaud was writing during the years of "The Star Wept Rose" were very different, even in those days. Compared to the Romantic archetypes, the speaker's place in the world remains unchanged because, unquestionably, there is a collective meaning in the subjective experience it evokes. What disappears is the balance between self-expression and stylistic composure that Romantic poetry managed to preserve. Rimbaud understands that it is possible to write lyric poetry in verse or in prose, to break to a new line at will, to mix different registers, and to use tropes that subvert the forms generally used to give order to the world through language. In short, he understands that to pursue immediacy, individual talent can now permit itself to ignore every shared constraint.

I would not know how to define this way of making poetry except by using a category that has a long history and many layers, that of *expressionism*. To avoid misunderstandings, for it is a notion worn out by polysemy, I will draw out the perimeter of its intended meaning. Among the documents generally used to explain the principles of figurative expressionism, there are letters in which Vincent van Gogh explains his idea of painting to his brother, Theo. In one of the most important of them, Vincent contrasts himself with the Impressionists: while the latter try to depict the way things look to human eyes, van Gogh uses "color more arbitrarily in order to express [him]self forcefully."[30] This definition lends itself to a wider use; indeed, we could call

---

29. Thomas Stearns Eliot, "Tradition and the Individual Talent" (1919), in *The Sacred Wood: Essays on Poetry and Criticism* (1920) (Mineola, NY: Dover Publications, 1998), 30.

30. Vincent van Gogh, *Verzamelde brieven van Vincent van Gogh;* English translation, *Ever Yours: The Essential Letters*, ed. Leo Jansen, Hans Luijten, and Nienke Bakker (New Haven, CT: Yale University Press, 2014), letter dated Arles, August 18, 1888, 572.

expressionist that form of mimesis in which artists give themselves the right to profoundly distort the sensible appearance of reality—the appearance shared by common sense—in order to express themselves more forcefully. Just as painters alter natural colors, so poets alter inherited customs and the ordinary way of saying things, by subverting the laws of meter and public syntax, for example, by rejecting poetic diction, and by using rhetorical figures with absolute freedom, even at the cost of becoming obscure or difficult. To this end, poetic expressionism submits mimesis to a strong subjective estrangement, but it does not erase the reference to reality, to the idea that the text talks about a common world. This is a continuation of Romanticism by other means, in an era in which the centrality of the self is no longer reconciled with respect for inherited norms and with the ordinary way of representing things through language. What remains unchanged is the central value that continues to be attributed to subjective experience, the aura of seriousness of the speaker's monologue. While it is true that great Romantic poetry already contained some expressionist elements, the new poetics became established primarily in the second half of the nineteenth century, when it became clear that in order for lyric egocentrism to be fulfilled, poetic form needed to be liberated from the boundaries imposed by conventions. This is what took place in English-language poetry after Whitman and in French-language poetry after Rimbaud.

The mirage of absolute authenticity did not act exclusively on form. Although egocentric, Romantic confessions in verse never went beyond a certain threshold of subjectivism in their choice of subject matters: rarely did they allow themselves to be carried away into the unregulated expression of the dark, unconscious, chthonic content that would invade the global language of modern poetry between the second half of the nineteenth century and the beginning of the twentieth; nor did they allow their personal lives to overstep the boundaries of dignity and decorum, as happens regularly in twentieth-century literature. From this perspective, some twentieth-century confessional poetry has an aggressive element to it when it tells its story as self-display, intended to challenge common sense and modesty. In talking about an expressionist development in modern subjective poetry, I would like to mention two intertwined processes: the conquest of formal anarchy, which allowed poets to transgress the stylistic limits still adhered to by the greater Romantic lyric, and the possibility of telling about aspects of one's inner life that early nineteenth-century literature ignored, censored, or restricted to the comic genre.

But this was not the only way for subjective poetry to adapt to a different era. It suffices to see how the "shame of poetry" theme evolved—a sure sign that lyrical Romanticism was in crisis. There are two versions of this *topos,* as we have said: one, euphoric and expressionistic; the other, dysphoric and ironic. Beginning in the 1880s, French-language literature (Maurice Maeterlinck, Francis Jammes, but especially Jules Laforgue), developed a poetry that was still Romantic in structure (a first person speaks about itself in an expressive style) but anti-Romantic in spirit, with the egocentric genre used to display the limits of the speaker in an ironic or pathetic way. These are poems that claim to speak to everyone solely because they flaunt a marginality that all readers are expected to recognize as their own. In Italy, Maeterlinck, Jammes, and Laforgue influenced the poets that Giuseppe Antonio Borgese, in 1910, called "crepuscolari," "the twilight poets," inventing a critical category that would be hugely successful. Guido Gozzano was the most prominent of them. The work of Laforgue influenced English-language modernist poetry, especially Eliot and Pound.[31] Thanks to the mediation of Arthur Symons and his book *The Symbolist Movement in Literature* (1899), Eliot discovered Laforgue in 1908, and the effects of his reading are discernible in the texts collected in *Prufrock and Other Observations* (1917). Pound discovered him a few years later, around 1914. Laforgue exerted an influence on the tone of "Homage to Sextus Propertius," (1919), on *Hugh Selwyn Mauberley* (1920), and on the construction of the poetic persona in the first *Cantos.*[32]

The introduction of an ironic element gave new life to the lyric, in part because the claim to truth made by the traditional Romantic lyric subject would be destroyed by irony. This process could thus mean many things, all of which were difficult to reconcile with the Romantic paradigm: the weakening of the speaker, its splitting into multiple voices, the irruption of a theatrical element, the irruption of a reflective element ("The ironist is one

31. Ina Dorothea Danzer, *T. S. Eliot, Ezra Pound und der französische Symbolismus* (Heidelberg: C. Winter, 1992).

32. Scott Hamilton, *Ezra Pound and the Symbolist Inheritance* (Princeton, NJ: Princeton University Press, 1992), chap 3. Laforgue is also one of the masters of the idea of poetry that Pound called *logopoeia* and defined as "the dance of intellect among words."

who suggests that the reader should think").[33] In any case, it is a sign that the balance out of which Romantic poetry arose no longer held, as happens when "men don't ask anything anymore from poets" (Palazzeschi, "So Let Me Have My Fun!") or they ask for something other than "obscure reveries | Of the inward gaze" (Pound, *Hugh Selwyn Mauberley*). In the prosaic years of the second half of the twentieth century, some great poets would incorporate an ironic element into their poetic persona, from Philip Larkin to Montale in his last phase, with which they would streak their desperate and ultimately tragic voices.

Expressionism and irony are mirror-image poetics. They are animated by a sort of pathology of self-expression: the idea that talking about oneself has become a gesture charged with latent violence. The expressionist poet experiences it as a provocation, the ironic lyricist as something from which one must shield oneself, either by putting one's diction in quotation marks, or by introducing an element of shame and passive aggression. For both, the confident and measured individualism of the greater Romantic lyric was irrecuperable.

Modern Lyric Classicism and Subjective Poetry

Although twentieth-century culture and poetry have in many ways distrusted Romantic poetry and Romantic discourse around poetry, "the romantic model of the lyric as an expression of the poet has remained very much in the horizon for poets in the twentieth century,"[34] both "as a model to be resisted or rejected"[35] and as a paradigm to be readjusted. From this standpoint, a substantial part of modern poetry can be viewed as an attempt to acclimatize a poetic subject that still functions according to a romantically inspired logic to new, more torn and skeptical times. The tendencies that oppose such a model tend to trivialize it by equating it to the most naive mainstream poetry (the "first person meditations | where the meaning of life becomes | visible after 30 lines" detested by Bob Perelman, or the *re-poésie*

---

33. Ezra Pound, "Irony, Laforgue, and Some Satire" (1917), in *Literary Essays of Ezra Pound*, ed. and introd. by Thomas Stearns Eliot (New York: New Directions, 1968), 281.

34. Culler, *Theory of the Lyric*, 85.

35. Ibid.

detested by Jean-Marie Gleize), but the lyric poetry of the twentieth century that followed in the wake of the Romantic paradigm cannot be reduced to this. Since a great deal of modern poetry continues to preserve a theoretical continuity with the Romantic stance, there are many examples from which to choose.

In February 1922, while Eliot was finishing his revisions to the manuscript of *The Waste Land,* Rilke completed the project of the *Duino Elegies* and wrote his *Sonnets to Orpheus.* The speaker in these works (whether *I* or *we*) constructs a *dichtende Denken,* a poetic thought that proceeds through allegories and figures: the angel, the animal, the hero, the artist, the lover, the mother, the maiden, the marionette (with reference to Heinrich von Kleist), the mask, the acrobat (with reference to Baudelaire and Picasso), the Rose of Contemplation, the inside, the outside, Orpheus, Apollo, and so forth. If the endpoint of both *Elegies* and *Sonnets to Orpheus* is the acceptance of the world's transience, it is significant that they contain many reflections on transience but few fragments of it, that is, few anecdotes. The greater Romantic lyric is nowhere to be found, except on occasion, and in any case there are much fewer of them than in *Neue Gedichte* (*New Poems*) and especially in the prose of *Malte Laurids Brigge.* Rather, there is an attempt to acclimatize the high-register lyrical voice that Novalis and Hölderlin had developed—absolute and vertical—by introducing a new philosophical vitality into traditional topics and genres. And it is no coincidence that of all his contemporaries Rilke felt particularly close to Paul Valéry, who, in many of his poems, starting from *La Jeune Parque* (1917) onward, pursued a poetics that was in some respects similar.

If Baudelaire, as Montale writes, was "the central, normative, entirely nineteenth-century poet"[36] of French literature because of his ability to adapt themes and forms of Romantic origin to the new urban world, then the central, normative, entirely twentieth-century poet of Italian literature was Montale himself. What made him so was his ability to adapt the forms of the greater Romantic lyric to the psychological and physical world of the twentieth century. In the poems he wrote between the second edition (1928) of *Ossi di seppia* (*Cuttlefish Bones*) and *La bufera* (1956, *The Storm*), his style maintains a bond with the premodern tragic lyric through its meter, syntax,

---

36. Eugenio Montale, "Variazioni" (1945), in *Il secondo mestiere: Prose 1920–1979,* vol. 1, ed. Giorgio Zampa (Milan: Mondadori, 1996), 620.

and vocabulary, and the everyday experience of an empirical person still has a world-historical value, just as it did in lyric Romanticism. This is a dynamic and dialectical continuity, which gives a measure of how much poets' habits changed after the triumph of individual talent, and it salvages the spirit of tradition by retracing it to the letter but without nostalgia. Montale's language is technical, concrete, and modern, with historical allusions, but it is also precisely chosen and stripped down to the essential: it is multilingual and open to the modern world but also monostylistic and cohesive, as the lexicon of high lyricism has always been. These two components, a vocabulary of literary origin and technical or prosaic terms, are held together by a search for precision, by the ability to convey the particular nuances of a particular experience.[37] Meanwhile, the meter recaptures or alludes to traditional verse and schemes without a trace of irony or blatant archaism. Thus, in an age when lyric poetry is subjected to the mimetic force of prose and the anarchic thrust of individual talent, it makes no assumption of an incomprehensible rupture between present and past, and it does not denounce the anachronistic character of prosody, the most ceremonial of rules. The form of experience evolves as well: Montale can attribute a universal value to segments of his life history only because the events he speaks about proceed in a discontinuous, epiphanic fashion. Romantic biographies are potentially continuous, because a personal life can be transformed at any moment into a universally human symbol; by contrast, the densely packed moments to which Montale's poems give voice are entirely random, surrounded by a time that is empty and senseless, by that "wearing-down | of threadbare facts" that each poem must interrupt in order to come into existence.[38] Therefore the continuity of the themes, every bit like that of the style, is not rigid but dialectical: the spirit of the greater Romantic lyric survives, the letter adapts to the times.

Rilke's and Montale's poetry are two different forms of *modern lyric classicism:*[39] "classicism" because it presents a continuity with the canonical

---

37. Pier Vincenzo Mengaldo, *L'opera in versi di Eugenio Montale*, in *Letteratura italiana: Le opere*, vol. 4, *Il Novecento*, vol. 1, *L'età della crisi* (Turin: Einaudi, 1995), 656.

38. "La vita è questo scialo | di triti fatti, vano | più che crudele" ("Life is this wearing-down | of threadbare facts, | more vain than cruel")—one reads in "Flussi" ("Flows") in *Ossi di seppia* (1925, 1928); English translation in *Collected Poems, 1920–1954*, 2nd rev. ed., trans. Jonathan Galassi (New York: Farrar, Straus and Giroux, 2000), 103.

39. It was Montale himself who used the notion of classicism (a classicism considered *"sui generis* and nearly paradoxical") when speaking of Saba and, indirectly, of his own poetry. See Eugenio Montale, "Umberto Saba" (1926), in *Il secondo mestiere: Prose 1920–1979*, vol. 1, 114–128.

tradition of high-style poetry, and especially with the entelechy of the greater Romantic lyric, which has become the canonical model of modern subjective poetry written in a tragic tone; "modern" because it adapts tradition to new times without nostalgically preserving the past. But lyric Romanticism becomes a standard even when it does not present a continuity with the tradition of poetry written in a tragic style. During the twentieth century, differential autobiographism broke down any remaining thematic or formal boundaries and became grammaticalized. In American poetry, this process became fixed in the critical category of *confessional poetry* and in the critical discourse accompanying it. In a review that M. L. Rosenthal dedicates to Robert Lowell's *Life Studies,* published in 1959 in *The Nation,* one page traces a genealogy that starts from the Romantic lyric and arrives at Lowell through Whitman's "Calamus."[40] Lowell distanced himself from what preceded him because he was not afraid to push his confession to the point of shame, and because his speaker did not seek the "cosmic equations and symbols" used by the Romantics to try to link the universal to the particular; he accepted, rather, to be himself, without masks or hidden meanings.[41]

Beyond the Lyric: Long Poems and Theatricality

Although the variants of lyric Romanticism differ from one another, they nevertheless retain a kinship because their texts never deviate from the basic form of subjective poetry: monologues by an individuated character that speaks to itself in a style expected to be laden with personal characteristics. But the history of modern poetry also includes attempts to overcome the unrestrained individuation to which lyric poetry seemingly tends. While expressionism, ironic diction, and modern classicism remain tied to the lyric form, the genre's peripheries arise from attempts to transcend its egocentric core. This overcoming takes place in diametrically opposed directions, producing contrary results. On the one hand, we find the intricate world of

---

40. M. L. Rosenthal, "Poetry as Confession" (1959), in *Our Life in Poetry* (New York: Persea Books, 1991), 109.
41. Ibid.

texts that recycle narrative, reflective, or broadly theatrical content, thereby overstepping the limits of autobiography; on the other, texts that attempt to shift the reader's attention from meaning to sound, from an interest in personal content to the play of form. One of these peripheries tends to go beyond the lyric monologue; the other, while proclaiming the elocutionary disappearance of the poet, ends up exacerbating the innate individualism of modern lyricism.

To regain objectivity, one can act on the content, on the form, or, as often happens, on both. Acting on the content means regaining an epic or essay pace that is alien to the lyric measure; acting on the form means escaping from the opacity of modern poetic style by adopting a more discursive diction, but without necessarily giving up on private anecdotes or personal opinions. Sometimes these two movements go together, and sometimes they do not: a work like Wordsworth's *The Prelude* adopts a relatively communicative style but tells the story of the author's life; a work like Pound's *Cantos* transcends lyricism in terms of subject matter but does so by adopting a highly personal and idiosyncratic style; Carson's "The Glass Essay" uses a transparent style to combine autobiographical content with essay writing in verse.

Narrative or essay poetry, an essential part of the modern literary space, is constantly reevaluated by those who strive to show that modern writing in verse does not coincide with the lyric.[42] Although subjective forms undoubtedly occupy the center of the territory, antilyric poets have earned a place of absolute prominence in the canon of modern literature. Among the many examples that could be cited, I will choose the most representative. T. S. Eliot is perhaps the most famous and influential of the twentieth-century authors who tried to renew verse writing by rejecting the centrality of the speaker. His works changed the way poetry was composed in English-language literature and also in Greece (Giorgos Seferis), Poland (Czesław Miłosz), and Italy (Mario Luzi, Elio Pagliarani). In the 1910s, Eliot exhorted poets to practice "the extinction of personality"[43]

---

42. Peter Baker, *Obdurate Brilliance: Exteriority and the Modern Long Poem* (Gainesville: University of Florida Press, 1991), "Introduction: Against Interiority"; Alfonso Berardinelli, *La poesia verso la prosa: Controversie sulla lirica moderna* (Turin: Bollati Boringhieri, 1994); Ronald de Rooy, *Il narrativo nella poesia moderna: Proposte teoriche & esercizi di lettura* (Florence: Cesati, 1997).

43. Eliot, "Tradition and the Individual Talent," 30.

and search for forms that are foreign to traditional lyrical egocentrism, such as dramatic monologues ("The Love Song of J. Alfred Prufrock," "Gerontion"). In the 1920s and early 1930s, he devoted himself to narrative poems in which a linear plot is replaced by a multilingual montage of voices, characters, and different situations (*The Waste Land, Ash Wednesday*), or texts with a theatrical structure (*Sweeney Agonistes*). Then, in the period of the *Four Quartets,* he invented a poetry that was classicist in style but antilyric in intention, introducing long passages of philosophical or theological reflection into the verse plot. What remains unchanged in Eliot's poetry, in both his experimental and classicist phases, is the rejection of poetic egocentrism: in different ways, the montage of voices in *The Waste Land* and the meditations in the *Four Quartets* show the reader that what is essential in life never occurs in personal and self-centered experiences.

Mutable and extensive, this antilyric periphery combines with the lyric center in many ways. For example, the works of Wordsworth and Pound mentioned earlier include phenomena of partial contamination, since *The Prelude* fits the most subjective of content into a transitive form, while the *Cantos* recount suprapersonal content in a strongly personal form. That said, stylistic expressivism is not something that can be eliminated, unless the poet rediscovers a premodern type of ornamental versification. The style of the modernist long poem incorporates a marked trait of subjective estrangement: *The Waste Land,* for example, is held together by a montage of parts, following a logic that is partially obscure to readers who lack guidance. The notes that Eliot added at the end of the book edition are a sign and symptom of this.

Another way to expand the boundaries of subjective diction is to introduce a strong theatrical dimension into the lyric monologue. European literature has always been familiar with what German critics call *Rollengedicht,* role poetry, in which the first person does not correspond to the poet or to the class of people to which the poet belongs but possesses the autonomy of a real character (the lover, the shepherd in love, and so on). After the Romantic turn, this tradition was enriched with new possibilities, the most important of which was the technique of the dramatic monologue. Alfred Tennyson and Robert Browning helped to develop and disseminate it in English-language poetry of the nineteenth century, while Mallarmé, Laforgue, and Valéry introduced it into French poetry of the late nineteenth and early twentieth centuries.[44] The speaker in the dramatic monologue is a historical or fictional character who publicly reveals the meaning of his or her destiny, as in a theatrical soliloquy isolated from the plot of the drama. Somewhat similar to this archetype is a changing, pervasive form that met with extraordinary success in the second half of the twentieth century: the poem for interposed persona,[45] in which the speaker is a kind of mask, a character who resembles but is not identical to the poet. Fernando Pessoa used it systematically, distributing his work among many figures of authorship, one of whom bears his name, as did John Berryman and Geoffrey Hill, who implicitly or explicitly adopted theatrical forms in most of their major works. From this point of view, the work of Wallace Stevens is extraordinary and unclassifiable. The subjective element is overwhelmed by the multiplication of reflexive and metapoetic parts, by the play of pronouns, by the plurality of personae. On the other hand, Stevens's work also has a lyric trait, especially his last two collections, *The Rock* (1954) and *Opus Posthumous* (1957). It is interesting to see how the theatrical aspect and estrangement that derive from talking about one's life using grammatical subjects other than the first-person singular allow the emergence of several topical themes of the great lyric tradition: lost time, the vanishing of the world that once was ours, the approach of death. This is the beginning of "Seventy Years Later," the first section of a long poem entitled "The Rock," "the most nihilistic in Stevens's work so far":[46]

It is an illusion that we were ever alive,
Lived in the houses of mothers, arranged ourselves
By our own motions in a freedom of air.

Regard the freedom of seventy years ago.
It is no longer air. The houses still stand,
Though they are rigid in rigid emptiness.

44. See Robert Langbaum, *The Poetry of Experience: The Dramatic Monologue in Modern Literary Tradition* (New York: Random House, 1957); Elisabeth Howe, *Stages of the Self: The Dramatic Monologues of Laforgue, Valéry, and Mallarmé* (Athens: Ohio University Press, 1990) and *The Dramatic Monologue* (New York: Twayne, 1996); and Culler, *Theory of the Lyric*, 263–275.

45. Enrico Testa, *Per interposta persona: Lingua e poesia nel secondo Novecento* (Rome: Bulzoni, 1999).

46. Helen Vendler, "Looking at the Worst: Wallace Stevens's *The Rock*," in *Last Looks, Last Books: Stevens, Plath, Lowell, Bishop, Merrill* (Princeton, NJ: Princeton University Press, 2010), 44.

Even our shadows, their shadows, no longer remain.
The lives these lived in the mind are at an end.
They never were . . . The sounds of the guitar

Were and are not. Absurd. The words spoken
Were and are not. It is not to be believed.[47]

We find this same ability to reinterpret the themes of lyric poetry through a gaze that goes outside itself, observes itself from outside, and deflates the pathos in one of the poets who learned the most from Stevens, John Ashbery. For example, many poems in *A Wave* (1984), one of his finest books, are about the most topical of lyrical themes—love—but in this fashion:

To have been loved once by someone—surely
There is a permanent good in that,
Even if we don't know all the circumstances
Or it happened too long ago to make any difference.
Like almost too much sunlight or an abundance of sweet-sticky,
Caramelized things—who can tell you it's wrong?
Which of the others on your team could darken the passive
Melody that runs on, that has been running since the world began?

Yet, to be strapped to one's mindset, which seems
As enormous as a plain, to have to be told
That its horizons are comically confining,
And all the sorrow wells from there, like the slanting
Plume of a waterspout: doesn't it supplant knowledge
Of the different forms of love, reducing them
To a white indifferent prism, a roofless love standing open
To the elements? And some see in this paradigm of how it rises
Slowly to the indifferent heavens, all that pale glamour?[48]

---

47. Wallace Stevens, "The Rock," in *The Rock* (1954), in *Collected Poetry and Prose*, ed. Frank Kermode and Joan Richardson (New York: Library of America, 1997), 445.

48. John Ashbery, "When the Sun Went Down," in *A Wave* (New York: Viking Press, 1984), 6.

Beyond the Lyric: Pure Poetry

Another anti-Romantic periphery that has played a significant role in the history of modern poetry is located on the other side of the literary space. It originated with French Symbolism, centered on the utopia of pure poetry, and was disseminated in countless variations during the twentieth century. I describe it starting from the theoretical writings of the poet who contributed more than any other to its diffusion—Stéphane Mallarmé. Ever faithful to the poetics he embraced during his school years, in all his programmatic reflections, from his youthful letters to his writings as an older adult, Mallarmé contradicted the cornerstones of lyric Romanticism. It is pointless for poets to express themselves with immediacy or describe the phenomenal world and visible reality, for all this is meaningless contingency or, in Mallarmé's vocabulary, brute *Matière* or *Hasard,* brute matter or chance. Rather, the authentic vocation of literature is orphic and suprapersonal: to strip language of its everyday use and bring it back to a hypothetical original fullness, by creating an absolute poetic voice, divorced from contingency, by making the form and content of human discourse coincide, and by describing the "pure notion" of things instead of external accidents.[49] The synthesis and supreme result of literature is *Le Livre,* "a hymn . . . , like a pure whole grouped in some dazzling circumstance,"[50] on which all true poets unconsciously work together, and to whose writing Mallarmé wished to devote himself consciously. Mallarmé's texts are actually distinguished by their rejection of any mimetic or expressive immediacy, both in content and form, since they ignore or sublimate the fortuitousness of everyday life. Instead, they tell about mythological subjects and recount allegories or emblematic scenes in which the primary conflicts of the human condition find a symbolic representation in a register that is vertical and absolute. Given that these "dazzling circumstances" are, as Mallarmé says, the revelation of an Idea, in both the psychological and metaphysical sense of the word, the style of the work must be the "exact spiritual setting"

49. Mallarmé, "Crise de vers" (1886–1896); English translation "Crisis in Poetry," in *Selected Prose Poems, Essays & Letters,* trans. Bradford Cook (Baltimore, MD: Johns Hopkins University Press, 1956), 75–76.

50. Stéphane Mallarmé "Quant au Livre (Le Livre, instrument spirituel)" (1895); English translation in *Mallarmé,* ed. Anthony Hartley (Middlesex, UK: Penguin, 1965), 189.

of this revelation;[51] and since the pure language of the essences, unlike the corrupted language of ordinary communication, does not distinguish between form and content, the true poet must strive to abolish the separation between sound and meaning, constitutive of the common way of speaking, and achieve that perfect correspondence proper to music.[52] In the practice of writing, a poetics of this kind makes it imperative to reduce referential elements in favor of evocative ones, by choosing words on the basis of the signifier or by following an illogical syntax. The goal is to dissolve the "words of the tribe" into the essential language of poetry, to which Mallarmé attributes orphic and collective meanings, as if it were the nucleus of a future popular religion built around art.[53] True poetry presupposes the eclipse of the poet, who yields the initiative to words, allows sound to speak, and relinquishes any claim to expressing his or her own irrelevant contingency.[54]

From this poetics descends, directly or indirectly, a long and frayed critical tradition that emphasizes the primacy of sound over sense, form over content. In addition to his immediate successors, Mallarmé's poetics has influenced authors very different from him in terms of their background and interests. The idea that the focus of modern poetry is play on language and not the communication of content is a topic we find in the essays of both Valéry and Sartre.[55] Usually, the reflections that accompany the development of pure lyric insist on the irreconcilable opposition between romantic subjectivism and symbolic depersonalization, between *Erlebnislyrik* and pure poetry. In reality, this conclusion is valid only if one accepts Mallarmé's aesthetics. Remaining instead in the realm of common sense affords an interesting perspective. Whoever reads Mallarmé's poems without knowing his assumptions finds a poetry that is introverted and solipsistic in its choice of subject matter and style. The texts describe the fragments of an individual metaphysics difficult to understand in its entirety; the style is based on a strong subjective estrangement, on the horror of something "said without being

---

51. Stéphane Mallarmé, "Préface" to *Un coup de dés* (1897); English translation in *Mallarmé*, 210. See also Stéphane Mallarmé, "La Musique et les Lettres" (1895); English translation, "Music and Letters," in *Mallarmé in Prose*, ed. Mary Ann Caws, trans. Jill Anderson (New York: New Directions, 2001), 39.

52. See especially Mallarmé, "Music and Letters," 39.

53. Ibid., 44–45.

54. Mallarmé, "Crise de vers".

55. Combe, *Poésie et Récit*, 15–18, 82–85.

put in order (*arrangée*)," as the young Mallarmé explained to his friend Eugène Lefébure.[56] As in all art forms that distance themselves from the lifeworld, the text makes sense if reader and writer share the underlying assumptions that make it possible to construct a world remote from the ordinary perception of things. When Mallarmé's poetry is separated from its legitimizing aesthetics, it takes on a different meaning. The death of the old lyrical attitude does not lead to the birth of an impersonal poetry but to the construction of a poetic super-world divorced from everyday prose—a world where allegories written on paper are shards from a personal *forêt de symboles,* and the form overturns the ordinary way of saying things, guided by a chain of associations, idiosyncrasies, and personal references. Symbolism is a form of lyricism without a confessional speaker, and in a certain sense it is the triumph of subjectivism in poetry. It communicates an inwardly oriented idea of the world and an egocentrism so strong that it eliminates the last residue of narrative objectification that Romantic and post-Romantic poetry had preserved—a character in the structure of the text who tries to tell or express something by saying "I." When literary subjectivity is communicated through style, the dominion of the speaker over the represented reality becomes total and imperceptible.[57]

Speaking of this, it may be helpful to revisit two concepts from Ortega y Gasset's ideas on modern art that Hugo Friedrich adapted to poetry in order to explain the development of lyric poetry in the second half of the nineteenth century and the twentieth century: dehumanization (*Enthumanisierung*) and depersonalization (*Entpersönlichung*).

> A basic feature of modern poetry is its increasingly pronounced divorce from natural life. Together with Rimbaud, Mallarmé brought about a radical withdrawal from personal and confessional poetry, a genre that was still being cultivated on a high level by Verlaine. Older poetry, from the troubadours to the preromantics was hardly ever an experiential or diarylike communication of private feelings; only the misconception of a few literary historians infected by romanticism

56. Stéphane Mallarmé, *Correspondance complète 1862–1871, suivie de Lettres sur la poésie,* ed. Bertrand Marchal (Paris: Gallimard, 1995), 228.

57. See Käte Hamburger, *Die Logik der Dichtung* (1957, 1968); English translation, *The Logic of Literature,* 2nd rev. ed., trans. Marilynn J. Rose (Bloomington: Indiana University Press, 1993), 242–272.

made it appear as if it were. But, on the other hand, this poetry, stylized and artistically varying the universal, remained within the range of the human and the familiar. Modern poetry excludes not only the private person but also normal humanness. None of the above-mentioned poems by Mallarmé ["Sainte," "Éventail (de Mme Mallarmé)," and "Surgi de la croupe et du bond"] can be explicated biographically—although for reasons of curiosity or laziness some critics have repeatedly tried to do so. But no poem by Mallarmé can be interpreted as an expression of a joy that we all know or a melancholy that we all experience and therefore comprehend. Mallarmé wrote from a center of gravity that would be difficult to name. . . . Mallarmé continued along the route that Novalis and Poe had recommended, the road leading the poetic "I" to a suprapersonal neutrality.[58]

Mallarmé, writes Friedrich, "perfects the view, current since Baudelaire, that by imitating reality, the artistic imagination does not idealize it but deforms it,"[59] thereby eliminating the speaker and allowing language to speak. Indeed, restored to their basic structure, Mallarmé's poems are nothing more than emblematic scenes represented in an estranged style and devoid of references to a recognizable lived experience; and yet the skeptical reader cannot help but distinguish between what the scenes are objectively and what they should be according to the aesthetics of Symbolism. For Mallarmé, the great orphic poetry, the supreme form of knowledge, communicates an image of the world that has a universal value, because it is not *a language* but *the human Language,* removed from its definitional use and brought back to its essence. By contrast, according to the logic of literary history, the works to which Mallarmé ascribes world-historical importance are not *the* Language but *a* language—one of the many poetic manners scattered throughout European poetry in the late nineteenth century. The only reason it differs from the others is because of the strong censure and estrangement to which it submits mimesis of the inner and outer worlds. To the eyes of a disenchanted

---

58. Hugo Friedrich, *Die Struktur der modernen Lyrik* (1956); English translation, *The Structure of Modern Poetry,* trans. Joachim Neugroschel (Evanston, IL: Northwestern University Press, 1974), 81.

59. Ibid., 70.

observer who does not take these poetics as a given, the style of Symbolist poetry—so remote from *doxa* and tradition—is anything but impersonal: writing by circumventing *verba propria* and the degree-zero of perception actually means introducing an entirely subjective image of the world, which is sedimented in the content and, above all, in the style.[60] To believe that the dehumanization achieved by this poetry is a form of "suprapersonal neutrality" (Friedrich), that it allows access to a deeper orphic, symbolic dimension, or that it alludes to regaining a utopian communitarian language removed from the equivalence of exchange value (Rancière),[61] one must accept the logic that governs Mallarmé's reflections, which has an objectively elitist aspect to it.[62] If, on the other hand, we place Mallarmé's poetry in its literary space, in the field of poetic possibilities that were practicable in the second half of the nineteenth century, we cannot fail to see that every type of opaque style distant from the lifeworld and based on a system of references shared only by a limited public is an extreme form of subjectivism, because the elocutionary disappearance of the poet at the level of content corresponds to the elocutionary triumph of the poet at the level of form. In this regard, symbolism is the true archetype of obscure poetry.

There are, however, other forms of intransitivity—of egocentrism without individuation—and they have a complex genealogical relationship with Symbolism. In Franco Fortini's essay "Obscurity and Difficulty," he had in mind a historical pattern that, although never made explicit, is alluded to more than once. In his opinion, literary writings have always been partially obscure or difficult, but only after Romanticism did the difference between modern and premodern poetry, and that between obscurity and difficulty, become understandable. It was Surrealism that would definitively clarify the terms of the problem:

> In the complex of tensions and experiments in the 1920s that united and separated the Symbolist heritage and the break with it, we can

---

60. Hamburger, *The Logic of Literature*, 249.

61. Jacques Rancière, *Mallarmé: La Politique de la Sirène* (1996); English translation, *Mallarmé: The Politics of the Siren*, trans. Steven Corcoran (New York: Continuum, 2011); and Jacques Rancière, *Politique de la littérature* (2007); English translation, *The Politics of Literature*, trans. Julie Rose (Cambridge: Polity Press, 2011), 80–98.

62. On the differing and conflicting political interpretations of this aspect, see Robert Boncardo, *Mallarmé and the Politics of Literature: Sartre, Kristeva, Badiou, Rancière* (Edinburgh: Edinburgh University Press, 2019).

now discern a tendency to saturate the figures of diction and rhythm, which press out from within the syntactic units, breaking them up or dissolving them into a continuous flow—in imitation of a consciousness that is inarticulate and therefore obscure to itself, even before being obscure to its intended readers. This tendency moved toward asyntacticism, interior monologue, words in freedom, a secret language, the dominion of the phonosymbolic, and finally to silence. Paradoxically, it brought parts of the poetic discourse that seemed completely irreconcilable into proximity, such as . . . Futurism, Expressivism, and late Symbolism.[63]

According to Fortini, a continuity exists between orphic Romanticism, Symbolism ("obscurity as Mallarméan darkness"[64]), Futurism, Surrealism, and certain experiments of the new avant-garde movements of the 1950s and 1960s. While very different on the surface, these tendencies were nevertheless united by the use of a self-referential and intransitive form: the "imitation of a consciousness that was inarticulate, and therefore obscure to itself, even before being obscure to its intended readers." Albeit motivated by different reasons, and with varying nuances, this schema is widely accepted in French- and German-speaking cultures: it can be found, for example, in the essays of Marcel Raymond, Barthes, Adorno, Friedrich, Hamburger, Stierle, and Rancière.[65] Certainly, while Symbolism rarefied subject matters and language, drawing them upward, the poetry of the twentieth-century avant-gardes opened poetry to prose, to blends, to antisublime content. But the criterion of openness to prose blunts other differences that are no less important than those it highlights: isolated from the other elements of the text, the inclusion of low or traditionally antipoetic registers is not really sufficient to define a poetics, since the

---

63. Franco Fortini, "Oscurità e difficoltà " *L'asino d'oro* 2, no. 3 (1991): 84.

64. Ibid., 88.

65. Marcel Raymond, *De Baudelaire au Surréalisme* (1933, 1947); English translation, *From Baudelaire to Surrealism* (New York: Methuen, 1970); Roland Barthes, *Le Degré zéro de l'écriture* (1953); English translation, *Writing Degree Zero*, trans. Annette Lavers and Colin Smith (New York: Hill and Wang, 1977), 41–52; Adorno, "On Lyric Poetry and Society"; Friedrich, *The Structure of Modern Poetry;* Hamburger, *The Logic of Literature,* 250–272; Karlheinz Stierle, "Möglichkeiten des dunklen Stils in den Anfängen moderner Lyrik in Frankreich," in *Immanente Ästhetik, ästhetische Reflexion: Lyrik als Paradigma der Moderne,* ed. Wolfgang Iser (Munich: Fink, 1966), 157–194; Rancière, *Mallarmé: The Politics of the Siren* and *The Politics of Literature,* 80–98.

form this inclusion takes must be factored in. When prosaic materials are held together by a totally subjective structure, their presence does not stop the text from being self-centered and impenetrable. Consider, for example, Breton's collection discussed in Chapter 3, *Clair de terre (Earthlight)*. A few pages before and after the text we read, "The Sun on a Leash," there are a few poems that report the data of reality with absolute immediacy, as verbal *objets trouvés,* using the cut-up technique, whose writing is nevertheless as intransitive as the Symbolist compositions. Take the opening of "PSTT":

Neuilly 1–18. . . . . Breton, vacherie modèle, r. de l'Ouest, 12, Neuilly.

Nord 13–40. . . . . .Breton (E.), mon. funèbr., av. Cimetière
Parisien, 23, Pantin.

Passy 44–15. . . . . . . .Breton (Eug.), vins restaur., tabacs, r. de la
Pompe, 176

Roquette 07–90. . . . . . . Breton (François), vétérinaire, r. Trousseau, 21, (11e)

Neuilly 1–18. . . . . Breton, model dairy, 12 Rue de l'Ouest, Neuilly.

Nord 13–40. . . . . Breton (E.), fun. Monum., 23 Av. Cimetière
Parisien, Pantin.

Passy 44–15. . . . . Breton (Eug.), wines, rest., cigars, 176 Rue
de la Pompe,

Roquette 07–90 . . . . . Breton (François), veterinarian, 21 Rue Trousseau, (11th).[66]

In this case too, the reader is faced with a partially incomprehensible text: one understands that Breton is reproducing a section of the Paris telephone directory with the names and addresses of people who have his surname, but his reasons for doing so remain indecipherable, especially for readers at the time, who were as yet unfamiliar with this kind of *trouvaille*. It is worth quoting an excerpt from the notes accompanying the text in the Pléiade edition of Breton's complete works:

---

66. André Breton, "PSTT," in *Clair de terre* (1923); reprinted in *Oeuvres complètes*, ed. Marguerite Bonnet (Paris: Gallimard, 1988), 156; English translation, "PSTT," in *Earthlight*, trans. Bill Zavatsky and Zack Rogow (Copenhagen: Green Integer, 2004), 57–58.

This seemingly gratuitous piece can be looked at from different and noncontradictory points of view. One can see it, as Aragon did, as a manifestation of poets' mindset in the 1920s, linked to the mental activity of which the work is a sign and not to the result that the work represents. Aragon writes: "André Breton made an exact transcription from an address list of everyone who turned their heads in the street when they heard 'his' surname. A mysterious, imposing bond; a reality with more power on us than fine poetry; an expedient of command."

At the same time, one can read in it a certain aspiration to efface oneself, similar to that of Jacques Vache, who refused to create a work. The 1930 note on the mysterious "Bois et Charbons" that closes *Les Champs magnetiques* testifies to this by then prevailing will to disappear into the masses, analogous to the will to silence and death.[67]

The flood of interpretations is proportional to the gratuitousness of the text: in this case too, the poet abandons the shared lifeworld and takes refuge in a personal forest of free associations. This is why the currents that Fortini mentions resemble one another to some extent, even when they are not related by a documented genealogy and despite obvious differences in the choice of materials. They share a form of solipsism, which blurs the connection with the public structures of the lifeworld and seeks forms of communication far removed from common sense.

The Egocentric Genre

I have attempted to map out our literary space, using a very large scale that overlooks details and, amid the forest of particulars, to trace out a hypothetical cartography. If the confident, measured egocentrism of Romantic poetry represents the archetype of our symbolic form, the forcefield of modern lyric poetry can be defined in relation to that model. The Romantic stance is prolonged by tendencies that, in different forms, adhere more or less closely to the archetype, others that seek to transcend it, and yet others that exaggerate

---

67. Breton, *Oeuvres complètes*, 1195–1196.

it. The first maintain the basic structure of subjective poetry but transform the nature and importance of the first person; the second transcend the limits of modern lyricism by recapturing narrative, essay, or theatrical forms alien to the most uncompromising poetic diction; the third reject the logic of the Romantic paradigm but communicate an egocentric worldview through the opacity of the writing. These are not closed groupings but fluid forms that intersect, overlap, and slowly fade into each other, as neighborhoods do in a city. A single work may include opposing elements, as happens when the border between the antilyric and ultralyric parts divides the axis of selection from the axis of combination, and a chain of totally intransitive associations assembles narrative, essay, or brutally mimetic materials: Pound's *Cantos,* for example, pursue the project of a new epic, but the structure that holds them together is almost always stream of consciousness; certain typically lyrical themes of the later Stevens enter the text through forms of theatrical estrangement, and so on.

The boundaries of modern poetry are as frayed as those of a city, and a single name defines texts that are very different from one another: lyrical poems, pure poems that work on language, poems that maintain a narrative or argumentative flow, poems of a theatrical nature, poems in prose form, and, in between, a congeries of complex hybrid cases. This swirl of currents and tendencies is held together by a common expressive element. Ever since prose became the natural medium of storytelling, and versification was no longer an ornament superimposed on degree-zero writing but a different language or the product of a particular sensibility, every form of writing in verse and every form of prose that seeks to unabashedly distinguish itself from the ordinary way of saying things appears charged with subjective opacity. While the novel places people in time, space, and in the midst of others, while the theater makes individuals act in the common space of the stage, modern poetry seems to tell us that the interesting, essential aspect of life lies in the estranged representation of reality, in the expression of subjective thoughts, passions, and states of mind, or in a work on language that distances language from its social use. What Adorno said about poetry applies perfectly to modern poetry as a whole: an art that, in the hope of attaining the universal through individuation, ends up in one way or another putting the writer's self at the center of the represented world.

This is a conclusion that applies to every sphere of our literary space, beginning with its lyric core. If we wanted to introduce an element of abstraction and consider this form in its ideal type, modern poetry seems to be made to censor or estrange the common image of reality, since its average form escapes from the degree-zero writing of prose, obscures the physical, psychological, and verbal presence of others, struggles to describe time as duration and its transcendence with respect to individuals—all things that a novel would have no difficulty putting on paper. We identify with a speaker who gives value to a few fragments of life, known not for what they really were but for how the first person represents them, subjectively employing materials that come from a ritual use. Marked by this double expressivism, modern poetry evokes a personalistic and monadic image of the world: the center of the representation is not staged action between human beings or the telling of stories and their entanglements but the way in which an isolated speaker reports some experiences that are mostly individual, unrelated, intense, and instantaneous. No other genre, not even autobiography, is so egocentric in content and form; no other genre so easily eliminates the levels of reality that transcend the self, nullifying the presence of time, reducing the external world to landscape, separating the first person from the fields of psychic and social forces that traverse it, destroying the constraints that tradition and common sense place on anarchic self-expression. Even more inherently egocentric is the symbolic periphery of modern poetry, composed of works that efface content in order to focus the reader's attention on the opaque beauty of words—because the moment there ceased to be any tradition limiting the play of individual talent, any style that displays itself and hides things ultimately expresses a vision of the world that is centered on the subject. But the other large periphery of our literary space, that of narrative and essay poems, does not escape lyricism of form either. The only kind of writing that the modern horizon of expectation judges to be servile and transparent is prose written in a simple style—not stories in verse, reflection in verse, or prose filled with figurative language.

Modern poetry is the literary genre that most closely resembles the figurative arts of recent centuries. Like painting and sculpture, writing in verse has reacted with extremism to the crisis in mimesis and to the dehumanization of art. In spite of the spectacular narrative experiments that dot twentieth-century literature, the average novel for educated readers has remained far more faithful to the common way of seeing things than poetry has. It is no accident that highbrow storytellers sell far more books and are far better known than poets. If a large number of readers understand the experience recounted in novels, even when some experimentation is allowed by the novelist, if irregular punctuation, interior monologues, or the deconstruction of the plot do not prevent those who are not literary professionals from admiring Clarice Lispector, José Saramago, Toni Morrison, Uwe Johnson, Alice Munro, Abraham Yehoshua, Don DeLillo, or Annie Ernaux, then to appreciate poetry one must be well versed in the language of the sector—one must, in other words, know a specialized system of signs. Like all arts that have undergone strong dehumanization, modern poetry divides the audience in two—a restricted niche that understands and a vast mass that does not—following the lines of a dialectic that has been running through the plastic arts since painters and sculptors were able to ignore the ordinary aspect of reality and transgress inherited norms.[68]

Invisible Choirs

Particular sensitivity, self-expression in the form, a qualitative difference in the way the world appears, and individual talent: the words used by Barthes, Eliot, and Proust to imagine the activity of the writer in a regime of stylistic freedom owe much to the Romantic vocabulary. But an overarching look at the history of art after the death of tradition shows us a different landscape from the one we would encounter if the Romantic schema corresponded in full to the reality of things.

I randomly open an anthology, *Poesia italiana degli anni Settanta* (1979, Italian Poetry of the Seventies), and find the work of Eros Alesi, who in 1971 committed suicide at the age of twenty:

> Caro Papà.
> Tu che ora sei nei pascoli celesti, nei pascoli terreni, nei pascoli marini
> Tu che sei tra i pascoli umani. Tu che vibri nell'aria. Tu che ancora ami il
>   tuo figlio Alesi Eros.

---

68. See José Ortega y Gasset, *La deshumanización del arte* (1925); English translation, "The Dehumanization of Art," trans. Helene Weyl, in *The Dehumanization of Art and Other Essays on Art, Culture, and Literature* (Princeton, NJ: Princeton University Press, 2019), 1–54.

Tu che hai pianto per tuo figlio. Tu che segui la sua vita con le tue
    vibrazioni passate e presenti.
Tu che sei amato da tuo figlio. Tu che solo eri in lui. Tu che sei chiamato
    morto, cenere, mondezza.
Tu che per me sei la mia ombra protettrice.
Tu che in questo momento amo e sento vicino più di ogni cosa.
Tu che sei e sarai la fotocopia della mia vita [. . .].

Dear Dad.
You who are now in the heavenly pastures, in the earthly pastures, in the
    marine pastures.
You who are in the human pastures. You who vibrate in the air. You who
    still love your son Alesi Eros.
You who have wept for your son. You who follow his life with your
    vibrations past and present.
You who are loved by your son. You who solely existed in him. You who
    are called dead, ash, garbage.
You who are for me my protecting shadow.
You who at this moment I love and feel closer than anything else.
You who are and will be my life's photocopy [. . .].[69]

This is an eminently lyrical poem, in the modern sense of the word: the
distance between the speaker and the author seems minimal, the first person
imagines speaking to his father and, following the logic of the text, expresses
what is most intimate to him and confesses in public; the meter, syntax, lexicon, and figures are free from rigid rules and charged with pathos, sup-
porting this self-expressive intent. However, it is not difficult to understand
that this sort of poem, which seems so personal when compared to the ordinary way of saying things, is in itself not personal at all. Eros Alesi blatantly
imitates Allen Ginsberg:

O mother
what have I left out
O mother

---

69. Eros Alesi, "Frammenti," in *Poesia italiana degli anni Settanta*, ed. Antonio Porta (Milan: Feltrinelli, 1979),
235; English translation, "Dear Dad," trans. Cristina Viti, in *Modern Poetry in Translation* 3, no. 3 (2005): 92.

what have I forgotten
O mother
farewell
with a long black shoe
farewell
with Communist Party and a broken stocking
farewell
with six dark hairs on the wen of your breast
farewell
with your old dress and a long black beard around the vagina.[70]

Ginsberg, in his turn, picks up on a way of making poetry whose distant archetype is Whitman's *Leaves of Grass;* and Whitman, in his turn, drew his inspiration from the Bible and the oratorical tradition:

Thou, laving, tempering all, cool-freshing, gently vitalizing
Me, old, alone, sick, weak-down, melted-worn with sweat;
Thou, nestling, folding close and firm yet soft, companion better than
     talk, book, art,
(Thou hast, O Nature! elements! utterance to my heart beyond the
     rest—and this is of them,)
So sweet thy primitive taste to breathe within—thy soothing fingers on
     my face and hands [. . .].[71]

This is a rule that applies to any art whose forms have become distanced from conventional wisdom and a heritage of accepted norms: the death of rules is not followed by a monadic swarming of personal styles but by a form of tribalism, as if the victory of individual talent over a centuries-old poetic diction were not resolved in pure subjectivism but in the birth of many small, local dictions. In this respect too, the history of poetry resembles closely the history of painting and sculpture after the crisis of imitation and rules: once the obligatory references to reality had disappeared and the customs inherited from the past had vanished, the theoretically infinite freedom of artists

---

70. Allen Ginsberg, "Kaddish IV," in *Collected Poems 1947–1997* (New York: Harper, 2006), 234–235.
71. Whitman, "To the Sun-Set Breeze," in *Leaves of Grass,* 458.

became crystallized and produced schools. It comes as no surprise that the arts which are most expressive and, in theory, most egocentric are also those which produce the most highly cultivated imitative behaviors: precisely because the authors' anarchy lacks any shared relationship with the lifeworld, it needs to lean on a solid collective support to reduce the anxiety-provoking risk of gratuitousness, a risk that weighs on all unrestrained individuation. What Bakhtin said about lyric poetry applies to the form of modern poetry as a whole:

> The authority of the author is the authority of a *chorus*. Lyrical pos-
> sessedness is, fundamentally, *possessedness by a chorus*. . . . In an atmo-
> sphere of absolute silence and emptiness, this [lyrical] voice would
> be incapable of sounding in such a way. An individual and totally ar-
> bitrary violation of absolute silence has a frightening and sinful
> character; it degenerates into a scream which startles and frightens
> itself and finds itself hard to bear—finds it hard to bear its own in-
> trusive and bare givenness. A solitary and totally arbitrary breaking
> of silence imposes an infinite responsibility or it is cynical without
> justification. The voice can *sing* only in a *warm* atmosphere, only in
> the atmosphere of possible choral support, where *solitariness* of sound
> is in principle excluded.[72]

The more objective limits that custom imposes on the artist's potential freedom are lifted, the greater the need for choral support; at every level, the subjectivism of modern art is in reality (to use an oxymoron) *a group subjectivism*. After obtaining the right to originality, the arts became a competitive field, shaken by continual revolutions and occupied by tribes that fight or negotiate among themselves for the conquest of economic capital or, more often, symbolic capital—precious finite goods such as prestige and memory.[73] Anyone who aspires to enter into this territory finds a set of already-fixed possibilities that form a sort of transcendental scaffolding, tracing out the

---

72. Mikhail M. Bakhtin, "Avtor i geroj v èstetičeskoj dejatel'nosti"; English translation, "Author and Hero in Aesthetic Activity," trans. Vadim Liapunov, reprinted in *Art and Answerability: Early Philosophical Essays*, ed. Michael Holquist and Vadim Liapunov (Austin: University of Texas Press, 1990), 169–170.

73. Pierre Bourdieu, *Les Règles de l'art* (1992, 1998); English translation, *The Rules of Art: Genesis and Structure of the Literary Field*, trans. Susan Emanuel (Stanford, CA: Stanford University Press, 1996).

horizon of forms that artists can reasonably adopt if what they desire is the support of a chorus. In other words, artistic fields are not dominated by an individualistic, chaotic anarchy but by a social, organized anarchy composed of tendencies, currents, manners, and schools that divide up the sphere of possibilities available in any given era. As complexity grows, so does the autonomy of each system that makes up the whole, and with it the tendency to develop languages that are distant from the lifeworld and incomprehensible to those who do not know the background that generated them. When we talk about individual talent, we are referring to individuals who associate in groups and remain caught in the internal logic of the space to which they belong. Similarly, when we say that modern poetry differs from premodern poetry because authors have conquered the right to self-expression, this is not to say that poets of the last two centuries imitate no one but themselves, as Leopardi said,[74] or that they repudiate all conventions so as to write in full autonomy and give voice to their own singularity.

More realistically, self-expression through style is a relative quantity that alludes to three historical changes, thanks to which the anarchic system of the modern arts distinguishes itself from the premodern arts: the theoretical possibility to violate customs inherited from tradition and to break lexical, metrical, syntactical, and figural norms that existed for thousands of years; the possibility to choose between many equal competing tendencies within a system that is no longer uniform, hierarchical, and static but competitive, fluctuating, and chaotic; the possibility to write in order to revolutionize the literary space and etch out an enduring trace of one's singularity. As will be explained more fully in the Conclusion, the aesthetic of originality *has a primarily theoretical and negative value*: it does not herald a real autonomy—something unattainable for anyone who depends on the judgment of others—but simply the right to step out of the rut of practices that have been handed down by tradition. In the 1810s, when Leopardi began writing his first adult poems, he knew that the impulse to imitate lived experience that runs through some of his shorter idylls could not go beyond the limits set by centuries-old rules: poetic diction, the laws of meter, the norms of grammar and syntax, an etiquette that governed the choice of rhetorical figures. In the 1910s, when Montale began to write his first adult

---

74. Leopardi, *Zibaldone di pensieri*, 4372–4373, September 10, 1828.

poems, he could in theory break every limit, choose among many competing poetics to gain prestige and memory in the domain of high-style lyric poetry, and aspire for his work to someday transform the layout of the poetic space. Although the stylistic freedom granted to Montale was markedly greater than that granted to Leopardi, Montale's poetry still had to pass through the mediation of a social language. Despite living in an age dominated by anarchy, the modern artist remains bound nonetheless to the territory of possibilities. The distance between a claimed autonomy and a real autonomy remains insuperable.

Conclusion

Modern Poetry as a Symbolic Form

The Self and Fragments of Time

Works of art owe much of their meaning to a form of fetishism. When the *illusio* shatters, when the collective belief that attributes spiritual content to certain images or texts breaks down, the works are reduced to inert, tautological objects, to mere *res* devoid of hidden meanings.[1] This need for credit is all the more necessary the more the works move away from common sense and from the languages considered valuable by the average educated public and tradition, as happens with the dehumanized art of the last hundred and fifty years. A visitor to a museum of contemporary art who regards the collection with the gaze of someone unfamiliar with the web of hidden meanings that invest those objects with value understands just how thick

---

1. The term *illusio* comes from Bourdieu's sociology. Bourdieu brings the term back to its etymological meaning, which he derives from Huizinga's *Homo Ludens: illusio* as *in ludere*, the ability to "play along," to accept as meaningful the assumptions and stakes of a social practice. See Pierre Bourdieu (with Loïc Wacquant), *Réponses* (1992); English translation, *An Invitation to Reflexive Sociology* (Cambridge: Polity Press, 1992), 98–101; and Pierre Bourdieu, *Les Règles de l'art* (1992, 1998); English translation, *The Rules of Art: Genesis and Structure of the Literary Field*, trans. Susan Emanuel (Stanford, CA: Stanford University Press, 1996), 227–231.

the patina of implicit conventions can be.[2] The same thing happens in some areas of modern poetry. If we were to ignore for a moment the assumptions that allow us to attribute a meaning to these texts, the credit granted to modern poetry could even seem excessive. Why give so much importance to these brief subjective fragments? Why do schools and scholars devote so much time and social energy to the study of "The Infinite," a text of only fifteen lines that, unlike *War and Peace*, *Middlemarch*, or *In Search of Lost Time*, contains so little experience?

The primary meaning of modern poetry's symbolic form lies in the answer to these questions: evidently only an individualistic society can attach so much weight to an art that conveys to readers a markedly subjective view of the world through its content and, even before that, its style. The egocentrism of modern poetry has no equivalent in any other literary form, not even in autobiography after Rousseau. Autobiographers are accustomed to situating personal content more or less obviously in a suprapersonal context, to telling the story in a prose not far removed from the language of ordinary communication, and to placing the first-person story in a time and space that are meant to be objective and in the midst of other people. Poets of recent centuries, on the other hand, use a style far removed from degree-zero writing that can ignore altogether whatever transcends or goes beyond the self: while the narrative form is made to show circumstances (etymologically, "what surrounds" individuals),[3] modern poetry can safely ignore them. No limits are placed on the speaker, because once the link with premodern ritualism had fallen away, the poem's form was interpreted as the author's expression.

The image of the world conveyed to the reader by most modern poems is a narcissistic one. I use this term with in the sense that Christopher Lasch gives it.[4] As an existential attitude, narcissism is characterized by the idea that meaning is not to be sought in the encounter with the outside world or

---

2. Howard S. Becker, *Art Worlds: 25th Anniversary Edition, Updated and Expanded* (Berkeley: University of California Press, 2008), 28–34.

3. On the role of *die Macht der Umstände*, "the power of circumstances," has in narrative, see Georg Wilhelm Friedrich Hegel, *Vorlesungen über die Ästhetik*; English translation, *Aesthetics: Lectures of Fine Art*, vol. 2, trans. T. M. Knox (Oxford: Clarendon, 1988), 1070–1071.

4. Christopher Lasch, *The Culture of Narcissism* (New York: Norton, 1979). Lasch takes his notion of narcissism from that developed by Béla Grunberger, *Le Narcissisme: Essais de psychanalyse* (1971); English translation, *Narcissism*, trans. Joyce S. Diamanti (New York: International Universities Press, 1979); and Grunberger, *Narcisse et Anubis: Études psychanalytiques, 1954–1986* (1989); English translation, *New Essays on Narcissism*, trans. and ed. David Macey (London: Free Association Books, 1989).

with others but by protecting oneself from centrifugal passions, by shifting energy away from human relationships, and by trying to "be oneself" or, at most, by "expressing oneself." The lyric center and the periphery occupied by pure poetry emanate a manifestly narcissistic image of the world: in lyric texts, the speaker describes subjective content in a form charged with expressivism; in pure poetry, the voice programmatically distances itself from the prose of ordinary life and from the common way of experiencing it. But, as we have seen, by now even narrative or essay poetry, which would appear to have different characteristics, is equally caught in subjective estrangement. Two centuries of antilyric long poems have failed to tarnish readers' commonsense idea that the mimetic genre of modern literature is the novel and not verse writing.

The vision of reality crystallized in modern poetry seems to be crossed by two deep cuts. The first, the most visible one, is the self's isolation, the *interruption of the social bond* that unites individuals in systems of mutual dependence, externally and internally; the second, less visible but equally important, is the *interruption of the chronological bond* that unites the instants of life in an abstract continuity captured by narrative in the form of plot. The poetry of the last two centuries, emphasizing a drift inherent in the structure of the lyric form, tends to reproduce the instantaneous and epiphanic nature of subjective monologue, as if the fragmentation had spread within experience itself, separating a few moments of meaningful life from the senseless course of a destiny that is perpetually the same. The image of the world conveyed by the ideal type of modern poetry is contrary to the image we usually associate with that of the nineteenth-century novel: on the one hand, a supposedly objective mimesis of social bonds, fashioned in the conviction that ordinary life is full of meaning and acquires its own significance thanks to the plot, that is, to a web of relationships between human beings that unfold over time; on the other, a subjective mimesis of personal and instantaneous experiences, fashioned in the conviction that the meaning of life resides in a few fragments, in a few lightning epiphanies, and that the poet is a "custodian not of years but moments."[5] Anyone who writes poetry takes it

---

5. "Passano—tornava a dirsi—tutti assieme gli anni | e in un punto s'incendiano, che sono io | custode non di anni ma di attimi" ("The years—he was telling himself once more—pass as one | and burst into flame at a point, which is me | custodian not of years but moments"). Vittorio Sereni, "Un posto di vacanza," IV, lines 19–21, in *Stella variabile* (1981, *Variable Star*); English translation, "A Holiday Place," in *The Selected Poetry*

for granted that a universal truth can be told by starting from oneself and somehow withdrawing into oneself. This means subscribing to the belief that the narrative, intersubjective dimension of life (being in time, being with others, being in a plot) is not primary. In this sense, modern poetry is also a giant historical symptom: if there is a genre that attains universality through unrestricted individuation, it is because individuation, a sense of not belonging, and solitude are all part of the modern condition.

Modern Poetic Anthropology

By looking at the literary space of poetry from the perspective of the long duration, one can try to sketch out an overall trajectory of the anthropology of modern poetry. When observed from the height of our day, Romantic first persons strike us with the confidence, measure, and wholeness that they preserve when they make themselves heard. The inner life of the speakers does not dissolve into a bundle of fragmentary perceptions, hidden drives, and obscure mental associations; they speak as if they had an audience before them that was ready to listen, as if they were supported by an invisible chorus. Although the form of modern poetry owes its deep structure to the Romantic paradigm, few of the authors remain faithful to the archetype. A portion of post-Romantic poetry tries to transcend the first person, as if the life of a human being alone were no longer enough to account for reality. Another, more extensive portion maintains the self-centeredness but lowers the pretensions of the lyric voice, staging an ironic, antiheroic, marginal, or theatrical self. Still another, the most extensive of all, keeps the first person at the center of the world but presents a self that is divided and opaque to its own perception, imprisoned in an uncertain or conflicting relationship with the invisible chorus of the poem.

Corresponding to this anthropological mutation is an analogous stylistic metamorphosis. Although the premises of the revolution that changed the form of writing in verse between the second half of the nineteenth century and the period of the historical avant-gardes are contained in the poetics of

---

and Prose of Vittorio Sereni, ed. and trans. Peter Robinson and Marcus Perryman (Chicago: University of Chicago Press, 2006), 237.

Romanticism, Romantic poetry is relatively conservative and—to use an oxymoron—classicist. While it is true that the theory of lyric poetry as immediate writing, as the "spontaneous overflow of powerful feelings"[6] or the "free and frank expression of any living and deeply held human feeling,"[7] was widespread between the second half of the eighteenth century and the beginning of the nineteenth, it is also true that the formal innovations of the greater Romantic lyric were relatively few when compared to what occurred after Whitman or Rimbaud. Compared to the revolution in meter, syntax, and rhetoric that took place in the second half of the nineteenth century, the free verse poems in German lyric poetry of the second half of the eighteenth century and the crisis in poetic diction in the lyric poetry of English Romanticism are preludes rather than definitive ruptures. The confidence and wholeness of the speaker are reflected in an analogous form, suspended in a reformist balance between self-expression and convention, narcissism and decorum, solitude and form, which are increasingly rare in recent lyric. The poetry of the last century and a half, on the other hand, is marked by a conflict that is difficult to reconcile with the invisible chorus and tradition, in part because the spectrum of objective possibilities available to contemporary poets when they write no longer sets limits to the anarchic expression of individual talent.

After the stylistic revolution in the second half of the nineteenth century, after the historical avant-gardes, and, definitively, after the new avant-gardes of the 1950s and 1960s, writing in verse accentuated the vocation for egocentrism inherent in modern lyric poetry. It definitively exposed itself to idiosyncrasy, to what Hegel called the "delirium of particularity": poetic personae who flaunt their marginality; theatrical personae who turn the poetic monologue into a play; narcissistic personae who, with apparent naiveté, tell their story in a simple style, with the air of those who do not question their social mandate; expressionistic personae who put no limits on self-confession; regressive personae who exaggerate the private, involuntary, and irresponsible nature of poetic diction. These lyric subjects have corresponding styles: irony, mannerism, experimentalism, and forms of naive lyricism.

---

6. William Wordsworth and Samuel Taylor Coleridge, *Lyrical Ballads*, 2nd ed., ed. R. L. Brett and A. R. Jones (London: Routledge, 1991), 246.

7. Giacomo Leopardi, *Zibaldone di pensieri* (1817–1832); English translation, *Zibaldone*, trans. Michael Caesar and Franco D'Intino (New York: Farrar, Straus and Giroux, 2013), 4234–4235.

The Dialectic of Expressivism

But idiosyncrasy does not exhaust the meaning of modern poetry. When this process is observed from the outside, the image of the world communicated by our genre shows another aspect. As we saw at the end of the previous chapter, the subjectivism that runs through our literary space is actually a group subjectivism: such an egocentric art can only be charged with collective meaning if an invisible chorus resonates behind the voice of the poem. This support, important for any text that aspires to have value, is absolutely decisive for arts that have distanced themselves from common sense and, for this very reason, risk appearing gratuitous or incomprehensible to a lay observer. From a logical and chronological point of view, the chorus does not limit itself to intervening after the writing by bestowing praise or criticism, but influences the artist's choices even before beginning to write, making it clear that only certain possibilities can reasonably be practiced and showing that the choices fluctuate in a space occupied by many heterogeneous choruses, by many literary tribes.

The logic of modern arts has much to teach those who reflect on the dominant ethos in Western societies over the last two centuries, for in a culture that places the meaning of life in the obligation to live up to one's originality, the behavior of the artist ultimately casts light on the dynamics of the self.[8] In this sense, lyric poetry, which involves some of the essential aspects of individualism, is one of the arts that best illustrates the forcefields that pulse around and within the modern identity. What does it mean for lyric poets, and for the artists of our time in general, to write at the height of their originality? What does it mean to "be yourself" and "express yourself"?

It certainly does not mean achieving full independence, autonomy from the past, from precursors, or from the expectations of others. Nothing so clearly exhibits the paradox of individualism itself as the logic inside

---

8. "In our civilization, moulded by expressivist conceptions, it has come to take a central place in our spiritual life, in some respects replacing religion. The awe we feel before artistic originality and creativity places art on the border of the numinous and reflects the crucial place that creation / expression has in our understanding of human life." Charles Taylor, *Sources of the Self: The Making of the Modern Identity* (Cambridge, MA: Harvard University Press, 1989, 376). "Aesthetics is the field par excellence in which the problems brought about by the subjectivization of the world characteristic of modern times can be observed in the chemically pure state." Luc Ferry, *Homo aestheticus: L'invention du goût à l'âge démocratique* (1990); English translation, *Homo Aestheticus: The Invention of Taste in the Democratic Age,* trans. Robert De Loaiza (Chicago: University of Chicago Press, 1993), 3.

the aesthetic sphere: the more each individual is granted the right to leave a trace of his or her own subjective difference, the more this difference turns out to be a social product. The conquest of a new autonomy is not followed by an anarchic explosion of individual talent but by the emergence of new forms of mutual influence, of tribal belonging, of tradition—a tradition that is mobile, local, polytheistic, and plural but no less binding than the network of norms, models, and *topoi* that accompanied the history of Western literature until the Romantic era. Compared to the relationship that premodern culture had with the customs of the past, the margins of freedom granted to individuals changed (brilliant, charismatic artists could, in principle, completely revolutionize their discipline), and the structure of the tradition changed (a relatively unitary system of rules was replaced by a plurality of schools, trends, and currents that divided up the artistic space and coexisted in conflict or indifference). However, the essential result did not change: for modern artists, too, self-expression means introducing a variation in the forest of languages that precede them, while the space of possibilities continues to transcend the singularity of the writer and exert an influence that is different, but no less important, than the influence of the premodern artistic *nomoi*.

This is a paradox that calls for reflection. The watchwords inspired by Romanticism have a literal meaning only when they are interpreted as signs of an abstract theoretical freedom; but, in actual fact, even in the epoch in which expressivism has become conventional wisdom, all artists find themselves caught up in a social network that precedes and determines them—a system made up of currents and tendencies that gives shape to their words and within which they must align themselves. If anything, these choral aggregations grow in strength and number when the arts become more egocentric, freer from the schemas of the past and therefore potentially more remote from common sense, and when the need to control the risk of gratuitous expression becomes urgent and dramatic. What Adorno and Bakhtin write about lyricism is true of all dehumanized art: the principle of individuation that guides creators does not guarantee the production of normative works that avoid ending up "within the contingency of mere separate existence"[9]—

9. Theodor W. Adorno, "Rede über Lyrik und Gesellschaft" (1957); English translation, "On Lyric Poetry and Society," in *Notes to Literature*, trans. Shierry Weber Nicholsen (New York: Columbia University Press, 1991), 38.

because "an individual and totally solitary violation of absolute silence has a frightening and sinful character."[10] When nothing remains to curb the theoretical anarchy of individual talent, there is the risk that every text will give voice to the tautology of a speaker that expresses itself without proving to be representative. It is difficult for a real text to fulfil the pretense claimed by modern poetry, to transform the particular into the universal and personal idiosyncrasy into collective singularity. In this sense, as Ben Lerner notes, "hating on actual poems . . . is often an ironic if sometimes unwitting way of expressing the persistence of the utopian ideal of Poetry."[11] Inevitably, in modern times successful poems seem to be—and are—rare, because when one starts from unrestrained individuation it is always difficult to create a text that means something to many people, and because modern society multiplies differences, distancing individuals and groups and making mutual understanding more complicated.

This intrinsic fragility also contributes to the crisis in the relationship with common sense becoming accompanied by the spread of "isms"—of schools and currents. These aggregations come to occupy the space once occupied by centuries-old rules, both written and unwritten, that ensured the value of the texts and the production of collective meanings. Although the field of poetry and modern art is stirred by a process of permanent revolution, it is not the chaos of isolated cells that a fully expressivist culture would be expected to generate. It is composed not of monads but of families, tendencies, and groups that struggle among one another to conquer prestige and memory. Romantic expressivism gives partial insight into the changes that have occurred in the modern artistic space, because it gives a platform for the authors' point of view without heeding the logic of the whole. The ideal of creative freedom, of individual talent, which was born to enthusiastically celebrate the end of the aesthetic Ancien Régime, had—and continues to have—a theoretical and negative value. Expressing oneself does not mean achieving full autonomy but being granted a right that the premodern poet had no knowledge of: *the right not to belong.* For two centuries, artists have been themselves because in theory they can behave like monads released from any binding constraint, ready to pass from one approach to another, willing

---

10. Mikhail M. Bakhtin, "Avtor i geroj v èstetičeskoj dejatel'nosti"; English translation, "Author and Hero in Aesthetic Activity," trans. Vadim Liapunov, reprinted in *Art and Answerability: Early Philosophical Essays,* ed. Michael Holquist and Vadim Liapunov (Austin: University of Texas Press, 1990), 170.

11. Ben Lerner, *The Hatred of Poetry* (New York: Farrar, Straus and Giroux, 2015), 76.

to experiment with endless variations on inherited forms. However, when we abandon the particular point of view of individuals and look at the general panorama of the modern artistic space, we realize that the Romantic watchwords do not describe the whole reality. The conquest of complete inner freedom is not matched by complete outer freedom; the monads that can subjectively claim their own originality are objectively bound together to form families that struggle with one another, systems of forces and counterforces. To be an artist means to stake out a position in a territory of possibilities: to accept a fashion, to imitate one's models, to preserve and surpass their approach, to vie with one's peers, with their genealogies and traditions. The more a system of art is dehumanized, self-referential, remote from the lifeworld, and lacking in a nonspecialist audience, the more it needs to reinforce its *illusio* and its logic as a system. Since a unitary *nomos* no longer exists, every value ends up becoming relative. The only certainty of prestige is that accumulated by schools, currents, and trends, by poetic fathers or poetic mothers to draw on or fight with.

A widespread critical *topos* has it that imitation was an important phenomenon only as long as the age-old culture of classicism retained hegemony over European literature; when artists assimilated the new imperative of originality, the relationship with precursors supposedly lost its importance. In reality, the problem of imitation gained philosophical import precisely during the period when universal canons died, the space of recognized values became frayed and, in theory, anything became acceptable. It is no accident that the idea of the anxiety of influence, a principle that applies to all modern art, began with poetry.[12] For artists trying to be themselves in a regime of permanent revolution, precursors, peers, artistic parents, and artistic siblings are figures charged with ambivalence. They are carriers of anxiety or confidence as the case may be, or even at the same time—because they can crush a writer's ego by occupying the territory of possibilities but also help it achieve an identity for itself. After the fall of the shared world consisting of relatively solid, centuries-old conventions, a cultural universe opened up composed of separate worlds that coexist or conflict with one another, in which there is no divine *nomos*, just many equivalent, earthly *nomoi* devoid of any legitimacy other than that based on the fragile consensus of one human group lost amid

---

12. Harold Bloom, *The Anxiety of Influence: A Theory of Poetry* (New York: Oxford University Press, 1973).

other hostile, friendly, or indifferent groups. In this age of polytheism and perspectivism, many models of beauty and truth share portions of a symbolic capital whose only foundation is a shifting social agreement, a collective illusion. In such a world, imitating individuals, works, and trends that have been given an assured value is crucial for developing an intellectual personality. The anxiety of influence represents the dialectical reverse of the charismatic and reassuring fascination that certain figures exert on artists in search of identity, creating a sense of belonging and value in an age in which belonging and values are no longer assured. Sometimes this feeling of aesthetic kinship reinvigorates an objective social and psychological kinship; sometimes it expresses what Freud called the ego ideal—what one would like to be or become. In both cases, it ends up counterbalancing the narcissistic wound that prestigious precursors inflict on egos in search of prestige. Proust is right in saying that we have as many worlds available to us as there are original artists, but he is wrong to depict them as "more different one from the other than those which revolve in infinite space."[13] However dissimilar they may appear, artistic worlds always stand in relation to families and systems; expressing oneself means entering into the ether of the languages that precede us, finding one's own genealogy, and introducing a variation into an already-formed path. For this reason, not only is there no immediate access to the "personal way of seeing things,"[14] but there is also no authentically personal way of seeing things.

Over the last two centuries, tradition has lost its unifying structures, and the conflict between incommensurable currents has torn the Western aesthetic space apart. This rupture has generated two diametrically opposed effects: it has allowed artists to depict the lifeworld with a new expressive freedom, and it has allowed them to create systems of signs far removed from the shared reality. Trends that retain a solid connection to common sense and speak to a nonspecialist audience coexist with trends that detach themselves from common sense and speak to a niche audience with a shared *illusio*—along the lines of an antithesis that runs throughout the system of the arts as a whole. Usually the novel, cinema, and photography are much

---

13. Marcel Proust, *Le Temps retrouvé* (1927); English translation, *Time Regained,* trans. Andreas Mayor and Terence Kilmartin, rev. D. J. Enright (New York: Modern Library, 2003), 299.

14. Ibid.

closer to the lifeworld than contemporary figurative arts. Writing in verse occupies an intermediate position, since modern poetry, while remaining as inherently mimetic as any other form of writing, is also the most egocentric of literary genres. It is the genre that lends itself more than any other to estrangement, obscurity, and *forêts de symboles*. Dehumanized artistic fields obey an entirely internal dialectic, similar to the dialectic governing how fashions develop. Moreover, since the most self-referential forms of the arts do not evoke experiences that everyone can understand, they age quickly. Sometimes a peculiar form of melancholy emanates from museums of contemporary art or anthologies of twentieth-century poetry: it is dismaying to think that thousands of artists have tried to "express themselves" by immersing themselves in a fashion that today seems outmoded. It takes little for their works to be reduced to inert objects, faded *trouvailles*. If the remote atmosphere surrounding premodern art takes on a heroic tone, the melancholy of dehumanized modern art is imbued with precariousness: the former speaks to us of the cultural earthquake that came with the birth of the modern world; the latter shows us how fragile the discursive ether is that contains us, and how dizzying the dialectic of expressivism. The larger the distance grows between individual talent and common sense, between the world of invention and the lifeworld, the more it becomes evident that individual talents are inserted in a game of systems: free to construct an autonomous identity for themselves, monads who have in theory achieved the right not to belong continue to behave gregariously, because belonging to a group, to a chorus, is the only way to ensure meaning. But even the systems turn out to be fragile and transitory, prey to an autonomous evolution that has lost contact with a shared public foundation and which wavers in a space where everything changes and anything goes.

The Marginality of Poetry

Art forms are therefore constantly in need of legitimation, especially those that are remote from the lifeworld and those that make the author's self central to the text: the former have to demonstrate that their world of invention is not an absurd oddity; the latter have to legitimize the gesture of pure hubris by which a human being equal to all others grants himself or herself a representative status. Modern poetry faces both these problems.

Picking up on the concept that Lenin used to explain the legitimacy of the political avant-garde, Marxist criticism defines *social mandate* as the power the public grants poets so that they will produce works with a collective value. In the mid-1800s, writes Benjamin, speaking about Baudelaire, the bourgeoisie stripped lyric poets of a social mandate that fifty years earlier seemed unassailable.[15] We will discuss the stages of this loss later; the fact that it happened is indisputable. For the last century and a half, poetry has no longer had a mandate. It has become an art that appeals to a very restricted public, composed mostly of poets, aspiring poets, and poetry scholars, confined to a protected reserve that survives, thanks to the prestige it accumulated over the centuries, the conservatism of school curricula, and the residual patronage of a few publishers.

The arts acquire a collective weight by virtue of a mechanism of meaning production similar to that which, according to Max Weber, governs the social life of religions.[16] It is ruled by a triangular logic based on a clear division of roles between the figures of *authors, commentators,* and *readers* or *spectators.* Just as in religions the revelation of the prophets is interpreted by priests and reaches the faithful, so in the arts the work of authors is mediated by cultural institutions (criticism, schools, universities, publishers, the press, museums, galleries) and reaches the public. When the charismatic authority of the creators no longer speaks to a real audience, and when the authority of the mediators loses all function, the mechanism goes into crisis. In the case of contemporary poetry, the logic according to which this vertical pyramid has been functioning in recent decades is horizontal and anarchic: since poetry readers are mostly aspiring poets, there is no longer a clear division between authors and readers, and cultural institutions matter less and less. The three clearest symptoms of this process are the disappearance

---

15. Walter Benjamin, "Über einige Motive bei Baudelaire" (1939); English translation, "On Some Motifs in Baudelaire," in *Illuminations,* trans. Harry Zohn (New York: Schocken Books, 2007), 156.

16. Nathalie Heinich, *Le triple jeu de l'art contemporain* (Paris: Minuit, 1998), 56ff. Heinich builds on the analysis of Weber's sociology of religion introduced by Bourdieu (Pierre Bourdieu, "Une interprétation de la théorie de la religion selon Max Weber," in *Archives européennes de sociologie* 12, no. 1 [1971]: 2–21). See also Eduardo de La Fuente, "La filosofia weberiana del profeta e il compositore d'avanguardia," in *Rassegna italiana di sociologia* 42, no. 4 (2001): 513–540.

of a real audience, the proliferation of amateur poets, and the invisibility of poets that critics deem important.

The data presented here come from Italy, the literary society I know best, but other Western countries present very similar situations. According to recent statistics reported in the press, 5 percent of Italians write poetry, although it must be kept in mind that these sorts of surveys are often unreliable.[17] Other facts and figures are more interesting to look at. In the late 1990s and early 2000s, the front page of one of Italy's most widely read newspapers, *La Repubblica,* regularly featured an advertisement from an unknown publisher soliciting unpublished manuscripts by poets. The advertisement did not say that the aspiring author would then be asked to contribute money for the printing of the book, but the fact that this sort of ad appeared in such an expensive advertising space means that the business was profitable, suggesting an abundance of amateur poets willing to pay. Starting in the 2000s, cultural websites and social networks would drastically change the way poetry circulated, making it easy to bring work into the public eye and eliminating the mediation of publishers. Nevertheless, the number of texts appearing in inconspicuous venues, online or in print, would not be matched by any real audience. Those who frequent Italian poetry circles (people who write, continue to buy poetry books, participate in readings, follow poetry websites) know perfectly well that there is a restricted number of readers and that the reason they themselves are interested in poetry is because they write it too.[18] The number of books sold is also minimal.[19] In recent decades the large Italian publishing houses, those that are responsive to market forces, have constantly cut down the number of new titles. Most of the works written by authors under the age of sixty who have received critical attention have been published by small or very small publishers: having your work appear in major poetry series, those that are distributed in bookstores, "no longer means anything in itself."[20]

---

17. Fabio Chiusi, "L'Italia, il paese con tre milioni di poeti," *L'Espresso,* January 31, 2017.

18. This has been the situation since the 1970s. See Alfonso Berardinelli, "Effetti di deriva," in Alfonso Berardinelli and Franco Cordelli, *Il pubblico della poesia* (Cosenza: Lerici, 1975).

19. According to official sales data provided to the Italian Publishers Association by the Nielsen agency, in 2018 poetry books made up about 1 percent of the Italian market, and they were largely classic texts.

20. Gianluigi Simonetti, *La letteratura circostante: Narrativa e poesia nell'Italia contemporanea* (Bologna: Il Mulino, 2018), 35.

This marginal status in the publishing world is a sign of its wider marginality in society, which, although difficult to measure with reliable statistics, is easy to perceive. I would like to tell an anecdote in this regard that serves as a small survey. For some years now, I have been teaching a course on twentieth-century Italian poetry for first-year students in the department of Literature and Philosophy at the University of Siena. To demonstrate how socially marginal the literary genre has become, I ask the class to tell me the name of five living poets. I have about sixty students in the classroom: no more than four or five usually raise their hands. I then ask if they know the names of five living novelists and five living filmmakers, and I already know that everyone, or almost everyone, will say yes. I repeat the same ad hoc survey in a preparatory course for secondary school teachers, and although I am addressing a group of university graduates in the humanities who are about to become high school teachers, few of them know the names of five living Italian poets. Over the years the number of positive responses has increased slightly, but only because names of the five living poets include some Instapoets—poets who publish mainly on Instagram. Today, people who are interested in traditional cultural works but who do not exercise an intellectual profession, people who do have an intellectual profession but are not directly involved with literature, people who teach literature but are not avid readers of contemporary literature—those whom we call educated people—feel no need or duty to buy books of poetry or to know at least the names of contemporary authors; and yet they still feel the need or duty to watch movies, buy novels, and know something about living directors and novelists.

The marginalization of poetry is a constant in contemporary Western literatures, and the same phenomenon can easily be found in many countries. In 1991 Bob Perelman was inspired by the title of a panel at the American Comparative Literature conference in San Diego to write a long essay poem in couplets of six-word lines entitled "The Marginalization of Poetry":

> If poems are eternal occasions, then
> the pre-eternal context for the following
>
> was a panel on "The Marginalization
> of Poetry" at the American Comparative.

Literature Conference in San Diego, on
February 8, 1991, at 2:30 P.M.:

"The Marginalization of Poetry"—it almost
goes without saying. Jack Spicer wrote,

"No one listens to poetry," but
the question then becomes, who is

Jack Spicer?[21]

Jack Spicer, whom Perelman refers to by alluding wryly to the fact that the
general public is unaware of his existence ("who is | Jack Spicer?"), had in
his turn put the loss of social mandate into verse:

> This ocean, humiliating in its disguises
> Tougher than anything.
> No one listens to poetry. The ocean
> Does not mean to be listened to. A drop
> Or crash of water. It means
> Nothing.
> It
> Is bread and butter
> Pepper and salt. The death
> That young men hope for. Aimlessly
> It pounds the shore. White and aimless signals. No
> One listens to poetry.[22]

In 2008, when Barack Obama decided to restore the tradition of having a
poem read during the presidential inauguration ceremony, an article by
George Packer appeared on the website of the *New Yorker* asking the president

---

21. Bob Perelman, "The Marginalization of Poetry," in *The Marginalization of Poetry: Language Writing and Literary History* (Princeton, NJ: Princeton University Press, 1996), 3.

22. Jack Spicer, "Thing Language," in *My Vocabulary Did This to Me: The Collected Poetry of Jack Spicer*, ed. Peter Gizzi and Kevin Killian (Middletown, CT: Wesleyan University Press, 2008), 373.

not to do it. In two pages, Packer summarizes what a substantial portion of contemporary culture thinks about poetry:

> Is it too late to convince the President-elect not to have a poem written for and read at his Inauguration? The event will be a great moment in the nation's history. Three million people will be listening on the Mall. Many of them will be thinking of another great moment that took place forty-five years ago, at their backs, when Martin Luther King stood in front of the Lincoln Memorial. Such grandeur would seem to call for poetry. But in fact the opposite is true.
>
> For many decades American poetry has been a private activity, written by few people and read by few people, lacking the language, rhythm, emotion, and thought that could move large numbers of people in large public settings. . . . On all these occasions [the Inaugurations], the incoming President seemed to be claiming more for his arrival than he deserved, and to be doing it by pretending that poetry means more in American life than, alas, it does.[23]

An art with no social mandate, a private activity written by few people for few people that means far less in collective life than it still claims to. Packer asks Obama to take note of this and to give up on an old ritual that, in his opinion, is now meaningless. It is true that in certain circumstances modern poems regain public significance (this happened with Auden's "September 1, 1939" right after September 11, 2001), but these are exceptional situations, after which the debate on how poetry can recover its lost central role inevitably begins again. True, a new form of poetry has been emerging with much greater visibility in recent years, such as the work of Kae Tempest, or that of Amanda Gorman, who caught the eye of a broader public during Joe Biden's inauguration in January 2021. This is a very different kind of poetry from that of the past though. It incorporates a performance element and revives popularity thanks to a hybridization with social networks and with arts that have a mass following, such as hip-hop and rap, while the forms of

---

23. George Packer, "Presidential Poetry," *New Yorker*, December 18, 2008, https://www.newyorker.com/news/george-packer/presidential-poetry.

writing that descend from the culturally hegemonic tradition of modern poetry remain confined to a niche.

Traditional poetry's loss of social mandate is the effect of a profound change in the cultural demography. It must be said, however, that in fact two losses actually occurred, and the most important one did not take place when it was announced, at the beginning of the twentieth century. When Palazzeschi wrote "men don't ask anything anymore | from poets" and Gozzano wrote "I am ashamed, yes, | I am ashamed to be a poet," in Italy universal suffrage did not yet exist (male suffrage would be introduced in the 1913 elections and female suffrage only in 1946), the illiteracy rate recorded by the 1911 census was 46 percent, and an authoritative statistic calculated that about one third of the literate population was actually semi-illiterate.[24] The society of the early twentieth century was still a society of notables based on cultural deference and political proxy.[25] In such a context, whoever is able to write and publish a book maintains solid social prestige: a loss of mandate with the reading public does not affect the writer's authority as an educated person among those who do not know how to read. This state of affairs continued into the early decades after World War II: in 1961, only about 25 percent of men and 15 percent of women continued into higher education after junior high school.[26] Change only came with mass schooling that began in the 1960s: in 1975 the percentages of men and women entering higher education were close to 55 percent and 45 percent; in the first decade of the twenty-first century the percentage for both sexes was over 90 percent.[27]

Poetry has twice lost its mandate. The first loss occurred wholly within the literary field of a society of notables. In Italy, it took place at the beginning of the twentieth century in a world where everything that happened in the cultural domain still possessed prestige regardless: it was therefore a

---

24. "Suffragio universale e analfabetismo: Appunti statistici," *Nuova Antologia*, 5th ser., vol. 93, file 946, May 16, 1911, 330–338. The calculation was made with an eye to the 1913 elections with universal male suffrage, so it does not take women into account. In the end, the final calculation was "three and a half million educated voters versus more than five million illiterate or nearly illiterate voters," but then it adds, "And this is the most favorable hypothesis: in reality the proportion of educated to uneducated will be worse." "Suffragio universale e analfabetismo," 333.

25. On the "society of deference," see Kenneth Minogue, *The Servile Mind: How Democracy Erodes the Moral Life* (New York: Encounter Books, 2010), part 2, chap. 1 ("Democracy Versus the Deference World").

26. ISTAT (Italian National Institute of Statistics), *L'Italia in 150 anni: 7. Education*, http://www3.istat.it/dati/catalogo/20120118_00/cap_7.pdf, fig. 7.3.

27. Ibid.

relative crisis. The second was much more radical. In Italy, its effects began to show at the end of the 1960s (we can use 1968 as an allegorical dividing line) and became rampant from the 1970s on. It took place in a more horizontal and leveled society, in which reading and writing were less valuable activities because they were much more common, and it was predicated on some of the large-scale democratic transformations of the second half of the twentieth century, starting with mass schooling. A further step has been taken with the change in the public sphere and culture made possible in recent decades by the Internet, allowing anyone to make their voice heard through sites and social networks.

The cumulative effect of this process has been the disintegration of poetry as a literary space. "We may think of a field as a space within which an effect of field is exercised," writes Bourdieu.[28] A social interaction forms a field when its constituent parts conceive of themselves as a system, when the actors in the system find themselves connected by objective ties and subjective ties of imitation, collaboration, and competition that prompt them to think of themselves and their works in relation to the actions and works of the other participants. A common idea of Italian criticism in the last four decades is that a unified history of poetry is impossible to write because the field has exploded: there are too many writers, too different from each other, and there is no external audience; there are no shared traditions (something obvious in the second half of the twentieth century), but neither is there any debate or conflict between different poetic currents, as there was until the 1970s. Poetry is the horizontal art par excellence, the form of writing that, according to commonly accepted aesthetic paradigms, deals with subjectivity, immediacy, and self-expression. Those who know it from the inside are aware that things are more intricate than how they are viewed by this *communis opinio,* but this does not fit with conventional wisdom, which is unconsciously post-Romantic.

It must be said that this widespread aesthetic *doxa* captures the general outlines of what the genre has become in reality. In poetry, the liberation of individual talent is accompanied by the awareness that, contrary to what happens in the figurative arts, strong institutional mediations no longer exist, that it has become very easy to make one's work public, that hierarchies seem

---

28. See Bourdieu (with Wacquant), *An Invitation to Reflexive Sociology,* 100.

relative because the field has exploded, and that the expressive medium—writing—no longer offers any technical resistance to the desire for self-expression. In this sense, one of the paradoxical and unintended results of the avant-garde attack on tradition is a passport to widespread creativity.[29] Today we tend to think that in order to practice poetry there is no need to know how to do anything, or anything qualified at least: to create a verse according to particular rules, or to possess a specific vocabulary, or a specific system of rhetorical figures. Nor is it necessary to have a story and know how to tell it, as one must be able to do in order to practice the art of fiction: in principle, anything goes in poetry. For the same reason, poetry struggles to communicate: in a regime of horizontal, self-expressive subjectivity, everyone wants to express their difference, but few people are able or wish to understand what other people's difference consists of, or to grant it authority. If the need for self-expression unites, the content of self-expressions divides: in an art founded on the liberation of subjectivity, worlds of invention can diverge until they defy understanding.

Poetry and Song

But if contemporary poetry is undergoing a crisis of legitimacy, its deep core, what Benjamin would call its "Muse-derived element," proliferates and spreads.[30] It does so, however, in an art other than poetry, which arose out of mass culture: the pop and rock song, and then rap and hip-hop. In Italy, one of the first people to describe this change was the writer who first gave voice and form to the youth culture that emerged from the movements of the 1970s, Pier Vittorio Tondelli:

> Entire generations have satisfied the need for poetry, an absolute
> and poignant need in the years of early youth, by memorizing song

---

29. See Arthur Danto, *After the End of Art* (Princeton, NJ: Princeton University Press, 1997). On the notion of generic creativity, central to the logic of contemporary art, see Gabriele Guercio, *Il demone di Picasso: Creatività generica e assoluto della creazione* (Macerata: Quodlibet, 2017).

30. Benjamin discusses the *musische Element* of an art—specifically, the *musische Element* of the epic—in his essay on Leskov: Walter Benjamin, "Der Erzähler: Betrachtungen zum Werk Nikolai Lesskows" (1936); English translation, "The Storyteller: Reflections on the Work of Nicholas Leskov" in *Illuminations*, 98.

lyrics: pop ballads, psychedelic, neo-futuristic, intimate, sentimental, dreamy, political, ironic, demented texts. . . . While learned poetry was stuck in the territory of interpretation, exegesis, and tedious unpacking at school desks; while the poetry of the neo-avant-garde was studied, in identical ways, in college classrooms; while the poets of the seventies tried to imitate singer-songwriters, climbing onto improvised stages in city squares and pinewood forests, attempting, like Allen Ginsberg, to accompany their verses with the music of a harmonica, an accordion, or a pianola, young people resurrected the classical figure of the poet, someone who unites words to music. . . .

Poetry and songs, then. An aspect too often given insufficient consideration by official and professional literary critics: the realization, in short, that the greatest poets of recent decades have been produced by the world of rock.[31]

This process of substitution, which Tondelli announces provocatively, using hyperbole ("the greatest poets of recent decades have been produced by the world of rock"), should be interpreted within a larger historical phenomenon, one that is part of the most important cultural metamorphoses the West has undergone in recent centuries: the birth and legitimization of a culture for the masses, called *popular* or *pop*. In the second half of the twentieth century, completing a process that spans the modern era, newspapers, television, commercial movies, songs, fashion, advertising, and the Internet built a culture quite unlike the one taught at school.[32] Originally aimed at consumption and the market, over time pop culture has gained authority, giving a voice to social groups that were excluded from traditional canons and claimed the right to memory. It is actually a new humanistic culture, a corpus of texts and discourses that aspire to explain or tell about life in entertaining or instructive forms, just as traditional culture seeks to do. From this perspective, the generations of writers and readers born since the 1940s have experienced a kind of cultural bilingualism: they have been trained

---

31. Pier Vittorio Tondelli, "Poesia e Rock (1987–89)," in *Un weekend postmoderno;* reprinted in *Opere* (Milan: Bompiani, 2001), 335.

32. For a comprehensive interpretation of this transformation in Europe, see Donald Sassoon, *The Culture of the Europeans: From 1800 to the Present* (London: HarperPress, 2006), part 5. Broadly speaking, with appropriate modifications, Sassoon's argument also applies to the United States.

in the humanistic canons of old and, at the same time, in pop culture. Indeed, in the lives of many, the latter often precedes the former, seeing as young people who do not come from educated families almost always absorb the former years before they do the latter. As long as society preserved hierarchies based on the authority of the intermediate bodies, that is, power structures based on notables, traditional culture carried direct political weight; but the more a society transitions from the hegemony of elites to a true society of the masses, the less political weight is carried by the forms of the past. Pop culture is true mass culture: it spread thanks to some of the great democratic processes that ran through the twentieth century (the expansion of public schooling, the diffusion of free time—the mass version of literary *otium*—and the possibility for everyone's voice to be heard). Its relationship with the traditional humanistic legacy is complex, metamorphic, changeable, consisting of clashes and mixtures, conflict and hybridization. What happened in the late twentieth century resembles, on a grander scale, the process that between the eighteenth and early nineteenth centuries revolutionized the system of literary genres, giving rise to a new middle-class audience and a new kind of intellectual. Forms that were once prestigious and canonical, such as epic poetry, tragedy in verse, and comedy in verse, founded on continuity with the ancient world and intended for an audience of literati, yielded to new forms that in the eyes of classicist intellectuals might have seemed crude, intended for immediate consumption of the general public and lacking any future because they had no relationship with the past: journalism, the novel, and the *drame bourgeois*. Compared to this phenomenon, what happened in the second half of the twentieth century is broader still.

The dialectic between poetry and song should therefore be seen within an overall cultural transformation. The relationship between the two arts is dual and ambivalent, consisting of competition and contiguity. The most visible aspect is competition: while modern poetry now seems to be a genre far removed from the culture of the masses, writes Tondelli, a "territory of interpretation, exegesis, and tedious unpacking at school desks," the "youthful need for poetry" is satisfied by rock music:

> at this point, only in the world of rock does the image of the Romantic poet survive, burning bright—that of the writer who lives tragically to the end, until death and dissolution, in the conflict be-

tween art and life, between the call of the imagination and the demands of everyday existence. The official poets hide behind their desks and their books. They mix and refine words and rhymes. They applaud each other and congratulate each other, praising each other for the twenty copies they've sold. You get the feeling that beyond a combinatorial ability, beyond formal perfection, there is no soul. In rock poets, however cursed they may be, this soul is eccentrically alive and pulsating.[33]

Rock and pop and today's hip-hop and rap have a social mandate that modern poetry has lost. The choruses that echo behind the voice of the singer and the poet are of different magnitudes, the former made up of masses, the latter comprising a few readers. When Tondelli claims that the new poets are rock singers, he is giving voice to a historical pattern shared by a portion of the youth public that has long ignored contemporary poets but perhaps buys pocketbook editions of the consecrated poets of the past and associates them with listening to indie rock. This new social chorus no longer recognizes the boundary between high and low culture that the traditional humanistic canon erected so peremptorily until half a century ago.[34] The change in power relations is accompanied by the transformation that the song genre underwent in the late 1960s, when pop music became the medium of the new youth culture that emerged after World War II. The generation that was decisive for this change was born during the 1940s and was between twenty and thirty years old around 1968. School curricula and university teaching of the future might very well reserve a larger space for the singers of that period than what they give to contemporary poets. On the other hand, if we look at the effects their works have had on the social history of culture, it is undeniable that the Nobel Prize winner for literature Seamus Heaney, born in 1939, has had and will have less influence than the Nobel Prize winner for literature Bob Dylan, born in 1941.

As a matter of fact, it was the Nobel Prize awarded to Dylan in 2016 that rekindled the debate about poetry and song. Participants often comment on

---

33. Tondelli, "Poesia e rock," 336–337.

34. See Jay David Bolter, *The Digital Plenitude: The Decline of Elite Culture and the Rise of New Media* (Cambridge, MA: MIT Press, 2019).

the nature of the art that Dylan practices. There have been questions about whether songs are literature or poetry per se, or whether poetry has entered a musical phase again, as it has at other times throughout history.[35] For me, the really important question is a different one, and it is not about the nature of the arts, which is structurally changeable and open to transformation, but about their social history. The prize given to Dylan is new for two reasons. To begin with, it is the first time the Nobel Prize in Literature has been awarded to an author who comes from a culture other than what, for as long as the Nobel has existed, has been the traditional humanistic culture. The Nobel committee has also shown in the past that it can have a broad idea of the concept of literature: it has given prizes to historians (Theodor Mommsen) and philosophers (Henri Bergson, Bertrand Russell); it has recognized the oratorical qualities of politicians (Winston Churchill) and hybrid works between journalism and literature (Svetlana Alexievich). However, it had never awarded an author who came out of popular culture, partly because until the 1960s pop culture did not exist in the form it does now; nor did it hold the weight it has for us today. While the Nobel Prize usually goes to authors known to minimal niches of connoisseurs (Herta Müller or Tomas Tranströmer, to name a few winners in recent years) or to medium-sized niches (Mo Yan, Alice Munro, Kazuo Ishiguro, Peter Handke), everyone or almost everyone knew Dylan's name, if not his work.[36] The only other winner known to the wider public was Churchill but for entirely different reasons. Second, the breach through which pop culture entered the fortress of a prize reserved for traditional literature was poetry, because it was clear to everyone that Dylan's work occupied the symbolic space once occupied by modern poetry. But while the 2016 Nobel Prize in Literature represents the sanction of a process that began decades earlier, one should not take the de facto judgment for a value judgment. The fact that songs have taken the place of poems for the educated lay public is a real and inevitable process that corresponds to the cultural logic of modern societies. The mistake made by many is to turn this into an aesthetic judgment: modern poetry's social minority

---

35. See Richard F. Thomas, "Conclusion," in *Why Bob Dylan Matters* (New York: HarperCollins, 2017); and Alexandre Gefen, *L'Idée de littérature: De l'art pour l'art aux écritures d'intervention* (Paris: Corti, 2021), 9–13.

36. See Jerzy Jerniewicz, "I'm a Poet and I Know It: The Nobel Prize and Bob Dylan's Literary Credentials," *Aspen Review* 2 (2017), https://www.aspen.review/article/2017/im-a-poet-and-i-know-it-the-nobel-prize-and-bob-dylans-literary-credentials/.

status does not mean that today's poems are worse than those a century or two ago, or that contemporary poetry no longer has anything to say. We will return to this point in the following sections.

Although competitive from the perspective of a sociology of the arts, the relationship between poetry and song is also a relation of contiguity. If we consider the history of forms, the two arts stand in a dual relationship: *archaeological* and *figural*. Archaeological, because the new genre rediscovers forms abandoned centuries earlier by the old one, for example, restoring the ties with music; figural, because the more recent art accentuates certain archetypal elements of the older art, thereby rediscovering some aspects of poetry that modern poetry tended to conceal. Songs have unearthed deep structures from the lyric form that the history of silent poetry had covered up. For example, the "choral invasion" that Bakhtin sees as the foundation of the lyric has been made fully visible in a mass ritual of the last fifty years: the rock concert. The thousands of people singing a lyrical text in unison and identifying themselves with the experience that the singer intones on stage illustrate Bakhtin's words with a force that literature had not experienced for some time. Another one of these figural embodiments can be seen in a recurring music video *topos:* the singer is in a public space surrounded by people with whom he or she would normally connect if it were a realistic scene; at this point the music starts, and the video star isolates himself or herself from everyone by starting to sing or staring straight ahead. None of the surrounding people notice anything and everything goes on as before, accompanied by the music and lyrics. Few examples so graphically illustrate the musical element of modern lyric poetry: the escape from objective reality and human relationships, the idea that the world acquires a sense only when it is veiled by a subjective patina, and that "the 'I' whose voice is heard in the lyric is an 'I' that defines and expresses itself as something opposed to the collective, to objectivity."[37] All this can become a mass choral experience, but it does not change the intrinsically subjective nature of what is shared: the mass of people who gather at a rock concert do not put aside subjectivity to enter into a suprapersonal meeting ground, but they do come together precisely because they collectively share a form of subjectivity.

---

37. Adorno, "On Lyric Poetry and Society," 41.

Contiguity and competition, then. The most interesting social phenomenon arises from the intersection of these two relationships: at a time when poetry is losing its mandate, its Muse-derived element is spreading among the masses, thanks to popular music. Today, millions of people enjoy works that almost always have a lyrical spirit, that start from the speaker and, because of their internal logic, overlay the implicitly subjective nature of the form onto the objective representation of the content, the music, or rhythmic delivery of the words onto the mimesis. We like songs even when their lyrics are banal or incomprehensible, thanks to the secondary meanings that the power of sound superimposes on words. An eternal law of sung poetry ensures that the most obvious or stupid themes acquire a new truth when they are transfigured by music. It is no coincidence that the simple, direct, and immediate passions that the learned arts censored in recent centuries have found representation in melodrama and pop music. In this sense, musical poetry is a pure example of estrangement, of transfiguration through form.

Monads and Systems

What is the truth content of modern poetry as a symbolic form? What image of the world and the modern condition does it convey to us?

The first spiritual content that is crystallized in its sensible signs is "the unexplained need for individuality . . . which is inherent in our age."[38] Mallarmé's formula referred to the formal innovations that mark the history of the genre: since binding stylistic conventions no longer exist, poets know they can behave, in principle, as monads, abandoning tradition, experimenting, and innovating to the point of obscurity. The content is marked by an equally pronounced individualism. Contrary to what occurred in the cultural system of the *Gesellschaftslyrik* and in the cultural system to which the autobiographical poetry of Horace or Petrarch refers, the first person that resonates in modern poetry is not only a collective subject or the subjective embodiment of exemplary qualities; it can also be an individuated self that has personal

---

38. Stéphane Mallarmé, "Sur l'Évolution littéraire" (1891); English translation, "The Evolution of Literature," in *Selected Prose Poems, Essays & Letters*, trans. Bradford Cook (Baltimore, MD: Johns Hopkins University Press, 1956), 19.

and unrepeatable experiences. In addition to being individual, these experiences are also egocentric. They are literally so: they happen *in interiore homine* and in isolated moments, far from others and from the plots that individuals weave when they intertwine their lives, when they spend time together. The most individualistic aspect of modern poetry is its hidden conflict with the aspects of life that transcend the sphere of the first person, since the form of modern poetry, as we have seen, seems to ignore the two things—the presence of others and the passage of time—that demonstrate the world's transcendence in relation to the self. Although modern poems obviously talk about this as well, because this is the stuff of life, the textual form tips so heavily toward the first person and passing instants that they reduce the other levels of reality to the mere content of an egocentric and instantaneous discourse. As the symbolic form of an era that has granted individuals unprecedented weight, modern poetry communicates, above all, the idea that society is a collection of separate monads immersed in a discontinuous flow of experience.

The importance that lyricism has had for the literature of the last few centuries is often underestimated. Studies on the system of modern genres sometimes include an idea that goes back to the writings of Friedrich Schlegel and that in recent decades has become a commonplace, thanks to the global readership of Bakhtin. According to this commonplace, the hegemony of the novel over modern literature prompted all other genres to become novelistic, that is, to incorporate polyphonic or diegetic elements that are partially foreign to their natural logic.[39] This is partly true: even without knowing Bakhtin, Brecht and Szondi showed why modern drama tends to imitate narrative techniques;[40] and as we know, there are many poems from recent centuries that try to escape from the limits of the short, subjective monolingual form. But the contamination of genre described by Bakhtin is not the only kind that recurs with a certain frequency in modern literature. The large number of poems written in a narrative style could in fact be contrasted with

39. Mikhail M. Bakhtin, *Voprosy literatury i estetiki* English translation, "Epic and Novel" in *The Dialogic Imagination: Four Essays,* trans. Caryl Emerson and Michael Holquist (Austin: University of Texas Press, 1981), 6–7.

40. Bertolt Brecht, *Schriften zum Theater: Über eine nicht-aristotelische Dramatik* (1957); English translation, *Brecht on Theatre,* ed. Marc Silberman, Steve Giles, and Tom Kuhn (London: Bloomsbury, 2014); Peter Szondi, *Theorie des modernen Dramas* (1956); English translation, *Theory of the Modern Drama,* ed. and trans. Michael Hays (Cambridge: Polity Press, 1987).

an equally large number of novels written in a lyrical style.[41] This is what happens every time the narrative voice (or the last word) is given to a hero who is always in the forefront, or every time the interest of the narrative does not arise from the story but from the way of telling it, and the way of telling it is a trace of the author's gaze. If a work accentuates diction and hides mimesis, if it attracts the reader because of the way it is written and not because of the story it tells, it appropriates a lyrical element even when the writer hides behind absolute impersonality.[42] It is also one of the most widely used expedients to overcome the problem that plagues novelists: how to create interest out of the everyday life of ordinary people, who are immersed in that "middle station of life" from which Robinson Crusoe had to escape to become the protagonist of a novel.[43] Flaubert's solution would establish the model: if the prose of ordinary life is completely devoid of aura, if the story to be told is pure nothingness, one can give meaning to a plot that in itself would be uninteresting by accentuating the weight of the form, by shifting part of the interest from the objectivity of the story to the subjectivity of the style, and thus inventing a kind of lyricism without a speaker that is no less egocentric than the personal lyricism we find in monological novels focused on a single hero. Starting in the second half of the nineteenth century, the subjective elements began to invade theater as well, as evidenced

---

41. See Ralph Freedman, *The Lyrical Novel: Studies in Hermann Hesse, André Gide, and Virginia Woolf* (Princeton, NJ: Princeton University Press, 1963).

42. See Gérard Genette, *Fiction et Diction* (1991); English translation, *Fiction and Diction*, trans. Catherine Porter (Ithaca, NY: Cornell University Press, 1993), 16–21.

43. At the beginning of the novel that bears his name, Robinson Crusoe is summoned by his father, who is old and sick with gout. This merchant from Bremen who had immigrated to England had already lost two sons; he knew that the third wanted to become a sailor and thought it fitting to give him a lesson in life. According to Robinson's father, the pursuit of adventure is suitable either for men of superior status or for the desperate; the son of a merchant, on the other hand, should be satisfied with what is offered by "the middle station of life," that is, middle-class life. Mr. Crusoe knows from experience that this station is the best of all, the most suited for human happiness, the most distant from uncertainty. He wants his son to remain faithful to it. Robinson will disobey. He will set sail several times, face dangers and uncertainties, and be shipwrecked on a desert island; but it is for this very reason that he will have an interesting life, a narratable destiny. If the young Crusoe had remained faithful to his initial station, he would never have become the protagonist of a book: not surprisingly, the part dedicated to the events of his father is only a few pages long. Since its earliest founding texts, the modern novel has been plagued by this ambivalence: bourgeois life seems interesting only when it is shaken up by something extraordinary. Only when the genre reaches the mature phase of its history does it manage to partially overcome this contradiction. While Defoe finds stories worth telling only in exceptions to the average, the great nineteenth-century novel would try to give a narrative interest to the ordinary life of ordinary people—to the middle station of life.

by the success of dramas built not on the staging of interhuman relationships taking place in the present but on the introspective analysis of the main
characters.[44] The lyricization of genres is almost as important as the "novel-
ization" on which Bakhtin insists: a clear sign that subjectivism is every bit
as essential to the present literary system as novelistic polyphony.

When we observe this apparent victory of the self and individual talent
over tradition and common sense from the outside, though, the triumph of
subjectivism shows its reverse side. The more the literary space of poetry
loses any relationship with the lifeworld, with a shared tradition and a nonspecialist audience, the more poets find themselves dependent on the small
social chorus and the small tradition from which they draw. An art born to
tell the story of monadic individuals who do not belong to the collective life
ends up showing that monads build their identity on imitation, that is, on
belonging. This leads to an apparently paradoxical but perfectly logical result: the crisis in *nomoi* and the triumph of individual talent do not imply the
birth of an anarchic literary domain in which monads apply to the letter the
theoretical imperative to express themselves freely. Instead, it entails two consequences that are apparently antithetical to the poetics of expressivism: the
spread of group behavior and the development of separate cultural systems
remote from the lifeworld that therefore produce extreme forms of obscurity in the eyes of those who do not share the assumptions of those systems.
In this case, modern poetry functions as an ideal type of collective social
behaviors governed by dynamics very close to those that govern the social
behavior of poets. Today, between the active and the passive side of contemporary narcissism, between the imperative of "express yourself" and "be
yourself," there lies an aesthetic dimension dominated by the pursuit of a
personal lifestyle. It is easy to understand, then, how the logic that inspires such
a pursuit resembles the dialectic of artistic systems ruled by self-expression,
as is modern poetry.

But if expressivism is indeed the extreme phase of modern individualism,
then contemporary artistic fields lend themselves to being understood as figures of a much bigger state of affairs. This swarming of monads who have
won the right not to belong and who tend toward an individual purpose, who
lack a shared world and a stable tradition but are embedded in small social

---

44. Szondi, *Theory of the Modern Drama*, chap. 2.

groups and small systems on which their identity and satisfaction depend, also represents an extraordinary allegory of life in the present age. It would be difficult to find a device that exemplifies the cultural logic of our time so aptly and powerfully: relativism; the lack of a collective framework of values; the fragmentation of interests, cultures, and groups; the dialectic between the achievement of subjective autonomy and the discovery that this autonomy is nevertheless embedded in a network of small or large dependencies; the dialectic between the right to individual expression and the risk that this principle produces, in the eyes of those who do not share our assumptions, idiosyncratic texts that do not communicate, that do not mean anything.

In his lectures on aesthetics, Hegel reflected on the future of the era he called Romantic and indicated the two directions in which the art of the future would develop: "the imitation of external objectivity in all its contingent shapes" and "the liberation of subjectivity, in accordance with its inner contingency."[45] And so it would be. The art of recent centuries seeks to reproduce contingent life with a mimetic precision never achieved by premodern art, delving into the meticulous representation of a differentiated society. At the same time, however, it gives unprecedented importance to the display of individual singularity, legitimizing content and forms that would have been completely inconceivable in other epochs. Although the supreme example of subjectivism in the reasoning of his aesthetics is the eighteenth-century humorous novel, the same principle can explain art forms that Hegel could not yet know, such as modern poetry or some of the modern visual arts. The dialectic that opposes objective realism to lyricism, humor, and subjective estrangement runs throughout all the arts, but there are genres whose structural characteristics lend themselves better to expressing one of the two principles. In the division of labor on which today's literary space is based, poetry usually takes the side of subjectivity, whereas fiction occupies itself with describing the relationship between individuals and other people, and between individuals and circumstances. While the novel still attempts to construct a shared world supported by the elementary and objective devices of plot and character, modern poetry remains the most egocentric of genres. In the majority of cases, it continues to have a lyric form; it collects texts in which a speaker recounts fragments of subjective experience in a style

---

45. Hegel, *Aesthetics*, 1:608.

that aims to be subjective, that is, far from the degree-zero of ordinary communication. But the egocentrism is just as pronounced in texts that do not have a lyric form, as we have seen, because it is transferred to the gaze and the style and takes the form of estrangement. This organic relationship to subjectivity as the content and form of experience makes poetry the most widely practiced art, the primary medium of amateur expressivism and generic creativity. In common perception, one can write poetry without reading poetry, without following contemporary poetry, and without possessing any technique. Other people interest us primarily as mirrors, as sounding boards of our life stories: when it is their turn to express their own subjective difference, the discourse they give is almost never of interest to us unless they resemble us, because it risks giving voice to a merely private or tribal idiosyncrasy that does not relate to a common ground. The image of the world that we draw from the literature of our time presents different points of view on the same historical landscape, marked by individualism, by the breaking down of large explicit bonds, by the strengthening of the small implicit ties that surround the self and guarantee only a local meaning for its expressions and desires. The forms of art tell the history of humanity with greater accuracy than do historical documents.

ACKNOWLEDGMENTS

The University of Siena, the Fulbright Commission, the University of Chicago, and the Italian Academy at Columbia University, New York, supported the writing and rewriting of this book. Reading Room U at the Bibliothèque Nationale de France in Tolbiac, Paris made it possible. My thanks go to those who contributed with their suggestions, comments, and help: Annalisa Agrati, Albert Ascoli, Irene Babboni, Corinne Bayerl, Luigi Blasucci, Lina Bolzoni, Daniela Brogi, Franco Buffoni, Barbara Carnevali, Pietro Cataldi, Tommaso Cavallo, Remo Ceserani, Tiziana de Rogatis, Raffaele Donnarumma, Georgia Fioroni, Céline Frigau, Carmen Gallo, Claudio Giunta, Emeralde Jensen-Roberts, Romano Luperini, Francesco Orlando, Thomas Pavel, Pierluigi Pellini, Mauro Piras, Lucia Prauscello, Guido Sacchi, Francesca Scollo, Gianluigi Simonetti, Barbara Spackman, Justin Steinberg, Alfredo Stussi, Mario Telò, and Antonio Tricomi. My special thanks to Emily Silk and Lindsay Waters, who believed in this book and the potential of its English-language version and who supported its publication at Harvard University Press. Finally, I am very grateful to Zakiya Hanafi for her meticulous translation.

INDEX

Abrams, Meyer H., 29, 54, 56, 58, 116, 119, 122, 125, 172

Addison, Catherine, 169

Adéma, Marcel, 139

Adorno, Theodor Wiesengrund, 5, 7, 22, 24, 25, 31, 117, 141, 170, 175, 197, 200, 214–215, 231

Alcaeus, 31, 40, 88

Alcman, 40

Alesi, Eros, 202

Alexievich, Svetlana Alexandrovna, 230

Alfieri, Vittorio, 66, 73, 81, 146

Alford, Lucy, 29

Anacreon, 40

Anderson, Andrew A., 164

Anderson, Jill, 193

anxiety of influence, 216

Apollinaire, Guillaume, 138–139

Archilochus, 43

Aristotle, 18, 37, 41, 42, 43, 44, 46, 47, 48, 49, 50, 51, 56, 58, 63, 82, 83, 87, 102, 117–119, 147

Arkell, David, 138

Arnim, Bettina von, 137

Arnim, Peter Anton von, 16, 35

art as fetishism, 208

Ashbery, John, 168, 191–192

Aubry, Jean G., 180

Auden, Wystan Hugh, 28, 30, 170, 223

Auerbach, Erich, 5, 7, 9, 81–85, 170

Augustine of Hippo, 105

author notes to poems, 157–159

autobiographism in poetry, three models of, 88–101

Bacchelli, Riccardo, 72

Bacchylides, 40

Bachmann, Ingeborg, 30

Backès, Jean-Louis, 28

Baker, Peter, 188

Bakhtin, Mikhail Mikhailovich, 7, 170, 205, 214–215, 231, 233, 235

Bakker, Nienke, 181

Bald, Robert Cecil, 100

Baldini, Antonio, 72

Balzac, Honoré de, 85

Barolini, Teodolinda, 99

Barrett Browning, Elizabeth, 28

Barthes, Roland, 85, 116–117, 120, 130–131, 164, 197, 202

Batteux, Charles, 56–58

Baudelaire, Charles, 33, 151, 158, 176, 177, 178, 185, 195, 219

Baumgarten, Alexander Gottlieb, 54

Bec, Pierre, 44

Beccaria, Cesare, 133

Becker, Howard S., 209

Behrens, Irene, 36, 38, 44, 54

Beißner, Friedrich, 141

Belitt, Ben, 143

Bell, Clive, 157

Bell, Daniel, 7

Bembo, Pietro, 55

Benét, Stephen Vincent, 61

Benjamin, Walter, 3, 4, 5, 7, 8, 15, 129, 177, 219, 226

Benveniste, Émile, 36

Berardinelli, Alfonso, 188, 220

Bergson, Henri, 230

Bernard, Suzanne, 150

Bernardelli, Giuseppe, 29, 36, 42, 49, 59

Bernardo, Aldo S., 44

Bernstein, Charles, 29

Berryman, John, 190

Bertolucci, Attilio, 169

Bertoni, Alberto, 152

Bertrand, Aloysius (Louis Jacques Napoléon Bertrand), 151

Bettarini, Rosanna, 132

Betteloni, Vittorio, 133

Biden, Joe, 223

Bidney, Martin, 16, 35

Bigi, Emilio, 78, 79, 109

Bishop, Elizabeth, 30

Blasucci, Luigi, 75, 76, 77, 78, 79, 81, 86, 109

Bliss, Matthew T., 123

Bloom, Harold, 173, 216

Bolter, Jay David, 229

Boncardo, Robert, 196

Bonnet, Marguerite, 162, 198

Book of Psalms, 56, 58

Booth, Stephen, 136

Borgese, Giuseppe Antonio, 183

Boschetti, Anna, 10

Bothe, Henning, 141

Bouhours, Dominique, 54–55

Bourdieu, Pierre, 6, 8, 10, 12–13, 130, 205, 208, 219, 225

Brandeis, Bob, 169

Braudel, Fernand, 9

Bray, René, 54

Brecht, Bertolt, 233

Breton, André, 128, 129, 161–162, 198–199

Brett, R. L., 115, 173

Brioschi, Franco, 76, 80

Brock, Geoffrey, 111

Brodribb, William Jackson, 42

Brombert, Victor, 113

Brontë, Emily, 30

Browning, Robert, 28, 189

Buffon, Georges-Louis Leclerc de, 124

Buffoni, Franco, 169

Burchiello (Domenico di Giovanni), 144

Burckhardt, Jacob, 7

Bürger, Christa, 137

Bürger, Peter, 137

Byron, George Gordon, 28, 113

Caesar, Michael, 59, 75, 133, 166, 212

Calin, William, 28

Callimachus, 155

Carducci, Giosuè, 133

Carlton, Charles M., 123

Carson, Anne, 30, 35, 168, 169, 188

Casanova, Pascale, 10, 31

Cascales, Francisco, 54

Cassirer, Ernst, 14, 25–26

Castelvetro, Ludovico, 46

Catullus, Gaius Valerius, 42, 45, 89, 90, 101, 104, 108

Cavalcanti, Guido, 99

Caws, Mary Ann, 193

Cesarotti, Melchiorre, 66

Char, René, 30

Cherel, Albert, 150

Chiabrera, Gabriello, 55

Chiusi, Fabio, 220

Church, Alfred John, 42

Churchill, Winston, 230

Claudel, Paul, 142

Clayton, Vista, 150

Cleophon, 82

Cohn, Dorrit, 10
Coleridge, Samuel Taylor, 65, 115, 117, 149, 172, 173, 212
Coletti, Vittorio, 132
Combe, Dominique, 168, 193
confessional poetry, 187
Contini, Gianfranco, 99, 101–102, 132
Cook, Bradford, 153, 192, 232
Corcoran, Steven, 196
Cordelli, Franco, 220
Cornelius Nepos, 2, 3
Couton, Georges, 120
Crescimbeni, Giovanni Mario, 53
Croce, Benedetto, 36, 49
Culler, Jonathan, 36, 63, 88, 105, 109, 173, 184, 190
cultural epochs, 7–10
Curtius, Ernst Robert, 9, 38, 43, 120, 123, 128

Damiani, Rolando, 1, 73, 74, 87
Dante (Dante Alighieri), 43, 44, 85, 89, 90, 97–98, 100, 101, 108, 121, 158
Danto, Arthur, 226
Danzer, Ina Dorothea, 183
Darío, Rubén (Félix Rubén García Sarmiento), 27, 142
Dauguet, Marie, 154
Davie, Donald, 139
Debauve, Jean-Louis, 138
DeBevoise, M. B., 10
de Bruyne, Edgar, 44
Décaudin, Michel, 139
de Courten, Maryke, 138
Defoe, Daniel, 234
dehumanization, 129, 194–195, 214
Dei, Adele, 178
de la Fuente, Eduardo, 219
Del Bene, Giulio, 45
DeLillo, Don, 202
Della Casa, Giovanni, 80
De Loaiza, Robert, 213
de Man, Paul, 116
Democritus, 118

depersonalization, 194–195
de Rooy, Roland, 188
De Sanctis, Francesco, 66–67, 88
Diamanti, Joyce D., 209
Dickinson, Emily, 27, 143–144
Dickson, Donald R., 100
Diderot, Denis, 2
Didymus, 41
differential autobiographism, 105–108
Dilthey, Wilhelm, 6, 7
D'Intino, Franco, 59, 75, 133, 166, 212
Diomedes, 38, 43
Dionysius, 82
Di Tarsia, Galeazzo, 76
Donne, John, 41, 90, 99–101, 108, 161
Doriott Anderson, Vanessa, 10
Dostoevsky, Fyodor Mikhailovich, 137
Dotti, Ugo, 73
dramatic monologue, 189–190
Dryden, John, 53
Duff, David, 20
Dujardin, Édouard, 137
Dupont-Roc, Roselyne, 119
Dvořák, Max, 7
Dylan, Bob, 229–230

Ecclesiastes, 158
Egerton, Thomas, 100
Egger, Victor, 137
egocentrism, 199–202
Eiland, Howard, 4
Eliot, George (Mary Ann Evans), 28, 209
Eliot, Thomas Stearns, 25, 30, 112–113, 128, 139, 157–159, 168, 170, 178, 181, 183, 184, 185, 188–189, 202
Emanuel, Susan, 6, 130, 205, 208
Emerson, Caryl, 233
Empedocles, 147, 155
Enfield, William, 148–149
Enright, D. J., 8, 9, 126, 217
Enzensberger, Hans Magnus, 170
Epimenides, 155
epiphany, 176

Ernaux, Annie, 202
estrangement, 165, 166–169, 193
Eutychius Proclus, 40
expressionism, 180–183
expressivism, 124–131, 173; dialectic of, 213–218
Ezekiel, 158

Färber, Hans, 38, 40
Febvre, Lucien, 9
Fénelon, François de Salignac de La Mothe, 2, 3, 151
Ferroni, Giulio, 49
Ferrucci, Franco, 76
Ferry, Luc, 213
Fineman, Joel, 90
Flaubert, Gustave, 137, 234
Flint, Robert Willard, 129
Flora, Francesco, 76
Flynn, Dennis, 100
Fortini, Franco, 159–161, 163, 196–197
Foscolo, Ugo, 66–67, 73, 81, 144–145, 174
Foucault, Michel, 6, 7
Fowler, Alastair, 21
Francastel, Pierre, 9
Frazer, James, 158
Freedman, Ralph, 234
free verse, 148–155
freie Rhythmen, 148
Freud, Sigmund, 12, 128, 217
Frezza, Guglielmo, 49
Friedrich, Hugo, 29, 80, 194–195, 197
Fubini, Mario, 36, 49, 76, 77, 78–80, 88, 109
Fuhrmann, Manfred, 155
Fumaroli, Marc, 123
Fusco, Enrico M., 77
Futurism, 138, 147, 154–155, 197

Galassi, Jonathan, 76, 94, 132, 146, 186
Galilei, Galileo, 123
Gambarin, Giovanni, 145
García Berrio, Antonio, 36, 46
García Lorca, Federico, 163–164

Gasparov, M. L., 152
Gefen, Alexandre, 230
Gehlen, Arnold, 7
Genette, Gérard, 17–18, 34, 36, 54, 234
genres, nature of, 20–25
genres, theory of, 15–25
genres, tripartition of (epic, drama, lyric), 33–35, 45–53
genres as symbolic forms, 25–26
George, Stefan, 27
Gerratana, Valentino, 13
Gesellschaftslyrik, 89–90, 104
Gessner, Salomon, 86, 150
Getto, Giovanni, 131, 132
Giles, Steve, 233
Gilson, Étienne, 103
Ginsberg, Allen, 203–204
Ginzburg, Lidiya, 103
Girardi, Antonio, 134, 135
Giunta, Claudio, 89
Gizzi, Peter, 222
Gleize, Jean-Marie, 29, 185
Glück, Louise, 91–93, 96, 100, 101, 103, 106, 136
Goethe, Johann Wolfgang von, 2, 3, 16–19, 35, 113
Goldoni, Carlo, 66
Gombrich, Ernst, 6, 7
Gorman, Amanda, 223
Gosse, Edmund William, 100
Gozzano, Guido, 179, 183, 224
Gramsci, Antonio, 13
Gravina, Gian Vincenzo, 53
Gray, Thomas, 27, 65
greater Romantic lyric, 172–173
Greene, Roland, 89
Greet, Anne Hyde, 139
Grierson, Herbert J. C., 100
Grossman, Vasily, 24
group subjectivism, 205, 216–218
Grube, G. M. A., 37
Grünbein, Durs, 141
Grunberger, Béla, 209

Guarini, Alessandro, 45–46, 50, 51, 57
Guarracino, Vincenzo, 78
Guercio, Gabriele, 226
Guerrero, Gustavo, 36, 42, 44, 49, 52, 59
Guillén, Claudio, 36
Guillén, Jorge, 30

Haller, Albrecht von, 65
Hamburger, Käte, 194, 197
Hamburger, Michael, 141
Hamilton, Scott, 183
Hanafi, Zakiya, 22, 71, 87, 121
Handke, Peter, 230
Harris, William C., 177
Hartley, Anthony, 192
Hathaway, Baxter, 46, 49, 51
Haussmann, Georges-Eugène, 23
Hays, Michael, 5, 233
Heaney, Seamus, 96, 229
Hegel, Georg Wilhelm Friedrich, 5, 6, 7, 12,
    25, 34, 39, 62, 64, 107, 209, 212, 236
Hegemon of Thasos, 82
hegemony, 13–14
Heinich, Natalie, 130, 219
Heliodorus, 22
Helvius Cinna, Gaius, 155
Herbert, George, 100
Herbert, Magdalen, 100
Herder, Johann Gottfried, 116
Herrick, Marvin T., 46
Hill, Geoffrey, 190
Hilles, F. W., 173
Hoare, Quintin, 13
Hölderlin, Friedrich, 63, 139–141, 173, 174,
    175, 185
Holmes, Anne, 137
Holquist, Michael, 205, 215, 233
Homer, 36, 43, 81, 82, 147
Horace (Quintus Horatius Flaccus), 38, 39,
    41, 42, 43, 44, 45, 46, 49, 54, 56, 63, 68, 85, 89,
    90, 97–98, 100, 101, 104, 108, 118, 119, 120, 232
Houdar de La Motte, Antoine, 53
Houssaye, Arsène, 151

Howard, Richard, 17, 85
Howe, Elisabeth, 190
Hugo, Victor, 65, 176
Huizinga, Johan, 7, 208
Hullot-Kentor, Robert, 5, 25
Huret, Jules, 153
Husserl, Edmund, 14, 128

Ibycus, 40
ideographic mode, 85
illusio, 208, 216, 217
individualism, 105–108, 125, 130, 154–155, 174,
    188, 199–202, 213, 232–237
interior monologue, 135, 137–139
irony, 183–184
Iser, Wolfgang, 144, 197
Isherwood, Christopher, 178
Ishiguro, Kazuo, 230
-isms, 215

Jackson, Virginia, 29
Jahier, Piero, 110–111, 113
Jameson, Fredric, 5, 7, 12
Jammes, Francis, 183
Jansen, Annemiek, 123
Jansen, Leo, 181
Jaucourt, Louis de, 151
Jauss, Hans Robert, 20, 36
Jerniewicz, Jerzy, 230
John of Garland, 44
Johnson, Randal, 130
Johnson, Uwe, 202
Johnson, Walter Ralph, 36
Jones, A. R., 115, 173
Jones, William, 57–59
Joyce, James, 24, 137

Kahn, Gustave, 154
Kaplan, Justin, 152
Kappl, Brigitte, 46
Keats, John, 41, 113, 174, 175
Kenny, Anthony, 82
Kermode, Frank, 191

Killian, Kevin, 222
Kilmartin, Terence, 8, 9, 126, 217
Kingsley-Smith, Jane, 90
Kleist, Heinrich von, 185
Klopstock, Friedrich Gottlieb, 27
Knox, T. M., 25, 34, 209
Köhler, Barbara, 141
Koolhaas, Rem, 5
Kramme, Rüdiger, 105
Kuhn, Tom, 233
Kuzmin, Mikhail, 152

La Fayette, Marie-Madeleine Pioche de La
   Vergne, comtesse de, 22
Laforgue, Jules, 137, 183, 189
Lallot, Jean, 119
Lamartine, Alfonse de, 173
Lamprecht, Karl, 6, 7
Landino, Cristoforo, 44
Lane, Helen R., 129
Langbaum, Robert, 190
Lansing, Richard, 99
Larkin, Philip, 184
Lasch, Christopher, 7, 209–210
Latini, Brunetto, 121
Lausberg, Heinrich, 123
Lavers, Annette, 116, 197
Lee, Charmaine, 15
Lefébure, Eugène, 194
Leithauser, Brad, 169
Lenin (Vladimir Ilyich Ulyanov), 13
Leopardi, Giacomo, 1–4, 26–27, 31, 59–60, 63,
   65, 66–67, 67–69, 70, 71–81, 85–88, 104, 105,
   107, 108–109, 113, 114, 127, 128, 130, 133,
   144–145, 146, 150, 166–167, 171, 173, 175,
   206–207, 209, 212
Lerner, Ben, 177, 181, 215
Levine, Herbert J., 177
Lewin, Jane E., 17, 34
lexicon, 131–135
Liapunov, Vadim, 205, 215
lifeworld (*Lebenswelt*), 14
Lispector, Clarice, 202

literary space, 1–5, 225
Lloyd, Rosemary, 180
long poems, 187–189; decline of, 61, 122–124
longue durée, 1–4
loss of social mandate, 177–180, 218–226
Lowell, Robert, 187
Loyola, Hernán, 143
Lucini, Gian Pietro, 152
Lucretius (Titus Lucretius Carus), 38, 43
Luijten, Hans, 181
Lukács, György, 5
Luzi, Mario, 188
Lycophron, 155
lyrical Romanticism, 169–180
lyric and modern poetry, 33–35
lyric I. *See* subjectivity, three models of
lyric in ancient poetics, 37–43
lyric in medieval poetics, 43–44
lyric in Renaissance poetics, 45–53
lyric in Romantic poetics, 55–62
lyric in the modern sense of the word,
   45–53, 62–64

Macey David, 209
Macpherson, James, 28, 148, 150
Maecenas, Gaius Cilnius, 39
Maeterlinck, Maurice, 183
Maggi, Cristiana, 112
Mallarmé, Stéphane, 27, 30, 152–153, 154, 168,
   180, 189, 192–197, 232
Mandell, Charlotte, 173
Manfredi, Eustachio, 54–55
Manganelli, Giorgio, 123
Manheim, Ralph, 25, 83
Mann, Thomas, 24
Manzoni, Alessandro, 3, 66
marginality of poetry, 177–180, 218–226
Marinetti, Filippo Tommaso, 128, 129, 138,
   147, 154, 178
Marino, Adrian, 123
Marino, Giovan Battista, 131
Marot, Clément, 55
Marx, Karl, 12

Mason, Wyatt, 156
Maurer, Karl, 67, 69, 86
Mayor, Andreas, 9, 126, 217
Mayröcker, Friederike, 141
Mazzoni, Guido, 22, 87, 121
McCue, Jim, 112
McKeon, Michael, 123
McLaughlin, Kevin, 4
McWilliams, John P., 28
Medina, Pablo, 164
Meek, Mary Elizabeth, 36
Meléndez Valdés, Juan, 27
Mengaldo, Pier Vincenzo, 174, 186
Meredith, George, 28
Metastasio (Pietro Trapassi), 67, 88
meter, 147–155
Michałowska, Teresa, 36
Michelet, Jules, 8
Mill, John Stuart, 106–107
Miller, Cristanne, 143–144
Miller, Paul Allen, 42, 89
Miłosz, Czesław, 188
Milton, John, 53
Minogue, Kenneth, 224
Minturno, Antonio, 45–47, 51, 57
modern lyric classicism, 184–187
modern poetic anthropology, 211–213
modern poetry, concept of, 65–70
modern poetry, definition of, 26–31
modern poetry and narcissism, 209–211
modern poetry and self-expression, 34, 39,
    55–62, 226
modern poetry and social bonds, 210–211
modern poetry and time, 210–211
modern poetry as a symbolic form, 209
Molière (Jean-Baptiste Poquelin), 120
Mommsen, Theodor, 230
Mondor, Henri, 180
montage principle, 135, 137–139
Montale, Eugenio, 30, 94–96, 101, 103, 106,
    132, 136, 156, 157, 161, 185–186, 206–207
Montanari, Franco, 155
Monte, Steven, 150

Monti, Vincenzo, 73
Moon, Michael, 142, 176
Moore, Marianne, 158–159, 179–180
Morando, Bernardo, 132
More, Anne, 100
More, George, 100
Moretti, Franco, 10
Morpurgo Tagliabue, Guido, 118
Morris, William, 28
Morrison, Toni, 202
Moschus, 86
Mo Yan, 230
Müller, Herta, 230
Müller-Zettelmann, Eva, 105
Munro, Alice, 202, 230
Murat, Michel, 151
Murray, Les, 168
Musil, Robert, 24

narrative poems, 28, 168–169
Neruda, Pablo, 142–143
Neugroschel, Joachim, 29, 195
New, Elisa, 177
Nicochares, 82
Nietzsche, Friedrich, 12
Norden, Eduard, 124–125
Nouvel, Jean, 23
Novalis (Georg Philipp Friedrich Freiherr
    von Hardenberg), 150, 174, 175, 185, 195
Nowell Smith, Geoffrey, 13

Obama, Barack, 222–223
obscurity and difficulty, 159–165
obscurity of modern poetry, 155–165
O'Driscoll, Dennis, 96
Orlando, Francesco, 15, 165
Orpheus, 155
Orsi, Giovan Gioseffo, 54–55
Ortega y Gasset, José, 128–129, 165, 202
Orton, David E., 123
Osborne, John, 4
Ottieri, Ottiero, 169
Ovid (Publius Ovidius Naso), 42

Packer, George, 222–223
Pagliarani, Elio, 188
Palazzeschi, Aldo (Aldo Giurlani), 178–179, 184, 224
Palma, Michael, 180
Panofsky, Erwin, 7, 25–26
Parini, Giuseppe, 27, 65, 73, 132–133
Parmenides, 155
partage du sensible, 84
Pascal, Blaise, 123
Pascoli, Giovanni, 27, 134–135, 145–146
Pasolini, Pier Paolo, 30, 35
Paul, Zakir, 84
Pavel, Thomas, 84–85
Payne, Roberta L., 178
Perelman, Bob, 29, 184, 221–222
Perryman Marcus, 211
Persius Flaccus, Aulus, 155
Peruzzi, Emilio, 71, 146
Petrarch (Francesco Petrarca), 44, 45, 47, 48, 49, 51, 55, 58, 63, 68, 76, 79, 80, 81, 88, 89, 90, 101–105, 108, 131, 175, 232
Pfeiffer, Rudolf, 40
Photios, 40
Picasso, Pablo, 185
Pigna, Giovan Battista, 45
Pindar, 31, 40, 45, 54, 56, 139, 155
Plato, 17, 18, 37–38, 40, 41, 42, 43, 44, 46, 47, 48, 49, 50, 117, 119
Plutarch, 2
Poe, Edgar Allan, 61, 123, 169
poetic diction, 65–67, 117, 131–135, 144, 149–150, 174, 182, 206, 212
poetry and paraphrase, 120–121, 157
poetry and prose, 115–124
poetry and song, 226–232
Poliziano, Angelo, 44
Polygnotus, 82
Poma, Luigi, 46
pop culture, 227–232
Pope, Alexander, 2, 3
Porphyrios, Demetri, 6
Porter, Catherine, 234

Pound, Ezra, 30, 35, 139, 183–184, 188, 189, 200
Praga, Emilio, 133
Proclus, 41, 43
Propertius, Sextus, 155
prose poem, 148, 150–151
Proust, Marcel, 7, 8–9, 24, 126–127, 129, 154, 209, 217
Pseudo-Longinus, 118, 121
pure poetry (*poésie pure*), 192–197

Queneau, Raymond, 28
Quintilian (Marcus Fabius Quintilianus), 42, 121
Quondam, Amedeo, 49

Rammstedt, Angela, 105
Rammstedt, Otthein, 105
Rancière, Jacques, 84, 173, 196, 197
Ranieri, Antonio, 73
Rankine, Claudia, 30
Rauhut, Franz, 150
Raymond, Marcel, 197
Redfern, Joan, 66
Reeve, C. D. C., 37
Rembrandt (Rembrandt Harmenszoon van Rijn), 126, 129
Richardson, Samuel, 22
Richardson, Joan, 191
Ricks, Christopher, 112
Ricœur, Paul, 12
Rilke, Rainer Maria, 142, 185, 186
Rimbaud, Arthur, 104, 117, 151, 156, 157, 161, 181, 182, 212
Ripa di Meana, Ludovica, 169
Roberts, John R., 90
Robinson, Edwin Arlington, 61
Robinson, Peter, 211
Robortello, Francesco, 44, 119
Robson, John M., 107
Rocca, Andrea, 180
Rockhill, Gabriel, 84
Rogers, William Elford, 36
Rogow, Zack, 162, 198

Rollengedicht, 189
Roloff, Michael, 170
Romani, Werther, 46
Rose, Julie, 84, 196
Rosengrant, Judson, 103
Rosenthal, M. L., 187
Rösler, Wolfgang, 89
Rossi, Luigi Enrico, 40
Rousseau, Jean-Jacques, 105, 113, 115
Rubik, Margarete, 105
rule of the division of styles (*Stiltrennung*), 81–85
Russell, Bertrand, 230
Russell, Lucy, Countess of Bedford, 100

Saba, Umberto, 186
Salinas, Pedro, 142
Santagata, Marco, 49, 86, 89, 102
Sapiro, Gisèle, 10
Sappho, 40, 90
Saramago, José, 202
Sartre, Jean-Paul, 193
Sassetti, Filippo, 45, 52–53
Sassoon, Donald, 227
Savage, Denis, 12
Scaligero, Giulio Cesare, 52, 53
Schaeffer, Jean-Marie, 17, 19, 36
Schmit, John, 144
Scholes, Robert, 36
Schumann, Detlev, 142
Scott, Clive, 151
Scott, Sir Walter, 3
Scott Moncrieff, C. K., 8
Seaver, Richard, 129
Seferis, Giorgos, 188
Segni, Angelo, 45, 48, 50, 51, 57
Seldes, Gilbert, 157
Sennett, Richard, 105
Sereni, Vittorio, 210
Seth, Vikram, 168, 169
Shakespeare, William, 90, 101, 104, 108, 135–136, 158, 175
shame of poetry, 177–180, 218–226

Shelley, Percy Bysshe, 113, 173, 174, 175
Sidney, Philip, 90
Silva, José Asunción, 152
Simmel, Georg, 105, 125
Simonetti, Gianluigi, 220
Simonides, 40
Singh, Ghan, 78
Smith, Colin, 116, 197
Smith, G. S., 152
Song of Songs, 156
Spaziani, Maria Luisa, 169
Spenser, Edmund, 90
Spicer, Jack, 222
Spitzer, Leo, 142
Spivak, Gayatri Chakravorty, 31
Stanciu, Virgil, 123
Statman, Mark, 164
Steele, Timothy, 149
Stempel, Wolf-Dieter, 36, 144
Stendhal (Henri Beyle), 85
Stéphan, Anne-Joelle, 36
Stesichorus, 40
Stevens, Wallace, 190–191, 200
Stierle, Karlheinz, 197
Stillinger, Jack, 107
Strozzi, Giovan Battista, 45, 52
style as ornament, 120–122
style as self-expression, 115–120, 124–131, 206–207
subjectivity, three models of, 88–101
Sulzer, Johann Georg, 60
Surrealism, 197–199
Symbolism, 192–197
Symons, Arthur, 183
syntax, 135–147; public syntax, 135–136; private syntax, 135–147
Szondi, Peter, 5, 7, 17, 36, 170, 233, 235

Tacitus, Publius Cornelius, 2, 3, 42
Tarlinskaja, Marina, 152
Tasso, Torquato, 46, 51–52, 53, 67
Taylor, Charles, 105, 125, 213
Tempest, Kae, 223

Tennyson, Alfred, 189
Testa, Enrico, 190
theatricality, 189–192
Theophrastus, 82
Thomas, Richard F., 230
Thompson, Gary Richard, 169
Tibullus (Albius Tibullus), 42, 98
Tiedemann, Rolf, 117, 141
Tilgher, Adriano, 78
Todorov, Tzvetan, 17
Tolstoy, Lev Nikolayevich, 22, 137, 209
Tomasi di Lampedusa, Giuseppe, 24
Tondelli, Pier Vittorio, 226–229
Torelli, Pomponio, 45, 51, 57
transcendental autobiographism, 101–105
Tranströmer, Tomas, 230
Trapp, Joseph, 59
Trask, Willard R., 5, 9, 38, 82
Tropes, 155–165
Tsagarakis, Odysseus, 41
Tucker, Herbert, 28

Uhlig, Claus, 128
Ungaretti, Giuseppe, 111–113

Valéry, Paul, 185, 189, 193
Van Delft, Louis, 103
van Gogh, Vincent, 181
Vendler, Helen, 190
Venerable Bede, 44
Vermeer, Johannes (Jan), 126, 127, 129
Vico, Giambattista, 58, 115
Viëtor, Karl, 36
Villon, François, 55
Vincent-Munnia, Nathalie, 151
Viola, Corrado, 55
Viperano, Giovanni Antonio, 45, 51, 57
Virgil (Publius Vergilius Maro), 39, 43, 82
Viti, Cristina, 203

Vogelweide, Walther von der, 31
Voltaire (François-Marie Arouet), 27, 65

Wacquant, Loïc, 208, 225
Wagner, Richard, 158
Walcott, Derek, 168
Waldrop, Keith, 151, 178
Wallerstein, Immanuel Maurice, 9
Walzer, Pierre-Olivier, 138
Waterhouse, Peter, 141
Watson, James Sibley, 157
Weber, Max, 219
Weber Nicholsen, Shierry, 5, 117, 141, 175, 214
Weinberg, Bernard, 46, 48
Werfel, Franz, 142
Weston, Jessie L., 158
Weyl, Helene, 202
White, Heather Cass, 159
Whitman, Walt, 104, 142, 151, 152, 153, 176, 182, 187, 204, 212
Wilmans, Friedrich, 141
Wolf, Werner, 105
Wood, Christopher S., 25
Woolf, Virginia, 22, 24
Wordsworth, William, 65–66, 70, 107, 115–117, 131, 149–150, 173, 174, 188, 189, 212

Xenophanes, 155
Xenophon, 2

Yeats, William Butler, 28
Yehoshua, Abraham, 202
Young, James O., 56

Zampa, Giorgio, 95, 185
Zavatsky, Bill, 162, 198
Zohn, Harry, 88, 129, 177, 219
Zumthor, Paul, 43
Zuradelli, Gianna Maria, 133